POET IN EXILE

Translated by Harrison Brown

POET IN EXILE

The Life of Heinrich Heine

by

ANTONINA VALLENTIN

KENNIKAT PRESS
Port Washington, N. Y./London

NOTE

The few quotations from Heine in this book are followed in each case by an English rendering. No attempt whatever has been made to *translate* the German : Heine is untranslatable. The intention has been to give the merest indication of Heine's meaning, for the benefit of those who read no German.

H. B.

POET IN EXILE

First published in 1934
Reissued in 1970 by Kennikat Press
Library of Congress Catalog Card No: 72-113327
ISBN 0-8046-1003-7

Manufactured by Taylor Publishing Company Dallas, Texas

CONTENTS

CHAPTER I

DESTINY IN THE CRADLE

"In my cradle lay my marching route for the whole of my life."
(From a letter to Varnhagen, *July 16th, 1833*)

"I AM NO LOVER of sentiment," wrote Betty van Geldern in January 1796, "for although I can easily forgive a certain warmth of feeling, I detest the so-called fashionable sentimentality." Betty, or to give her her full name, Pereira van Geldern, who thus proclaimed her freedom from emotionalism with all the pride of a rationalist age, could not foresee that before the year was out the neat planning of her life was to be upset by her falling passionately in love.

She was twenty-five years old, no longer quite young therefore, even by present standards, and for those days of early marriage she must be reckoned almost an old maid. But the special circumstances of her family, her relationship with her father and brother, and her education, had combined to make her different from others in the narrow circle of Jewish bourgeois families. Like the golden shimmer of a legend there lay across the background of her childhood the traditions of the fabulous riches of her grandfather, the ducal Chamberlain Juspa van Geldern, who had possessed and lost again the palaces, Persian carpets, and massive silver plate, together with the favour of the Duke. This background of the past gave her a special importance in the eyes of her kinsfolk, who in this respect, like the feudal aristocracy, were apt to make a cult of heredity. The position of her father, who, after taking his degree at the University of Duisburg, had settled down as a doctor in Düsseldorf, added to this importance, and assured her the privilege of being judged by special standards.

Her education, according to the new learning of a

rationalist age, also raised her above the average woman. As a young girl she had had to read Latin prose to her father, but Gottschalk van Geldern had considered music a waste of time, and had forbidden her to practise the flute. She joined in the studies of her brother, who also chose the medical profession, and made a name for himself in Munich before returning to Düsseldorf to help his ageing father with his practice. The scientific training, constant association with men who recognised her intellectual maturity, and a well-grounded knowledge of the new literature of an age of enlightenment, all combined to give her a superiority over the other women in her circle, and at the same time set a distance between herself and the men with whom she came into contact. Pereira van Geldern, like all daughters who grow up in close association with the strong personality of their father, compared the daily contacts of her environment with the exceptional figures of father and brother. From this habit of comparison there developed in her a strong aversion to all ties which did not do justice to herself and to her ideal of manhood.

When Samson Heine came into her life, her vision of a proud spinsterhood vanished. Perhaps the blows which fate dealt her about the same time had already weakened that intention and softened her ; in 1794 her brother Joseph had died, and the death of her father in the following year had confronted her with the prospect of a life of loneliness. Or perhaps the mere fact that Samson Heine's qualities were the opposite of intellectual proved particularly dangerous to a woman somewhat isolated in her intellectual superiority. In any case we find her already engaged to Samson Heine in August 1796, although Heine had only arrived in Düsseldorf the previous month. "I have an ordinary face and an ordinary figure," said Betty van Geldern about herself. Samson Heine, on the other hand, was of that blond, delicate type which contrasts strongly with the more usual dark-haired characteristics of the Jewish race. At this time he was thirty-two years old, with fair powdered hair, soft as Chinese flock silk, hanging round the fresh-coloured features of a somewhat empty face. His melodious voice was soft too, like his hair, and like the white hands interlaced with delicate blue veins, which he took an almost childish delight in displaying. His whole personality was in keeping with his outer appearance.

He was Betty's fate, as it is the fate of many another strong, self-possessed woman, to fall in love with, and have to fight for, a good-looking man, whose only distinctive feature it is to be good-looking. In the view of her bourgeois world her marriage was a *mésalliance*. The family van Geldern was far higher up in the social scale than that of the son of Heymann Heine from Bückeburg. To the Jews especially, where differences of caste are so much finer than those of Christian society, these small differences appear far more important. In addition to this, Samson Heine was without means, and Betty had to use all her energy in order to obtain for him the right to work in Düsseldorf. The small Jewish community resisted the new-comer with energy, for it was already fully occupied with the care of its poorer members, and considered that the daughter of Gottschalk van Geldern had no need to marry a nobody who had appeared out of the blue. Betty van Geldern had to use all the connections which she owed to her father in order to obtain permission from the Government to settle down. "Would you really believe that I could make so many enemies through my engagement?" she wrote to a friend in November 1796. "But my Heine amply repays me for all that by his devotion and loyalty."

Handsome and easy-going, in some ways almost simple-minded, Heine managed the ordinary affairs of life so badly that he was constantly obliged to have recourse to others to get him out of difficulties. But he possessed to a high degree the indefinable quality of charm, and that instinctive tact, born of true sympathy, which forges the bonds of friendship more surely than any superiority of intellect can do. "With his mental antennæ he felt at once that which clever people only realised after long reflection. He thought less with his head than with his heart, and he had the most lovable heart one can imagine."

" He was the person I loved most of all on earth," wrote his son, twenty-five years after the death of his father, and the confession was no afterthought of reminiscence from one whose devotion to mother and sister was always unstinted. Rather was it the expression of a bond of sympathy between two creatures each of whom lived in a world of his own imagining. The marching route which Heinrich Heine found in his cradle was mapped out for him, in so far as the formation of his intellect and character was concerned, by the widely differing personalities of his parents.

In the character of Heinrich Heine the most conflicting traits dwelt side by side as peaceably as they did in the couple at No. 602 Bölkerstrasse. He had reasoning power combined with an instinct for emotion ; the enjoyment of the present with keen anticipation of the future ; an indestructible capacity for illusion, which sprang from his innate optimism and invariably led to confusion of issues ; a shrewd ability to judge both men and circumstances, and, above all, a capacity for plunging into the joys of life whilst still retaining the full vigour of ambition.

It was not merely dissimilarity in his inherited characteristics which was to determine Heinrich Heine's future, however. In the phrase about his destiny being formed in the cradle, he himself must have referred more to the period in which he was born and to his status in a particular class. He was born into a strictly circumscribed caste, whose peculiar position in society bound its members together in unusually close contact. Samson Heine brought up his son to the strict observance of religious customs, for he himself had not travelled so far from unquestioning faith as had the daughter of Gottschalk van Geldern, with her more modern education. In the same year in which his son was born Samson Heine had become President of a newly formed and very pious association—the " Society for the Practice of Humanitarian Actions and for the Recitation of the Psalms." As for the mother, so long as her son remained a child, Betty Heine left his upbringing to her husband.

Two anecdotes of his childhood well illustrate the

atmosphere of strict observance of Jewish articles of faith in which the boy grew up. Once, when asked to help put out a fire on a Saturday, the nine-year-old Harry flatly refused. " I may not, I will not, do it," he said ; " to-day is the Sabbath." But before long the child seems to have found means of interpreting the strict letter of the Commandments to accord with his own desires, for, on another occasion, we find him picking grapes from a vine on the Sabbath. And it is with a piece of sophism that he answers the horrified reproaches of his orthodox playmates : " It is true that I may not pick them with my hands, but the law does not forbid us to bite them off with our teeth and eat them." As the weak authority of his father became undermined the link with tradition slackened and, even in his early years, almost disappeared under the influence of his mother's lack of dogma and her " indulgent Deism."

Even without the contradictory influences of his earlier years, Heine would inevitably have broken away from religious tenets at a later period. This would have led to spiritual conflict in adolescence, and eventually to the security of his own intellectual conception of things ; the price he would have had to pay being determined by the gravity of the crises undergone between the inculcated beliefs of tradition and his own budding power of reasoning. But, as it was, Heinrich Heine learnt to doubt without such growing pains ; he felt no need either to fight for his belief or to overcome it, and in this his situation was similar to that of the youth of to-day. For him an easy readjustment between the contradictions of religion and rationalism replaced the usual intellectual commotion of adolescence. One other experience of his early life helped to force the precocious boy towards an exceptionally early intellectual maturity. The boy attended a Franciscan school the headmaster of which, a certain Schallmeyer, had been a friend of his uncle's, and looked upon Gottschalk van Geldern as having saved his life during a serious illness. Schallmeyer took special interest in young Heine, and allowed him, when only thirteen years old, to attend the upper classes, where all the theories of the free-thinkers came under discussion. " The latest developments can be explained by the earliest beginnings," Heine once wrote about the education he received from Schallmeyer. There he had observed how the venerable priest combined an unprejudiced intellectual pre-eminence with an observance of his priestly duties without hypocrisy. This co-existence of religion with scepticism drove Heine into a far more dangerous attitude for his age than atheism would have been—an attitude of " completely tolerant indifference."

But it was not only in religious matters that the childhood of Heine was influenced by an unusual degree of tolerance, nor was the possibility of a smooth reconciliation between two worlds experienced only in the intellectual sphere. He was born in that brief period when two nations also realised a temporary harmony, during which the frontier barriers separating the two peoples faded for a time from the consciousness of both. Doubtless the child understood little of the new religion of humanity, the echoes of which were wafted across the Rhine from France. But, in a period when an armistice between jarring nationalisms had been so openly declared, it was inevitable that his environment should provide quite other intellectual food in such matters than that absorbed by children at other periods or in other parts of the country. As a result, Heine early developed a tolerance in national affairs which he found difficult to reconcile with later developments.

It was a period in which the French were changing all frontiers, and when " the fixed soul of textbook learning was so altered and confused that the Devil himself would have recognised it no longer." Thanks to this, he entirely escaped the limitation of being able to think only according to rules, which is often acquired with such fatal ease in early days.

Harry Heine came into the world in a Düsseldorf occupied by French troops. His earliest recollection was of the day when the Kurfürst abdicated in the melancholy atmosphere of a funereal morning. He had been a lenient ruler, and his subjects mourned his exodus as much as they feared the arrival of the foreign conquerors who were now to occupy the city, for Düsseldorf was still in those days a fortified place and subject to the fortunes of war. Silently the inhabitants slunk about the streets, or stood in the market-place to read the long proclamation which had been posted up on the Rathaus, by which the late ruler released his subjects from their allegiance. Among the crowd before the notice stood many of the Duke's old soldiers, tears running down their scarred cheeks and mingling with their beards. The atmosphere of grief was so intense that it upset the boy. He returned home early, and cried himself to sleep, dreaming that the world had come to an end.

But the next day the whole town was once more bathed in sunshine and full of the sounds of rejoicing. The lad puzzled over this startling transformation, knowing nothing of the ease with which mass psychology can adapt itself to a political *fait accompli*. On the following morning the streets were gay with trumpeters heralding the march-in of the French troops, and in place of the weeping veterans, the old aldermen with bright new faces stood in front of the Rathaus. Women leaned from every window, and an idle, curious crowd followed the procession of marching troops. Thus an impression of the past he had never really known sank into the child's mind, to be quickly eclipsed by the excitement of the moment. Treitschke writes : " The history that lived in the hearts of the oncoming generation of Rhinelanders began with the French invasion."

The homeland of Harry Heine was now to be officially known as the Principality of Cleve and Berg. It was formed by a decree of Napoleon of March 15th, 1806, and presented to his brother-in-law Joachim Murat. It consisted of the old Prussian Dukedom of Cleve including Wesel, Duisburg, and Emmerich, together with the Bavarian Dukedom of Berg, which comprised Düsseldorf, Solingen, Elberfeld, Mühlheim, and Siegburg.

On the very first day of the French occupation of Düsseldorf, Murat gave the population his assurance that he had " vowed to make his people happy," a promise which he later repeated before the assembled governing bodies. Tired out with excitement, Harry Heine came home that evening to sum up his impressions of the eventful day by saying: "They want to make us happy, so there was no school to-day." It did indeed seem at first as though the new rulers seriously meant to try to content the people.

The inauguration of the laws of 1802 relating to the sale of national domains completely changed the previous serf-like condition of the peasants. In some parts of the Rhineland two-thirds of the land belonged to the aristocracy and the clergy; there were even parishes in which 1,500 out of 2,000 acres were in the possession of one or the other of these two privileged classes. Under the new laws a feverish activity in the disposal of ducal lands and clerical estates began to take place, and this continued until 1814. Shrewd men, well supplied with capital, formed large companies, which purchased the estates, divided them up, and resold them again to the land-hungry small farmers at a profit. "For the first time the abolition of tithes, which had been proclaimed some time before, began to take on real significance for the peasants," writes Perthes, "for they could now cultivate their land in peace and security. The continued high price of corn and the greater mobility of capital brought them in a good deal of ready money. Fortunes grew, and the population increased on the land. The peasants were not merely satisfied, in many districts they became extravagant and luxury-loving. They sat about in the inns, throwing dice for stakes of kronentaler or even gold, and they boasted of their riches."

Nor was it only the peasants who thought that the golden age had come. The Code Napoléon created a new conception of freedom also for the minor aristocracy, the bourgeois, the younger sons, and disinherited daughters. All individuals became equal before the law, there was new regulation of the rights of inheritance, and the right of paternal authority over children who had come of age was abolished. Out of submissive soldiers the new law made honoured citizens, said Johannes von Müller, and, he continued, "However new the many laws may seem, their spirit is an old one ; if they were translated into German, and if the strange foreign names of the officials were replaced by good old German names, people would be astonished to find how Germanic it all is."

Not only were the new laws clear, their application was also impartial. The discipline and sense of justice of the officials, as well as the understanding they showed and the affability of their manner, all acted greatly in favour of the foreign rulers. The establishment of public order was wholeheartedly welcomed by the population ; under the Napoleonic administration this was ensured by the infliction of rigorous punishment for all attempts on the life or goods of law-abiding citizens. After the execution of the notorious Schinderhannes, robbery with violence seemed to cease immediately, and people related with amazement how even a tax-collector now dared to go home at night along a lonely road.

The *gendarmerie* was recruited, almost without exception, from men who commanded respect by sheer force of personality. "The sureness and brevity of their reports astonished the German officials," says Perthes, who certainly cannot be accused of excessive affection for the French. The foreign soldiers also behaved in exemplary fashion. The passage of troops through the country inevitably caused a certain amount of friction, but the presence of soldiers with wages to spend brought an increase of trade to the towns, turnover was speeded up, and luxury trades in particular benefited greatly. The house in the Bölkerstrasse was likewise made aware of these cheerful signs of the new era. Samson Heine became an army purveyor, and the velveteens which were his speciality must have sold well. As a member of the Citizens' Guard he was able to parade the streets of Düsseldorf decked out in a well-fitting uniform, and that, to the light-hearted vanity of such a man, must have made the times seem like one long carnival. It was, in short, a good and well-ordered world in which the child lived. Reduced to the narrow sphere of his existence, this time of convulsion and upheaval on the chess-board of Europe became a period of security ushered in by the unwonted moderation of its legislation and the abolition of social barriers. Probably it was this new social tolerance which made the most marked impression upon the boy's mind, for it touched him at his most sensitive spot—his feeling of kinship with his race.

Aided by the gradual loosening of religious ties, and the peaceful rejection of traditional custom, this feeling of union with the Jewish race increased in the young Heine and remained with him as a realisation of the exclusive place held by his people in society. In this problem too, as also in regard to nationalism, the temporary armistice between two distinctive elements was to form in his mind a wrong impression of the realities of the situation. If he had had to find his own way out of the ghetto, as other gifted Jews had done before him, and if he had had to fight through the difficulties of belonging, at one and the same time, to a racial minority and to a united nation, then he would have retained no illusions as to the limitations set upon those of his racial origin, nor as to the extent of opposition which remained to the assimilation of the Jews into the life of the nation. But the shadow of the ghetto was fading, and it is natural that Jewish children who were born at this period should have mistaken the rosy hues of dawn for the light of an eternal day. Here again Harry Heine had no struggle of his own to pursue ; that also was postponed until later years, when he could no longer adapt himself easily to compromise. He could never forget that a boundless free world had once lain open before him, nor did he ever recover from the loss of that world.

The reflection of history in the tiny mirror of a single life is always difficult to observe. It becomes especially so when the reflection is that thrown upon the mind of a boy still young enough to be influenced by the false perspectives of childhood. Gropingly the young mind seeks to assimilate the meaning of events without the aid of that feeling for proportion which only comes from experience.

But at that time history itself seemed to conspire to that simplification and exaggeration of events which is necessary to the young mind, and inevitably the mighty figure of Napoleon became the hero of all young people in those days. The application of the grand principles of freedom to the everyday affairs of life seemed to find its embodiment in him. It was not until much later, when the passage of years had reduced him to truer proportions, that the champion of the new Equality came to be seen as the vanquisher of the Revolution. In Heine's case the glorified figure of Napoleon rose above a fourteen-year-old boy's horizon. Hero-worship naturally added the glow of legend to a great personality. But, in addition to this, Napoleon's instinct for publicity saw to it that the most refractory of his new subjects should be impressed by his passage. To this end he employed the oldest as well as the most up-to-date methods of stimulating the imagination, and even his flying visit to Düsseldorf left a permanent impression on the minds of the inhabitants.

On the day of his arrival Napoleon allowed himself no sleep until he had fully prepared himself for his first contact with the new environment. Count Beugnot, who governed the Grand Duchy of Berg for the son of Queen Hortense, was subjected to a fusillade of searching questions. Violently, and for hours on end, the great man quarrelled with the unhappy Count, even about financial questions, on which Napoleon was well aware of his own deficiencies. At last the Governor was exhausted by the battle of wits, and dutifully admitted that "the Emperor was better informed concerning the interests of the country than he was himself." The next day Napoleon showed off his newly acquired knowledge before the city council. "Il accable sous l'admiration ces bons Allemands," wrote Count Beugnot, with gentle irony. But the good Germans, who could not guess how the Emperor had obtained his knowledge, were amazed at the extent to which he had mastered the details of their affairs. "As we left the Council Chamber," goes on Beugnot, "Fuchsius said to me, 'I have read much about the Emperor, and have heard still more, but until now I had not met him. He is more than a man—*c'est plus qu'un homme.*'" And Beugnot, remembering the inquisition of the previous night, replied, " You are right, sir, he's a demon." The story came to the ears of Napoleon, who smiled grimly and remarked, " Perhaps. At any rate I kept him on hot coals for long enough."

Young Heine's recollections of these days were not confined to the characteristic picture of the Emperor in his dull grey uniform and famous little hat. He saw him thus as he rode through the Hofgarten, a kindly smile playing over his smooth, pale features, whilst his sunburnt hand quietly patted his horse's back. What most impressed the boy about that incident was the fact that the Emperor dared to ride down the forbidden central path of the Gardens, at the risk of a fine of five thalers.

Another event, however, must have aroused a more gratified excitement amongst the Jewish community. It was an event which demonstrated very practically to the isolated Jewish world the meaning of the new Equality, and it was an example of Napoleon's custom of leaving no stone unturned in his attempt to win over all sections of the population. He summoned to him the representatives " of all religions which are permitted to practise in the Grand Duchy." They stood humbly before him, the rabbi in the centre ; on his right hand, in the absence of the bishop, stood the doyen of the Catholic diocese, and on his left the oldest of the Protestant pastors. For the aged rabbi, whose long white beard flowed down over his black silk robes, the greatest hour of his life had come.

" Sire," proclaimed the rabbi, " the priests of the religions which recognise the same God, preach the same principles, and strive with the same aim, if by different means, to make men virtuous on earth and worthy of a better life in Heaven, come together to render homage to him who, like a new Cyrus, has rebuilt our altars and restored to us the old honour of our cults. They vow to you, sire, to teach their flock the love of your sacred person, the observance of your laws, and the recognition of your good deeds." " All men are brothers before God," came slowly from the lips of the Emperor, almost like a command. " They must love each other and help each other, without regard to the differences of their religions." "All men are brothers before God." The simple sentence, proclaimed so often and so often mechanically, was given a new significance by the practical example of the equal status of the men standing before him. It seemed as if the oldest of men's laws, so buffeted by floods of injustice as to be almost unrecognisable, was here revived with the breath of new life.

Nor was it only spiritual emancipation which the dawn of the new era of fraternity brought to those who had hitherto lived beyond the pale of legal citizenship. In the everyday world of practical opportunities it meant that all doors were now thrown open to the ambitious amongst the Jews, and that they could actually plan their aims higher than even their hopes had hitherto dared to soar. In this practical world Betty Heine felt at home. All the repressed desires and unfulfilled urge for recognition which survived in her, and which had been disappointed as a result of her marriage with the handsome, careless man whom she loved, were now centred in her ambition for her son. The time of boundless opportunity seemed indeed to have come. A friend of her girlhood, the daughter of an iron manufacturer in the district, was now the Duchess of Soult. She wrote letters to the ambitious little woman living her narrow life in the Bölkerstrasse, describing how her husband had won many battles and would soon be given a kingdom. "Ah!" wrote Heine. "My mother dreamt of me wearing golden epaulettes and the most richly embroidered uniforms at the Emperor's Court. For it was to the Emperor's service that she fully intended to dedicate me."

It never entered the head of this fanatic of pedagogy to ask to what extent her son possessed the qualifications for such a future. She was convinced that talent and quickness of mind could be trained to whatever goal was desired. This woman, who was good sense itself in all other matters, felt that she had done her duty towards her son's education if only she prevented him from wasting his intellectual capabilities in romantic dreaming. To this end she snatched all books of fiction from him, kept him from going to the theatre, and strictly controlled his circle of acquaintances. Any form of intellectual stimulation which was allowed to reach him must first have passed through the sieve of her sober mind.

The study of geometry and statics, of hydrostatics and hydraulics, was made to replace things of the imagination or poetic flights. The fact that scientific study was foreign to his temperament, and slipped from his mind like water from a duck's back, mattered less than that hours of concentrated effort were lost to him. But by far the most important of all was the fact that, by her exaggerated hopes for the boy's future, Betty Heine brought an element of instability into his character which proved disastrous in later life. She did not realise that by forcing his mind into conflicting desires she made herself largely responsible for that capacity for illusion which helped so much to form his zigzag path through life.

Time, education, and his own temperament conspired to separate Heine's boyhood into two parts. Mother and son dreamt of different things—the mother of an improbable future for which she thought she was preparing the lad by a commonplace daily existence, and the boy of a past which seemed to him a marvellous escape from his barren world of tutelage. Every child has his own secret island of refuge from the uncomprehending interference of adults. Harry found his world of make-believe in the attic of the home of his strange old uncle, Simon van Geldern. The old man lived in the house called "Noah's Ark," which had belonged to his father. There he spent his days writing endless articles for political papers and obscure magazines. The attic, as Heine later described it, was "a hospital for incurable household effects, and an asylum for old furniture." There the boy played with his grandfather's rusty ornamental daggers, with the map-rolls and astronomical charts, and the old flute with faded pink ribbon which had belonged to his mother. Or he would rummage in the chests where the old books were kept which had been cleared out of his grandfather's library—tomes on medicine and philosophy, and exciting works on occult science.

One day as he played amongst the litter he came across a real treasure, the diaries of his great-uncle, Simon van Geldern, known in the family as "the Oriental." In the dawning imagination of the youngster this ancestor now came to take the place of the heroes of fiction. He had been an adventurer who had travelled in the East, and had become the sheik of a bedouin tribe. There in the desert he had amassed a fortune as a robber chief, and after his return to Europe had still gone about in rich oriental robes, seeking to exploit the credulous of his time, like a small-scale Cagliostro. The books themselves were scrawled in Syrian, Coptic, or Arabic characters, but in the margins were scattered notes in French. From these notes, helped out by such tales of hearsay as he could coax from his unwilling family, a legendary figure came to take shape in the boy's mind. The thrill of personal discovery, and the realisation of kinship with the old robber, added to the mysterious magic of the Orient and enabled the lad to indulge in one of those games of identification with his hero which are common to all imaginative youngsters.

Such frivolities would have found little sympathy with his mother, but to his father Harry confided that he felt himself to be his dead ancestor, who was reincarnated in him. His father smiled indulgently, and said that he only hoped the great-uncle had not signed any bills which could be presented to him for payment some time.

In later years the poet wrote of his life at this time that it was "like a big newspaper, the upper portion of which contained the news of the day, all the items of topical interest, whilst in the lower half of the page there was a succession of tales about the romantic past interspersed with fantastic dreams."

Nevertheless this inclination to play with the impossible, which was so often to throw him off the track in later life, was not due solely to his dabbling in an imaginary past. To at least as great an extent it originated in the actual occurrences of his early years. In the upper half of the newspaper, as he called it, there occurred events scarcely less fantastic than those of the wildest novel.

In the poet's memoirs of his childhood there is no mention of one matter which, at the time, caused no little commotion in the family circle. This was the rumour of a legacy of several million gulden, which arose in 1809, and which kept the whole family on tenterhooks for years. By the receipt of a letter from Nymwegen, Betty Heine learnt that the fortune of the millionaire Moses Adolphus van Bueren, who had died in London, was being claimed by the Dutch family Bock, a branch of the German family of the same name. Since Gottschalk van Geldern had married Sarah, the daughter of Pinchas Bock of Siegburg, the descendants of the van Gelderns felt that they were entitled to the vast fortune. The letters exchanged between the heirs presumptive and their legal advisers throw more light on the atmosphere in which young Heine grew up than any contemporary account could do.

Heine's uncle, Simon van Geldern, had been educated in a Jesuit college, and, according to his nephew, expressed himself "in that stilted, formal fashion which is taught in Jesuit colleges, where Latin is the chief language." Nevertheless, his letters were strongly coloured by the Jewish jargon of the time. "Despite the fact that I write but seldom, I often think of you and seek to safeguard your interests," writes Simon van Geldern to his "highly respected uncle, Pinchas Bock at Siegburg." "In proof of this take note of the news with which I hasten to acquaint you. As you will see from the enclosed missive, the family may expect a large legacy." Simon proposes that his uncle should accompany him to Amsterdam. Betty Heine confirms her brother's story; "they say that the legacy amounts to thirteen million florins—I repeat thirteen million. A man from here, who was in Amsterdam last week, swears it is true." And her sister Chana adds a humorous note to the collective letter by asking, "What will happen when it comes to dividing the money?" The two families Bock and van Geldern made desperate efforts to prove their relationship to the Bocks of Holland, even to the extent of risking their money in the doubtful business. Samson Heine plunged in with that naïve delight which every fresh event aroused in him, and at length he persuaded the cautious cousin from Siegburg to accompany him to Amsterdam. " That my dear husband should leave his business here in order to discuss the matter with you, and fulfil the necessary formalities, shows that the affair of the legacy is serious," wrote Betty Heine, still under illusions as to the business capacity of her fascinating husband.

The mirage of fortune seemed to be about to materialise. In August 1809 Samson Heine wrote to the lawyer in Amsterdam who was charged with the estate : " I shall be obliged if you will inform me of what has transpired and whether the matter has now reached the point where I may soon expect to receive the benefits of my just claim to the inheritance of the deceased." But the just claim was non-suited, and the resulting disappointment in the Bölkerstrasse proved to be only the prelude to many others, which unfortunately proved to be the normal result of Samson Heine's commercial activities.

Perhaps it is because of those far-off years, shot through with the hope of fabulous wealth, that there arose in the poet the fatal habit which we find recurring so often throughout his life, the expectation of a miracle, of some help from outside, the constant waiting for the intervention of some *deus ex machina*, which later on was to take the form of his rich uncle, Salomon Heine.

The boy's first contacts with life were all the more difficult because he had been raised in an atmosphere of affection and adulation. He was very wide-awake as a little boy. His figure and his features were regular. His large eyes and perfectly formed mouth, the peculiarly beautiful shade of the fair hair which framed the perfect oval of his face, were combined with vivacity of manner and ease of self-expression. All these things helped to make him the idol of the family circle. The very austerity of his mother was due to her boundless faith in his ability ; she never hesitated to show that he was the favourite, and not one of his brothers, Max or Gustav. As for his younger sister Charlotte, she of course became his adoring slave, like all little girls with a clever elder brother. To this plethora of devotion was added the pride of aunts and great-aunts, who, with that partiality peculiar to the higher aristocracy—and to Israel—bestowed their favours on the male heir, on him who would recite the benediction of the dead.

Thus there was formed in the child's mind the conviction that he was an exceptional personality, destined for great things. But no sooner was he launched into the battle than he learnt the danger of being original, and came to recognise the hostility of his fellows to all that does not conform to the low average.

He received his first lesson in such matters through his foreign name, Harry, given to him by his father in remembrance of an English business acquaintance. As soon as attendance at school threw him amongst other children possessing ordinary names, his own became a pretext for the usual cruelties of youngsters. Pure chance gave the young barbarians a welcome opportunity—a chance which, to do him justice, Heine's father may be pardoned for not having foreseen. It happened that a rag-and-bone man of Düsseldorf, in his efforts to encourage his donkey, used a cry which came forth in a sound not unlike " Harry." What his schoolmates made of this coincidence may be imagined ; suffice it to say that the unhappy parody on his name pursued him relentlessly throughout his career. The best years of his young life were poisoned by what he himself called " the most painful hurt of his childhood." So unhappy did the recollection of it make him that a whole life of suffering and of triumphs did not succeed in effacing it. As he lay on his deathbed, immured in the silence of his room, the famous poet thought to hear again the mocking cry which had poisoned his boyhood. " It is only now, when I am no longer of the living, when all vanity of this world is dead within me, that I can speak of it without bitterness."

He had inherited the same need for affection and flattery which he notes in his father, and which he himself described as that of a child begging his mother to flatter him—to flatter him more than enough, even. This inherited tendency, deepened by his upbringing, made it impossible for him to live unless surrounded by flattery. And his sensitiveness exaggerated every interference with this crying need of his being. He was not of those born fighters whose strength is increased by the obstacles which they encounter. Cradled in affection and admiration, he either lay defenceless when opposed by spite or indifference, or he would plunge into paroxysms of hatred and wild schemes of revenge.

It was this tenderness of susceptibility which led him early to seek in the admiration of women its most easily attained satisfaction. In later years too he frequently soothed his acute susceptibility by consorting with that class of women which is most prodigal in the bestowal of its flattery. A precocious sexual instinct is not uncommon amongst Jewish boys, and Harry Heine was no exception in this respect. It seems, too, that he must have experienced that sexual impulse which exists before puberty and is now recognised by psycho-analysts, for there is evidence in one of his last poems, "Citronia," that even at the age of six vague erotic desires were stirring in the child's mind.

Heine himself has described in his Memoirs the awakening of his regard for the other sex. The story, however, is placed in a setting of such wild romanticism that its truth must be doubted. It is the tale of "red-haired Josepha," the executioner's daughter, an apparition surprising enough in the bourgeois world of Harry Heine's Düsseldorf, even without the dramatic description he gives of the girl. Her clothes clung to her long thin body, her face of transparent pallor was framed in a mass of the deepest red hair, which she drew together under her chin, so that her white face seemed to float in waves of blood, like the head of a beheaded person. The whole account of this first love-affair is in similar strain, and appears rather to resemble the early efforts of a romantic novelist than the first adventure of a Don Juan.

There are secret visits at night to the house of an old witch, Josepha's aunt, mixed up with references to the paraphernalia of superstition, and a vision of the girl standing with her father's shining sword in her hands. Except for Heine's own account in the Memoirs no trace whatever has been found of Josepha, or of any daughter of an executioner in the neighbourhood, although the local archives have been ransacked at various times by painstaking biographers. It seems indeed to the highest degree improbable that the boy of sixteen could have concealed from the sharp eyes of Betty Heine a liaison with the niece of a witch.

For the origin of the pale, flower-like face in its sea of red hair we must search rather in the poet's mind than in the parish records. Josepha is a creation of that vague borderland between the real and the imaginary, where dwell the creatures born half of book memories and half of fleeting moments of true emotion which pass too swiftly to be captured in their entirety.

Other feminine figures float through the poet's Memoirs which also seem to belong to that border-country of dreams. There is the beautiful but foolish Gertrude, the beautiful, gentle Catherine, and the beautiful and pious Hedviga.

The truth is that Heine throughout his life jealously guarded the real secrets of his early passions. The poet who sang most eloquently of love is, with few exceptions, the poet who is most careful to hide the identity of those to whom his lyrics are addressed. It would seem that he thought to generalise the character of his sentiments the more by veiling the actual sources of his inspiration. The most indiscreet of men where hate is concerned, he is in love the most secretive. The very way in which he speaks of the objects of his passion seems intended to make us doubt of their existence. Whereas, without a moment's hesitation, he delivers to posterity every detail of his early enemies, down even to their names—indeed of all his enemies, early or late—the least little incidents of his experiences in love are locked in silence.

But there can be little doubt that it was some real and

early love-affair, sprung from the precocity of his desires, which awoke the urge for self-expression in the immature boy, and thereby vaguely indicated his vocation as a poet.

One part of his " Dream Pictures " is based on the last years he spent at Düsseldorf, and on that first experience of an unhappy passion which bears the mysterious sign of Josepha. It is romantic poetry with all its attendant features —ghosts, churchyards, lost souls, evil temptation, and so on— expressed in the language of the period by a Heine still in his late teens. In later editions these poems were included in the larger collection as *Sorrows of Youth.* What is there expressed is only the vague, general unhappiness of youth with its intolerable surcharge of love ; but, despite the banal theme and borrowed metaphors, the extraordinary intensity of feeling clearly bears the mark of the later Heine. One note recurs throughout, and it is the note which eventually becomes the *leit-motif* of all his work :

Narren waren wir im Leben
Und mit toller Wut ergeben
Einer tollen Liebesbrunst.

" We were mad, and we madly surrendered to a mad passion."

But the hour for his real poetical work had not yet struck. Meantime great historical events were to sweep away the worldly ambitions of young Heine. Napoleon's defeat on the Beresina brusquely reduced the range of opportunity which lay open to the sons of the middle-class Jews of the Bölkerstrasse. Nevertheless his mother, that tireless dreamer in the field of realism, merely changed her aim. The rising star of Rothschild replaced in her mind the setting sun of Napoleon. Betty Heine promptly substituted a faith in the power of money for her late faith in political power. " My mother declared that the time had come when an outstanding brain could bring gigantic schemes to fruition in the sphere of business, and that by this means a man could raise himself to the very pinnacle of worldly power." The success of her husband's brothers seemed clear proof of her theory. The sons of Heymann Heine of Bückeburg, " the little Jew with the big beard," had become widely scattered. The eldest was established in Bordeaux, where he founded a dynasty of famous French bankers ; another brother, Salomon Heine, was amassing a huge fortune in Hamburg.

With the same disregard for her son's qualifications which she had previously shown, Betty Heine now sought to turn Harry into a business man. He was despatched forthwith to the technical school at Vahrenkampf. But the " apprentice-millionaire " showed no more aptitude for commerce than he had done for science. He wasted his time in such frivolous occupations as the translating of Homer and Ovid into Yiddish. He wrote satirical verse—schoolboyish amusements which are the only authentic examples we have of the poetry he wrote during this period. Then he arrives at the threshold of manhood, troubled and hesitant, stripped of all that life had bestowed upon him or had taught him. Vast events were taking place around him, but, since he understood nothing of them, since he discerned neither their causes nor their aims, he began to adopt an attitude of prejudice with regard to current happenings ; an attitude of indecision couched in terms of mockery of which he was never able to rid himself.

And, moreover, the years which followed upon the collapse of French hegemony drew him into the whirlpool of nationalism. Such changed conditions called for a serious effort of mental adjustment. At the same time, while a world fell all in ruins about him, he threw himself body and soul into a personal adventure, his first great love-affair. Everything in his character is still indecisive and malleable, but a first flash of his poetic genius shows already in these few lines :

Die Engel, die nennen es Himmelsfreud'
Die Teufel, die nennen es Höllenleid,
Die Menschen, die nennen es Liebe.[1]

[1] " Angels call it heavenly joy,
Hell proclaims it torture,
But men know it as love."

CHAPTER II

THE CASTLE OF AFFRONT

Da gab es nirgends eine Staette
Wo nicht mein Herz gekraenket ward
Wo nicht mein Aug' geweinet haette.
(" Affrontenburg ")

FROM TIME TO TIME, though at rather long intervals, Harry Heine was invited to visit his uncle, Salomon Heine, at his château at Rainville. Harry was just nineteen years old, straight from a middle-class environment which had never known luxury and was soon to experience actual want. He felt very conscious of being the poor relation.

The old château, with its castellated towers, stands on a hill overlooking the Elbe. In the grounds are marble statues, and heavy stone sphinxes, from whose mouths water once gushed, guard the approaches. Beyond the gardens, great avenues of grand old trees lead down to where a wide terrace gives a magnificent view towards the sea.

Salomon Heine spent the greater part of the year in this old château. The lofty towers and noble architecture seemed to him to provide the most tangible evidence of wealth and position, even though his Hamburg mansion was in the most fashionable part of the city, the Jungfernstieg, a quarter in which Jews were nominally forbidden to reside.

The family in Düsseldorf appreciated the interest which Salomon showed in their eldest son's career as the best possible augury for the future. The rebuffs which Harry had up till then experienced, however, argued ill for his ability in commercial matters. Profiting by a visit he was obliged to make to Frankfurt Fair in 1815, Samson Heine had taken his eldest son there to be apprenticed to a banker friend. But the only accomplishment Harry had retained after his wasted years at the commercial school was the ability to write a good hand. He must indeed have shown an astonishing ineptitude for the work to make the banker Rindskopff pack him off home after only a short three-weeks' trial. The next effort had been as an apprentice in a large grocery store, where he spent his time perched on a high stool dreaming over the account-books, and with satisfaction sniffing the spiced and scented odours which came from the piled merchandise. After a month he was informed that his apprenticeship was over, and he promptly returned home, happy as an escaped prisoner.

After the fall of Napoleon, Germany sank into a severe economic crisis, and the family in the Bölkerstrasse felt the whole brunt of it. Samson Heine had always been the victim of circumstances ; he possessed neither the character nor the imagination necessary to adapt himself to the narrowed conditions of German economic life after the wars of liberation. In addition his health was not good. With the family income dwindling and the education of two younger sons to be paid for, it became an urgent necessity for the eldest boy to earn his own living. As for Harry himself, he had his own reasons for wanting to go and live in Hamburg ; it is even possible that his ignominious failure to make good at Frankfurt had partly been a pretence so as to secure that end. However that may be, he arrived in Hamburg, thrilled and happy, and with no presentiment that he was running to meet the great misfortune of his whole life—his dependence in material matters upon Salomon Heine. Towards the end of his life the poet spoke of the old millionaire as his *fatum*, but at this early stage the young man could not foresee that the Jewish clannishness which had prompted his uncle to help a young nephew would one day be the cause of his bitterest suffering, so that the generosity of Salomon Heine would poison his life with each successive year, until it became a demoralising force which changed or impeded all his best impulses. His uncle, on the other hand, came to consider himself as a long-suffering benefactor who reaped nothing but ingratitude. The suspicion never entered his mind that even after his death he would be considered his nephew's worst enemy.

Salomon was a self-made business man. He owed his wealth and his influence alike entirely to his own shrewd judgment and his indomitable perserverance. He had started in Hamburg without a penny, and he knew every street in the city from having toiled up and down delivering bills from house to house, often until he was ready to drop with fatigue. In 1816, when Harry Heine came into his life, Salomon was already governor of the bank Heine & Heckscher. Two years later he bought out his partner and became sole proprietor. In character he was a mixture of hardness and generosity, of egotism and sentimentality not uncommon amongst parvenus, and to these traits was added the choleric disposition of the Heine family, all of whom were subject to fits of sudden passion followed by no less sudden appeasement. He possessed nothing of the fascination and good looks of his younger brother Samson. " I have never been able to claim good looks," he once wrote in his uncultivated German under a photograph which he gave to his nephew. His features were hard, with eyes set wide apart, a prominent nose over a broad, thin-lipped mouth and obstinate chin, and he had the searching look of the money-grubber. The kindness of heart which he certainly possessed was hidden under an armour of distrust and suspicion formed by the hard struggle of his early days, and also under the domineering manner which came from his rapid success.

Young Harry instinctively felt in this man, still only in his late forties, the maturity of great force of character hardened by struggle. Through all the crudities of his speech and the inelegance of his manner there shone an original personality ; he even recognised certain characteristics in common with himself : " We have the same obstinate daring, the same bottomless capacity for affection, and the same latent strain of madness," he wrote many years later. Salomon Heine could not, as a Jew, become a citizen of the Free City of Hamburg. But he received at his house the notabilities of the town and all the distinguished foreigners who passed through. In addition to his wealth he had a reputation for great generosity and straight dealing, and he gave liberally to all religious philanthrophic works. It was in this atmosphere that Harry Heine made his début in society life.

Although the owner of Rainville was somewhat of a rough diamond, the interior decoration and furnishing of the château did not in the least show that lack of taste which we are accustomed to associate with great riches newly acquired. Luxury was not there for mere display ; it simply found a natural setting. The great actress, Therese Devrient, wrote after her first visit that " the whole style of the place was so harmonious that at first one did not realise its beauty." In these great *salons* Harry met " the whole mob of the diplomatic world, millionaires, and senators famous for their wisdom," and on one occasion he even encountered Field Marshal Blücher, whose deep voice and loud, jolly laughter called echoes from the panelled walls.

Salomon Heine took no pains at all to adapt himself to the ways of the society into which he had pushed with such ease. His position was assured, and society accepted him as he was. He had no hesitation in admitting his humble origin ; on the contrary, his pride in his attainments led him rather to accentuate the difference between his modest past and his resplendent present. Fundamentally he despised all that did not help towards success in life, and therefore he was not ashamed to admit his ignorance in all other matters. He possessed to the full the arrogance of the self-made man who only recognises as valuable such qualities as can be transformed into cash. And, like many another, he was firmly persuaded that those values which intellectuals place higher than all others were only invented to conceal weakness of character and indolence of mind.

With such views, it was not unnatural that his nephew came to be regarded with a mixture of contempt and pity. After a month or two he even regretted taking into his bank this incompetent young fellow who would never do anything in life. For his own children it was different. After all, it was largely for them that he toiled ; they were the natural heirs to his fortune, and therefore a dreamy eye and a total incapacity for business were luxuries which they could afford to allow themselves. But this penniless lad was in much the same plight as he himself had been ; he should do as he had done, pull himself together, show initiative, and take an interest in his future ! Instead of which, he merely ambled about the office day-dreaming.

This, in all conscience, was irritating enough to the banker, but the young man's air of disdain, which was so ill seconded by his awkwardness and general shyness, was a thousand times worse. Not only was there a complete absence of that becoming servility which Salomon Heine expected from the poor relations and other hangers-on who sat at his board, but, when disturbed from his dreaming, the boy had a disconcertingly ironical way of looking at people and a rather aggressive smile. The two temperaments were wholly incompatible, and Salomon never had the slightest glimmer of understanding for his nephew, nor did he ever see in him anything more than a young fellow who had failed completely as a business man. Even many years later, when the famous poet Heinrich Heine had attained the height of celebrity, Salomon Heine would shake his head disapprovingly and say, " If the boy had only learned something he would not be driven to writing books."

At the time Harry Heine came to Hamburg his haughty reserve and superior airs were nothing more than an instinctive defence against his own feeling of helplessness. He was acutely aware of his position as the poverty-stricken nephew, allowed into the family circle on sufferance and out of racial solidarity, and at the same time being made to feel the gulf that separated him from his cousins. Whilst he is full of resentment, other visitors and strangers to the house envy him his relationship with " the great and wealthy Heine." It was during this period of humiliating experiences that he fell a victim to his first violent love-affair.

Harry was seventeen when he met the eldest of his cousins, Amalie—or Molly, as they called her—during one of his uncle's visits to Düsseldorf. The girl was then just fourteen, and in many ways they were alike. Both were of a delicate, fair type, with regular features and a high-pitched, rather metallic voice. In addition, the boy probably sensed the same early maturity in the young girl which he himself possessed. In any case, he built up a whole romance on this first fleeting encounter, and, during the two years which followed, his love for her took such hold of him that the imprint never faded from his mind.

"A golden star draws me northwards," he wrote in a poem, towards the end of 1816, when his parents had decided to send him to Hamburg. At the moment of his arrival Amalie was away from home. On her return, when the long and ardently awaited meeting took place, her cousin realised with a shock that his hopes had deceived him. During the two years in which he had been dreaming of her, Molly had forgotten his existence. She had grown up, become a true daughter of her father, and, as such, fully conscious of her social position. She was coldly polite but unapproachable. Her fascinating bluish-green eyes glanced at him from under their arched brows and met his challenging gaze with faint surprise and something like disdain. The rather long aquiline nose accentuated her haughty manner, and her thin, firm mouth would have been forbiddingly cold but for an occasional fleeting smile, which Heine likened to "the tail of a disappearing lizard." It was a face which had not yet made up its mind whether to be distant and reserved, or vivacious and seductive, and therefore tried both expressions with disturbing frequency. Molly well knew the effect she had upon her cousin, but the knowledge meant nothing to her. Harry was for her just a poor relation, something half way between a human being and a piece of the furniture. She used him as she used her mirror—to reassure herself of her charms. She herself felt in no danger, for she possessed all her father's proud assurance, the same virile character, and the same calculating temperament which kept her normally affectionate nature well under control.

The life she led corresponded with her position as daughter of the house. She felt at home amidst all the luxury, and knew how to shine in brilliant company. Harry, on the other hand, fresh from the middle-class environment of his own home, felt clumsy and out of place in his uncle's mansion. " Everything that is done here is so stiff and formal," he wrote plaintively to a friend, and, with a characteristic touch of mingled pride and humility he added, " The independent poet is often guilty of sinning against etiquette." It is more than likely that it was this wretched experience of society which sowed the seeds of bitterness which later coloured so much of his work, alienated his friends, and turned opponents into mortal enemies. In his uncle's *salons* the unhappy boy was left alone to struggle with his awkwardness ; he was ignored when he was not used as the butt of his cousins' raillery. One person alone showed him occasional sympathy—Betty Heine, his warm-hearted but vaguely preoccupied aunt.

In such surroundings Amalie was more unattainable than when distance had separated them. Harry sought refuge in correspondence with Christian Sethe, a friend from his Düsseldorf days. The letters show clearly the agony of mind of which the sensitive and precocious boy was capable. Through page after page he pours out his heart in terms which vary between touching sincerity and literary affectation. " To spend years far from her sight, with passion for her tearing at one's entrails, that is the torment of the damned. But to be near her and yet still have to languish for her company, craving it the while as a benediction from heaven, and . . . and . . . ah ! Christian, it would force curses against God from the purest and most pious soul on earth." " She does not love me," he writes another time. " One must murmur this ' not ' softly, very softly. In the words ' She loves ' me is hidden the paradise of eternal life. That other little word contains the whole of Hell, which is also eternal."

Harry has sense enough to see in the first few weeks that

she does not love him. Nevertheless, the magic of her charm continues to hold him under its spell. It is a faculty of illusion common in one of his years, consisting partly of the urge to love but caused chiefly, perhaps, by the coquetry of the girl herself. Amalie gave him no peace and used her mirror recklessly, one moment smiling upon him, the next mocking him heartlessly. If she bestowed upon him a lock of her hair or a light kiss, the gift would be followed at once by retreat into an icy reserve. One must see in Heine's frantic struggle to make Amalie love him more than just a young man's efforts to woo the heart of a girl. Unconsciously, he felt her to be symbolic of all that he desired most in life—acceptance by the society which spurned him, and, even more, the attainment of a regular, ordered existence, which he instinctively felt was beyond the reach of his unaided efforts. The turmoil of all this, added to a passion which he felt with the vehemence of his twenty years, left marks upon his mind and character so indelible that their effects can be distinctly seen throughout his life.

In the midst of this fever of perturbation there came another blow, which, added to the first, made all seem poison. His uncle pronounced him inept and incompetent in the work he had been given. A failure everywhere, he resigned himself to defeat, and gave up all attempt to force a passage to success.

Germany at this time was a prey to a fever of awakening national consciousness, and a tremor of indignation spread through the country at the recollection of the recent foreign domination. During the French occupation there had been two Germanys, one of which, the Rhineland, together with the kingdoms and principalities of the south, had managed to adapt itself comfortably to the rule of the foreigners. The lower classes there, in particular, were better off under it than they had been under the old feudal system. But in Prussia throughout this period there had still smouldered the spark of national pride lit by Frederick the Great. These Prussian irredentists had everywhere been active, inciting peaceful districts to revolt, as in the case of the insurrection led by Schill. After the defeat of Napoleon these elements naturally won over the entire country. And, as usual, the vehemence of national feeling and hatred of the French was strongest amongst those very sections of the population which had most easily accepted the foreign rule. The fires of nationalism burnt most fiercely where the disgrace of past dealings with the enemy most needed purifying. As Treitschke put it : " It was fatal to our political life that the idea of our national unity should not have ripened slowly through the centuries, as in France, but should have been suddenly and violently aroused after a long sleep."

The older generations, for whom the French occupation had been but an interlude, experienced little difficulty in erasing the period from their memories and returning to things as they had been. But those who, like Heine, had been born under the foreign regime, and who therefore had no other past to revive, could only base their experience on that which their own years had brought them.

Nevertheless, the impulse was so fierce that it swept all before it. An entire people became drunk with the spirit of national independence, and found in it a spiritual and moral unity which they had hitherto never known. A new type of heroism was born that affected to despise prosperity and material well-being. The lives of individuals must be sunk in the destiny of the collective whole ; the individual alone is nothing, the nation is all. It was the youth of the country above all that flung itself headlong into this delirium of idealism.

For the rationalist, Betty Heine, this clamour in favour of a principle did not fall on deaf ears. But her practical nature drew from it a lesson which her maternal instinct adapted. Since Napoleon could no longer supply a ladder in the social scale for her son, she must look elsewhere. The fervour of patriotism seized her, too, and she remembered that she was descended from several generations of Jews for whom Germany had been a home. But Samson Heine, for once the more far-sighted of the two, shook his fair head at the idea of the return of the old taskmasters. He thought with foreboding of his own affairs and of those of his co-religionists. The promises of the restored rulers to maintain the conditions granted to the Jews by the French inspired him with no confidence. He feared, too, the impending economic crisis and the re-establishment of frontier barriers. His face bore witness to his unwonted anxiety, and when he heard people uttering the now customary curses on "the Corsican brute," he was apt to murmur, "Ah! yes, Napoleon, I could wish we had him here again."

The son, however, followed the mother, and was carried away by the enthusiasm of the younger generation for the new discipline and the shouted words of command. Heine was just eighteen years old, and felt deeply stirred by the note of patriotism to which a whole people was thrilling. In 1815 he tried to enlist as a volunteer with the other graduates of his school in Düsseldorf. But his sight was not good enough and he was refused. The war, in any case, was in its last stages, and only the strongest were being passed. Failing in this satisfaction, he indulged at second hand in the stimulation of heroism and shared the contagion of melodrama with one of the recruits, Joseph Neunzig, the son of a Jewish baker of the Bölkerstrasse whom he had known since childhood.

Harry, indeed, possessed nothing to enable him to withstand the current infection. All that he had learnt, or had come to believe during the years of his adolescence, had crumbled to dust before his eyes. All that he had felt to be true, to be good, to be worth having, became useless, or worse than useless, in this exciting period of national revival. Emptied of all that he had been, he became for the moment a mere reflection of the period through which he was living.

The first result of this wholesale wiping out of his immediate past was an overwhelming desire to believe in something else. There was a vacuum to fill, and for Heine, as for all the young folk of his generation, the new truths which were now proclaimed became a dogma, and the enthusiasm which they aroused a religion. It was a creed whose articles of faith were as ill defined as were the objects of the religion itself. Reactionary in origin, the faith became of necessity one of negation and riveted attention upon the necessity of opposing the principles of the previous epoch. Since it had been in the name of progress that the conqueror had occupied German soil, the nationalist movement inevitably harked back to the ideals of the past. Since the French invaders had marched under the banner of liberty, that alone sufficed to condemn the humanitarian ideas which they had brought with them.

But the rapidity of developments left no time for the careful elaboration of a new system of ideas. The ideal behind the wave of nationalism was as vague and old-fashioned as the French scheme of things had been precise and dangerously adapted to the needs of the day. Nevertheless, it was necessary by some means to disarm the criticism which would inevitably arise. To go back only a short way was dangerous ; in the immediate past there had been much which would fail of appeal for the future. The past within living memory must, therefore, be avoided ; must, indeed, be denounced. After all, it had been a period of national disunion, and therefore detestable to all good patriots ; a prosaic, unromantic period too, worthy of the contempt of all poets. Back then, became the cry, to the heroic age of the far-distant past, remote from human memory and therefore safe from false prophets and mean comparisons. With this cry on their lips the *élite* of Germany marched back to the Middle Ages, leading the German nation, like sheep, in search of the German soul.

Treitschke wrote of this period that " enthusiasm was inflamed by vague historical images and the people became intoxicated with the idea of a mighty Fatherland in the clouds which, somehow or other, would re-create the splendour of the Ottos and the Hohenstaufens." And, he continues maliciously : " Amateurishness predominated. The word German became synonymous with mediæval. The decisive periods of mediæval culture were indiscriminately mingled. These zealous patriots forgot that it had been the

French they so abhorred who had set the tone and created the culture of the Age of Chivalry." The aim of this cult of the past was not merely to evoke hatred of a conqueror who had claimed the monopoly of progressive ideas, and, with it, the right to form the future of other peoples. There was also in it a belief which the Germans have held consistently, and more or less consciously, in all their spiritual crises—that their racial history is a sort of magnetic charm which can awake and galvanise the strength of the nation. This appeal to the past is believed to be the surest means of attaining to national unity, a method far superior to any appeal to the future for uniting the classes and welding divergent elements and differing aims into one harmonious whole.

This moral legacy from the wars of liberation became the purpose of the new generation. In order to restore the national soul to Germany it is, so the argument ran, first necessary to revive the qualities which have been traitorously sapped by the enemy. That the nation should not have resisted invasion, and that it should have supported so long the domination of the foreigner, is shown as proof that it was riddled with corruption and physical decadence. It follows naturally that the first commandment of the revivalists should concern the education of the young—the physical culture of the body must prepare the regeneration of the mind. A man appeared who formed a doctrine from the confusion of the current desires and thereby became the prophet of the hour. Vater Jahn, a peasant from the Priegnitz, a long-haired giant whose hair had whitened in a day over the defeat of Jena, captured the imagination of the young generation by means of his rough vehemence, his fanatical hatred of the French, and his eloquent—if arbitrary—appeals to the Glorious German Past. Uneducated but impassioned, he unearthed from this past the long-dead bones of Teutonism and established a place for himself in history by his doctrine of *Volkstum*—a word as untranslatable as the conception itself is incomprehensible, but which nevertheless is destined to reappear whenever the German nation is shaken by one of its periodic paroxysms of nationalism. It was this Jahn who first proclaimed that a people without arms is a people without honour, a notion now enshrined in the German language in the proverb "Wehrlos, ehrlos." The man's influence on the ignorant and weak-willed was magnetic. The very puerility of his programme was its best defence, for reason could at no point come to grips with it, and it was proclaimed with a vehemence which brooked no reply. Jahn possessed that form of oratorical genius which seems to transform the dullest platitude uttered into a vision inspired from on high. He spoke the language of the people ; nothing that he said was beyond the understanding of the most uneducated ; his words and clichés, tirelessly repeated, sank into the minds of the masses as surely as a nail is driven into wood by the repeated blows of a hammer.

He was obsessed by his mission ; his hatred was a sacred passion and his faith was invulnerable, for it was never embarrassed by considerations of feasibility. Jahn was a primitive creature born to be the conduit-pipe of one of those sudden, mad floods of popular sentiment. In times such as then prevailed, when the German nature was seeking to regain its element after wandering too far towards the civilisation of the West, such violent appeals to the deepest instincts of the race naturally raised such a creature as Jahn to the level of a national saint. He himself believed that he was destined to be the moral regenerator of his country ; he boasted of having given it *Ertüchtigung*, a spiritual weapon, by cultivating the physical strength of its youth. His famous gymnastic association, the "Gymnastic Movement," grouped round him immense numbers of exuberant young people, who enthusiastically accepted the strict discipline he imposed. He was followed as a prophet by a veritable army of youngsters, all in a kind of uniform of grey cloth with open necks, and wearing their hair long. When Jahn led his followers to Breslau for the first time, half the population of the city turned out to meet him ; for hours the streets resounded to the tramp of the young heroes, as they marched under the admiring gaze of the wondering citizens. The thoughts they awakened were similar to the uniforms and actions. It was the triumph of brawn over brain, aroused by one who was teaching his followers that brutality was a Teutonic virtue. Not a few parents who hesitated to send their sons to the training-camps were finally persuaded to do so in order to protect them from the savage bullying of their school-mates. To the mystical attraction of the herd was added an intense propaganda, intimidation and spying to both. Paragraph seven of the gymnastic regulation required each " Gymnast " to " report immediately to his superior any attitude of hostility towards the Movement, in order that the individual in question may in due time be punished." And as cement for this new-found unity there could, of course, be nothing better than hatred of the foreigner. A deputy of the time demanded that, in order to intensify their nationalism, journeys abroad should be forbidden to Germans. But Father Jahn found such mild measures absurdly inadequate. He had at first proposed the erection of a Chinese Wall round Germany, in order that all communication with the plague-spot of France should be cut off. But he soon found a more attractive solution. He demanded that a great forest should be planted along the frontier, an impenetrable jungle bristling with rocks and criss-crossed with precipices, into which no Frenchman, nor any German traitor seeking to journey abroad, would dare to venture. To make assurance doubly sure, he suggested that starving wild beasts should be turned loose in the forest. At this period nothing seemed strong enough to express the profound anxiety of the anarchic German mind !

The minor poets of the day hastened to acclaim Jahn as the only true apostle of the Holy German Empire. The Universities of Jena and Kiel bestowed upon him the degree of doctor *honoris causa,* solemnly holding high festival in honour of the founder of *lars tornaria*—this regenerator of youth, this second Martin Luther and saviour of the German tongue. The Greek scholar Thiersch dedicated his translation of Pindar to him, declaring that with the Germans, as with the ancient Greeks, the cult of the body is the father of the mind ; and the learned lexicographer, Passow, defined the Gymnastic Movement as " the formula for humanity's evolution towards the heights."

" The vulgarity of this movement," writes Treitschke, " is rooted in certain ineradicable qualities of the German character ; our people have always yearned for the formless simplicity of primitive life. As soon as the blood of Germans begins to stir, this yearning boils over with impetuous brutality." Treitschke was an ardent nationalist, but he was also an honest historian, and he recognised " the unhealthy condition which permitted the sons of a cultured people to worship a barbarian as their master."

The conservative element in the ruling class soon became alarmed by certain revolutionary aspects of the movement. Father Jahn applied a form of equalitarianism which accorded ill with the views of social policy prevailing in the Europe of the Holy Alliance. The prophet was thrown into prison, and kept there long enough for his followers to lose patience. Finally, the members dispersed and the movement collapsed in ridicule.

It was succeeded, however, by more lasting developments, which came in time to carry on the patriotic outburst born of the wars of liberation. At first the emotional crisis which shook the German people after the national revival was merely a natural reaction against foreign domination. A contemporary of the time, Count Beugnot, who was well placed to judge, remarked : " It may be that we have played the victor too clumsily in regard to Germany, and that we must reproach ourselves with having wounded those innermost feelings which should be sacred even amongst enemies." In any case, this spontaneous outburst of national feeling, which should normally have subsided when its aim of liberation had been attained, developed instead into a great movement which drew its strength from the stream of romanticism then flooding the literary world. The movement spread until it involved not merely the political world, but the fields of philosophy, art, and religion also.

The movement of romanticism had originated as a protest

against the cold objectivity of the classical school, a kind of individualistic expressionism which at first was not opposed to the doctrine of the Rights of Man. But in Germany it quickly became identified with the stirring of popular imagination, which resulted in the revival of the old national sagas, and this alliance became, in the political sphere, of considerable importance. German romanticism—*Die Deutsche Romantik*—placed its mystical power and its fervent vocabulary at the service of German nationalism. Besides, the revolutionary wave was subsiding. " There are times," says Novalis, " when youth is irresistibly attracted by the idea of revolution, by the surge of democratic ideas and the bursting forth of new forms of strength : but with the majority of men those years pass quickly." Thus it came about that, in the Germany of the years following 1815, political reaction and literary revolution joined hands and emerged as one great nationalist movement, a movement which was to contain within it the essence of the intellectual and moral characteristics of the German people.

Harry Heine was eighteen years old, an age when young people usually feel the necessity of reconciling their developing intelligence with their political opinions, and of identifying their lives as individuals with that of the society around them. With Harry this impressionable period was one of complete receptivity, and he plunged headlong into the mysticism of the time. Thus, when the junior employee of Salomon Heine had time to remember his vocation as a poet, the verses he wrote were no more than an exact reflection of the world in which he was living. The boy whose childhood had been dazzled by the glory of Napoleon now nurtured intense hatred of the French. He was as closely imprisoned in the closet of nationalism, as firmly determined to rid himself of all foreign taint, as any of the super-patriots whom he was one day to ridicule.

In the years which followed, his poetry bears all the characteristics of the period—old-fashioned phraseology, similes drawn from history and coloured by the Middle Ages or even by Catholicism.

So completely did he lose himself in this mimicry that he expressed even his passion for Amalie in the jargon of the period, with results that are often comical. His adoration for the blonde Jewess of Hamburg becomes " German love," this *Deutsche Minne* which rests on two unshakable pillars, the " dignity of Man and Faith." The lock of hair which Molly had given him he carried about in an iron cross, the sharp angles of which pricked into his chest, the iron cross being a patriotic emblem then much in vogue. He seeks a refuge from the despair into which he is plunged by his " German love " in the Catholic faith, as the fashion of the day demands. " I must have a Madonna. Can the divine take the place of the earthly ? " At times the cry rises near to hysteria, as when he exclaims, " I want to drown my senses ! " ; or, again, " infinite sorrow can only be assuaged by the infinite depths of mysticism ! " In a style which he imagined to be mediæval, but which is borrowed from Schenkendorf, he wrote in rhyme the legend of the Madonna of Pity, who bends over the pale youth wasted by his holy passion and, to console him, gives him a strand of her long sun-kissed tresses.

In the poetry of this period of his life—his " troubadour songs," as he called them—Harry Heine sought revenge for all the humiliating experiences in his uncle's house. As balm for his injured feelings he created an imaginary world in which his commonplace troubles assumed the dignity of deep tragedy. Later on he wrote that all his verse of that time bore " the sombre imprint of the cruelties which threw their malevolent shadows across my youth." Alas ! these cries from the heart found no favour with her to whom they were addressed ; their florid exaggeration shocked the hard common sense of the banker's daughter, and the clumsiness of his first efforts only roused her laughter. The children of Salomon Heine had no pity for blunderers. Amalie seems to have shown her cousin's poetic confessions to her friends, and to have laughed with them over the verses which he had copied out with such care. That, at least, is the conclusion one draws from a note he wrote at the time : " Truly it wounds me to the heart that she should have so cruelly jeered at the fine poems I wrote for her alone ; she has done me an evil turn by that."

The " fine poems " nevertheless appeared in an obscure review, signed with the laborious anagram " Sy Freudhold Riesenharf "—Harry Heine Düsseldorf. The pseudonym was probably chosen to elude the reproaches of his uncle, or perhaps even to avoid shocking the rather anti-Semitic readers of the journal by the name of a Jewish family so well known in Hamburg. But even the glory of this first appearance in print failed to impress Molly. One day she gave him a volume of Müllner's poems, ruthlessly pointing out the distance which separated them from his own. "Write something like that," said the girl pitilessly. Heine had not forgotten the wound when, some years after he had become famous, he related the story to Müllner. He had nothing with which to protect himself from the scorn of Molly, not even confidence in his vocation. When he writes, " All the same, my muse is dearer to me than ever," one cannot help feeling it is rather a reaction from wounded pride than the heart-felt cry of a poet confident in his star.

A long interval is to pass, longer still when compared to the pace of his earlier development, before Harry Heine succeeds in unearthing from under the barren environment of the period a note of self-expression drawn from the fruits of his own experience. At first all those qualities which are to bring him fame serve only to hinder the development of his creative personality. His faculty for adapting himself, his sensitiveness to beauty and rhythm, and his lightning susceptibility to impressions, only added to the misery of his three years in Hamburg. For Heine the years 1816 to 1819 were years of failure, made up of an unhappy love-affair, a daily occupation which he loathed, and a general atmosphere of hostility. His detestation of Hamburg was shown in his first letter from there, and it grew on him with the years : " It is a corrupt commercial hole, full of strumpets but with never a muse." He admitted later that his judgment was not impartial. All the humiliations which gored him are attributed to the commercial atmosphere of the city. For him Hamburg is a town inhabited solely by Philistines, whose portrait he drew later in picturesque terms : " As for the men, they are mostly squat and dumpy, with cold eyes, low foreheads, and red jowls that hang in folds ; their eating apparatus, that is to say their jaws and teeth, are exceptionally well developed ; the hat is worn glued to the head, the hands thrust deep into the pockets, as though to say : 'What do I owe you ?' " Another time he wrote : " What a grand town, this city of Hamburg, full of nothing but worthy folk. Here is no ignoble Macbeth ; here reigns Banquo."

But, for all that, he never found the courage to flee an atmosphere in which he suffocated. As early as October 1816 he was writing, " My uncle would like to send me away ; my father grumbles that I do no business, despite all the expenditure, but, *coûte que coûte*, I shall stay here." When his incompetence can no longer be hidden and he is obliged to leave the bank, he still continues to batten on the generosity of his uncle. In 1818 Salomon Heine set him up in business as a dealer in cloth, under the name Harry Heine & Co. The firm was meant to be a branch of his father's business in Düsseldorf, and it was hoped that it would help Samson Heine to restore his own dwindling fortunes.

Despite the bitterness of repeated failures in a field which certainly was entirely unsuitable for him, Harry Heine could shake himself free neither from financial dependence on his uncle nor from his passion for Amalie. The more intolerable the situation became, the more he temporised. The truth is that he lacked the courage, not merely to accept hardship, but even to put up with a few privations. Whether this moral cowardice was due to physical causes, or whether it was sheer lack of discipline which kept him from mastering his over-sensitive nerves, the result in either case was a persistent shrinking from the battle of life. It is possible, too, that he was affected by the enervating atmosphere of the luxury amidst which he lived. But, whatever the reason, the fact remains that his naturally indolent disposition and his love of good living were accentuated during these years in which he acquired the habit of depending upon Salomon Heine for every penny he spent. Henceforth and throughout his career, Heine the writer needed to have the material cares of life solved for him before he could begin to work.

His stay in Hamburg left another legacy scarcely less baneful. By way of escape from the despair into which he was plunged by frustrated love, daily humiliation, and the anxiety of his uncertain future, he developed a mode of life which speedily became a disastrous habit. He divided his life into two distinct parts, thus rendering permanent a tendency to temperamental disharmony which was already sufficiently marked. "My secret inner life," he wrote, "sank in an abyss of dreams whose obscurity was relieved only by fitful lightning flashes ; in my other, external life, I became mad, dissipated, cynical, and disgusting : in fact I formed it consciously, to be the opposite of my inner life, lest the latter should destroy all the rest." In point of fact, he sought to take revenge for the suffering caused by his passion for Amalie by giving himself up to petty amorous adventures. He forsook the "*Affrontenburg*" and the "poisoned garden" of Rainville for Winterhude. There he discovered a French *émigré*, M. Charaux, living romantically in a garret made gay by the beauty of his young daughter. As soon as the stern parent perceived the attraction of the banker's young nephew for his daughter, he forbade him the house. But Harry managed to pay one more visit. In the dead of night he climbed to the girl's bedroom window, on the glass of which he scratched with his ring : "Moi, je n'existe que pour vous chérir."

But these years in Hamburg were not taken up entirely by adventures with young girls of good family, jealously guarded by their fathers. Harry had already acquired a taste for the cheap and tawdry pleasures of the brothel, which flourished in such profusion amidst the bourgeois respectability of Hamburg. His remarks concerning the morality of the city are not merely academic. It was a misfortune for him that his first love should have been named Amalie Heine, a cool-headed young woman endowed to excess with that protection against her own temperament which is often possessed by young Jewesses of good family. Because she was made thus, Heine learnt sensual indulgence divorced from passion, and sought only as a relief from her. In this way it came about that this great writer of love poetry never himself experienced the harmony which comes from the union of body and soul. He also learnt to dissimulate both his disappointed love and his more disreputable adventures at an age when it would have been far better for him if he could have poured out his heart to a friend. In Heine this facility for dissimulation, so quickly acquired, lived on into his maturity, and caused him much unhappiness.

During these years Molly became lost to him completely. All the actors in this little Hamburg drama seem to have been entangled in the threads of infelicitous affection. Amalie Heine fell in love with a man who made her suffer from that same indifference which she herself showed to her cousin. Her infatuation was also too strong to remain hidden, and in her turn she suffered the humiliation of blunt refusal. One day, when the young man turned up at the house with his wife, Salomon somewhat tactlessly gave him to understand how much he would have liked him as a son-in-law. The banker had no more understanding for the feelings of his own children than he had for those of his nephew.

Es ist eine alte Geschichte,
Doch bleibl sie immer neu ;
Und wem sie just passieret
Dem bricht das Herz entzwei.

" It is the same old story, though it is always new ; and it still breaks the heart of him to whom it has just happened."

In these words, relating a common episode in general terms, Harry Heine began at last to attain simplicity of style and showed himself capable of rejecting romantic hyperbole for a sincere expression of emotion. . . . But at this very moment material disaster overtook him. The firm of Harry Heine & Co. went into bankruptcy in its first year, and proved to be the end of his abortive experiences in the world of commerce. Salomon Heine flatly refused to come again to the aid of such an incompetent man of affairs. At the same time, as if to emphasise the family failing, his father's business also collapsed. Samson Heine had no alternative but to go into liquidation and leave Düsseldorf, seeking humble obscurity in a small town near Hamburg.

More than ever was Harry Heine dependent upon his rich uncle. After much supplication, Salomon Heine at last consented to make his nephew an allowance which would enable him to continue his studies at a university. But he laid down the condition that the studies should have a utilitarian purpose ; since medicine and law were the only liberal professions which were open to Jews, and those only open in part, Harry must train to become a lawyer.

One would have imagined he might have been overjoyed to escape from the atmosphere of Hamburg, and still more to be put in the way of earning his own living. But his only thought is of his separation from Amalie. He would probably have pleaded piteously to be allowed to stay near her but for the fact that, with her usual devastating bluntness of speech, she herself insisted on his going.

Doch du drängst mich selbst von hinnen
Bittre Worte spricht dein Mund.

" But you yourself thrust me away and your mouth speaks bitter words."

He is not yet twenty years old. He leaves Hamburg disillusioned and disgusted : disillusioned without having really hoped, disgusted without having experienced satisfaction. The proceeds of his youth are but a stock of bitter precocity. Nevertheless, a poem is born of this sad leave-taking :

Schöne Wiege meiner Leiden,
Schönes Grabmal meiner Ruh,
Schöne Stadt, wir müssen scheiden.

" Lovely cradle of my sorrows, lovely tomb of my repose, lovely city, we must part."

Despite everything, the three years have not been entirely wasted, for Harry Heine has begun to find himself.

On the day of his departure from Hamburg he was seen off by his uncle's manager, perhaps in order to make sure that he actually went. The good man lamented unceasingly that the great banker's nephew should have thus thrown away his chances of living under his uncle's protection, and that he should now be obliged to sally forth alone towards an uncertain future. But, distraught though he is, Harry finds words to console his uncle's honest henchman : " Do not worry, my good Hirsch ; you will hear of me yet."

CHAPTER III

VAIN ASSIMILATION

"My forefathers were not the hunters, they were the hunted."
("Nordsee")

"HE HAS LEARNT no Greek, in Latin he is unsure and unpractised, which is why he did not hand in a Latin essay. He was unequal to the mathematics paper. He is not without some knowledge of history. His German essay, although written in an unusual style, shows promise." Such was the report of the board which examined Harry Heine when he was twenty-two years old. He had not finished his studies at the gymnasium, and thus had to take this examination in order to gain admission to the university. Despite these poor results Harry Heine was admitted. The examiners were mostly dealing with recruits who had interrupted their studies, and they were therefore particularly indulgent. In the final criticism of Harry Heine's German essay they wrote that he "is apt to wander from the subject, but shows a remarkable aptitude for satire."

Such was the intellectual equipment with which Harry Heine arrived in Bonn. Until then he had had no contact with university life—he had been too much occupied with himself to become greatly interested in young folk of his own generation. In his uncle's bank, and in his own cloth warehouse, he had heard only the distant echoes of the furious struggle which had broken out between the students and the new regime, in the name of liberty against reaction. Heine still cherished the grand illusion of the new national unity. He had no idea of, and was unable to imagine, the depths of disillusionment into which the student world had sunk.

The years which had just passed had brought German patriots to a rude awakening from their orgy of nationalism.

The first sessions of the Bundestag had seen all the old squabbles revived to the accompaniment of the creaking of the same old outworn diplomatic machine, and had been a severe test for the most enthusiastic believers in German unity. At the conclusion of these debates, Luden cried : " We have lost our faith in the honesty of any prince or monarch."

The general disillusion was increased by the economic crisis. The old hungry years returned with the old injustice. No sooner were the soldiers home again from the wars of liberation than they were singing a song with the refrain : " When we hunted the French from the land, they told us all would be well. Now we are treated like dogs. God grant us our daily needs, lest we regret having exchanged French bread for German hunger ! " The change of sentiment was seen most quickly, and in its most acute form, in the Rhineland. An emissary from the Prussian Government admitted in 1815 to the Chancellor that, in his native district of Coblenz, " there is not a single man who would not fall on his knees and thank God if the country were to return again to French rule."

The young people in the universities were morally worse off than men of a riper age, who at least were able to make comparisons before forming their judgments. The youthful volunteers who had returned to take up their studies had nothing behind them save years of glory spent in a noble adventure. For their present sustenance they had only their unbounded self-confidence and their passionate love of country. The transition period from war to peace would have been difficult for them even under more normal conditions. But they had to cope in addition with the ferment created in their minds by men such as Fichte, whom they had chosen as their spiritual leaders. They boasted of having within them that " fundamentally new self " which Fichte demanded from the German people. They felt themselves to be the anointed guardians of the new Teutonic conscience for which they had given their blood. Vague ideas about liberty and equality, unconsciously taken over from the French, mingled in their souls with *Furor Teutonicus*, and hatred of " Gallic falsehood." They had thrown themselves heart and soul into the fray, not only in order to free the soil of the Fatherland from the invader, but also to relieve their people from oppression, to bring about unity between the classes, and between the masses and their rulers.

As soon as the war was over these young people discovered that they had been cheated. They thought they were overthrowing one tyrant and found they had helped to reinstate twenty tyrants. No sooner were the German princes firmly seated on their thrones again, than they at once began to break all their most solemn promises. When they no longer had reason to fear their enemy, they proceeded to rid themselves of the young heroes who had become inconvenient allies.

" From every throat rose the bitter plaint that the blood of Leipzig and Waterloo had been spilt in vain," wrote Treitschke. Such profound deception could not merely dwindle away into silence : so much spirit, developed in what Treitschke calls " noble barbarism," could not simply be absorbed by docile absorption in daily routine. After all had not Fichte proclaimed, " Better life without science, than a science without life " ? The students became turbulent, and formed new university groups, called the Burschenschaften, adopting Vater Jahn's flag of black, red, and gold. The colours were symbolic, and represented the progress from the night of slavery through bloody struggle to the " golden dawn of liberty." They rose in revolt against those who had thwarted national unity, against Metternich's conservatism, and against the social reaction of Prussia. They set out to remind the governing classes that they themselves were the rightful heirs to the national heritage. On the anniversary of the Battle of Leipzig—the " Battle of the Nations "—October 18th, 1817, the new students' unions gathered together at Eisenach. Fiery speeches were made against those " who forget the common weal in the abject baseness of their egotism . . . who conceal their own miserable cowardice by mocking at our most sacred beliefs, and who insolently declare our patriotism to be a figment of the imagination, the mere invention of a sick brain." The gathering consisted of several hundred students, a few professors from the University of Jena, and Vater Jahn with his faithful lieutenant, Massmann, accompanied by their mob of young physical-culturists. The whole body was inflamed with "the German spirit," with an attitude of aggression the natural expression of which is hatred. Hatred of the French above all, to which was added hatred of the Jews as profiteers under the Napoleonic regime. And naturally the memory of Martin Luther was present with the assembly, especially there on the Wartburg, so near his birthplace. They had climbed up the famous hill at night, with torches in their hands, and it was in Luther's name that Massmann called upon the crowd to apply the purifying flame of their torches to those books which offended their patriotism. Such a crowd of hysterical youngsters, in such circumstances, asked nothing better than to express their feelings in the most melodramatic fashion possible. When Massmann cried to them that "the hour has come to make our desires clear to the German world, and to show them what they may expect from us," the excited students dashed about in all directions, collecting wood for the bonfire, and papers and books to be burnt on it. As copies of all the offending literature were not available, the names of many books of which they disapproved were scribbled out on pieces of paper, which were then cast to the flames.

The dancing light of the flames died down, and the throats, worn out with shouting, became silent at last, but the effects of the gesture were not so ephemeral. The commotion on the Wartburg woke enthusiastic echoes throughout the country, and pompous professors wrote that "the demonstration is an event which will stimulate the pride of Germans for centuries."

Neither the German authorities nor their masters in Austria felt disposed to belittle the incident. Court circles in Vienna became alarmed, and Metternich fanned their apprehension whilst he rejoiced in secret. The outbreak proved his warnings to have been well-founded, and once more he could boast of having known all and foreseen all. Once Napoleon was laid low, Metternich had only one idea in his head—the re-establishment of the *status quo ante*. He knew that the Austrian Empire had no chance of survival unless it could retain its position in the then existing balance of power and maintain the social system unchanged. To him the new outbreak of nationalism was as much to be dreaded as the equalitarian ideas of France. Everything, in fact, which did not accord entirely with the existing regime was, for him, hostile to it and but the spectre of revolution in another form.

He utilised the alarm caused in Vienna by the Wartburg episode in order to open a frontal attack on the rebellious younger generation. Demonstrations of any kind were forbidden to students. Those rectors of universities who were in agreement with the Government, watched them strictly, and took note of all they said and did. Metternich threw one of his famous nets of espionage over the younger generation of Germany, who, for the most part, did not even realise what had happened. Nor was this surprising, seeing that it was a change of face on the part of the authorities ; for the students, what one day had been a matter of patriotic pride became the next a crime of incitement against the regime.

As the months went by, the police inquisition became more and more galling, and the hot-headed amongst them were exasperated beyond endurance. The chief cause of their resentment was the intrusion of foreigners into the internal affairs of the German States ; their animosity against Metternich's spies and the agents of the Tsar became intense. One day it was learnt that a dramatist named Kotzebue, who was counsellor of the Russian Legation at Weimar, was sending reports on German university life to his sovereign. The " Union of Irreconcilables " decided to assassinate him, in order to teach a lesson once and for all to the other lackeys of reaction. Kotzebue was stabbed to death, by a young student called Sand, in March 1819.

"I wanted," cried the young fanatic, "to punish the man who was attempting to stifle what is divine in me, my conviction."

Inevitably this crazy act played straight into the hands of the reaction. Metternich no longer found any difficulty in persuading even the constitutionalist members of the Bundestag that rigorous measures must now be taken. "We must follow up the incident to the best possible advantage," he declared; and, with increasing pride in his own clairvoyance, "I cannot refrain from repeating twenty times a day—how right I have been and how hopelessly wrong all the others!"

At the conference of the Federal Diet, in Karlsbad, he succeeded in obtaining authority for measures even more severe than he had hoped. The students' unions were dissolved, and a Government representative appointed to each university, whose duty it was to inspect the tendencies of the curriculum and to watch over the opinion of both professors and students. The universities themselves were placed under police supervision, and to these measures was added the introduction of a rigorous censorship. This last blow at the rising tide of democracy was a flagrant violation of the Federal Constitution.

Metternich's right hand, Gentz, boasted that the resolutions passed at Karlsbad represented "the most retrograde step which has been taken in Europe in the last twenty years." The measures were put into force throughout all German States under the direct supervision of the Austrian and Prussian Ministers. A storm of persecution fell upon Germany—"like a plague," as Treitschke put it. The scum of the land united under the banner of reaction: professional informers, or those with personal grudges, job-seekers, and adventurers of all kinds who would betray either side for money. There were grovelling professors to prove in the name of science that the thraldom of thought was legitimate; respectable civil servants became executioners, and servile judges the tools of those in power.

At the University of Bonn, professors such as Welcker, the historian of art, and his brother, were pestered by the police, and had their houses searched from floor to ceiling. The same happened to Arndt, the patriotic song-writer and idol of the students. Ridiculous charges were levelled against the latter, and he was suspended from his functions, only learning many years later that the legal proceedings against him had been dropped.

Soon after his arrival in Bonn, Harry Heine also had occasion to learn of the methods employed to stifle the current of university life. As soon as they were enrolled at the university, Heine and his friend Neunzig became members of one of the " free unions " which had replaced those dissolved by the Government, and which were open for membership to all students. On October 18th of the same year, the members of the union known as " Allgemeinheit " decided to celebrate the anniversary of the founding of the university. The date coincided somewhat dangerously with that of the Battle of Leipzig, but otherwise the demonstration was a very harmless affair. A few moderate and non-political speeches, a few songs sung in chorus, and, in the evening, a climb up to the Drachenfels, where a bonfire was lit. There the young men sat round the crackling wood fire which flickered against the ruined walls of the castle. In the valley below, the Rhine was hidden in mist. For an hour or two they sang to dispel their depression, and then returned quietly down the hill to their beds.

But a few days later all the participants were summoned to appear before the authorities to undergo a rigorous cross-examination. They were accused of having conspired against the security of the State. Harry Heine's replies to the questions of the Academic Tribunal showed the aptitude for satire to which his original examiners had attested. When the presiding enquirer asked him if he could recall the logical sequence of the speeches, he shook his head, and replied : " In the first speech I was able to discern no logical sequence at all ; as to the second, I am unable to say, for I cannot remember what it was about." Heine was intensely amused by the contrast between the innocent nature of the event and the absurd pomposity of his interrogation.

Nevertheless he could not remain blind to the enormous change which had come about since the young volunteers of the Grammar School at Düsseldorf had gone about feeling themselves the saviours of the Fatherland. All that is past, and now the idea of liberty is anathema, the very word, indeed, forbidden. So literally was this true that when the students gathered in the evenings for the choral singing, which has always been a prominent feature of German university life, they were obliged to paraphrase the last stanza of one of Arndt's songs which was an invocation to liberty. When those lines were sung, the voices dropped, and the singing became like a dirge chanted in unison :

> " Sweetest of all things ! To thee I raise my glass in silence . . ."

It was not to be wondered at that experiences such as those which occurred during his very first weeks at Bonn should speedily have led Heine to revise his ideas of patriotism. The effect is seen in a poem, written quite early in his stay, in which observation of the present is mingled with his sentiments of the past :

> " Son of folly, ever dream when thy heart swells in thy breast, but never in life look for thy dream's likeness ! "

A dream ! That is all the past had become, that happy time " when custom and virtue were united in simplicity." A dream, too, the peace of victory which had been so dearly bought with German blood. And youth had awoken from the dream. It saw itself put in chains by " cunning tyrants who have created a system out of falsehood."

> " O the pity, that they should go hungry who liberated the Fatherland while idlers go about in silk, rascals wear jewelled decorations, and mercenaries pride themselves on being masters ! "

" A pygmy people grovelling on the tomb of a giant " is Harry Heine's description of the era—" this epoch of deception "—in which he lived. The poem is still inexpert and hesitant, composed of ill-matched ideas which grate together, but it reveals a chapter in his life. He is already at variance with his age. Every day provided some opportunity for the sharpening of his critical faculties, and his discontent grew on him.

Harry Heine might normally have expected to find some compensation for the loss of his own illusions in the society of others who were suffering from the same blow. But his very first contacts with his fellow-students showed him there was no possibility of relief in that direction. Truth to tell, it is probable that his earlier infatuation for the patriotic ideas in vogue was only due to the fact that he never came into actual contact with the holders of those ideas. For, however worthy of sympathy these young men were as victims of persecution, they themselves were no less cruel and narrow than their oppressors. Their idealism was pure enough, but they added to it an arrogant pride in their own virtue, and a brutal violence which rendered them strangers to all finer feelings. Treitschke himself held that the way this generation lived was modelled too closely on the slogan of their master, Fichte, who had said : " The doctrine of gentleness is an invocation of the Devil." In such an atmosphere Heine had no alternative save to retreat within himself : the period of savage moodiness in which he indulged speaks volumes on the rebuffs he must have endured. The pale reserved youth with the impenetrable gaze, and with lips always formed in a bitter smile, soon came to be considered by the other students as a creature for ridicule—" a kind of idiot who was only good to be the butt for their fooling," as Johann Baptist Rousseau wrote, he himself having been a friend and fellow-student of Heine's at the time. Heine was indeed alone in that world ; he did not share the partiality of the others for noisy gatherings ; he did not smoke, drank no beer and little wine, whereas they staked their prowess on the number of tankards they could empty. He did not believe in hollow demonstrations of revolt, and found no pleasure in bellowing songs at the top of his voice ; he just sat quietly in his corner, an irritating and rather superior smile playing over his face. " We made great fun of Heine," said Wolfgang Menzel, later to become the " Pope of literature," but then President of the " Allgemeinheit," and an excellent example of rough and noisy youth. In those early days Menzel had not yet become the " devourer of Frenchmen " animated by " a holy Teutonic rage," but he already possessed his overweening self-assurance and his raucous laugh. He was the personification of ruthless brutality, and his appearance did not belie his nature. A wide energetic mouth with a thick underlip, a boorish expression stamped on a flat face, with prominent eyes and long straight hair falling to his shoulders, such was the Menzel of those days.

Nevertheless the attitude adopted towards Heine by students of the type of Wolfgang Menzel was not solely due to their superior physical strength or the mood of the time, nor to contempt for his intellectual gifts. If Heine himself was not responsible for it, he certainly did all in his power to aggravate it. He early developed a characteristic which got him into endless trouble in later life, a sort of obstinate pride in behaving as though all that his enemies said about him was true. He was like a child who has been wrongly accused, and who therefore insists on doing all the things for which he has been reproached. His morbid sensibility induced him to allow a legendary reputation about himself to grow up, and he professed to see a kind of protection in the very falsity of the legend. This curious trait did not escape the notice even of Johann Baptist Rousseau, who was by no means unobservant. " He is one of the best-hearted and most loyal people I have ever known," wrote Rousseau, " but he seems to be ashamed of his good-nature, while his tendency to show himself in the worst possible light amounts to a vice."

In reality he had nothing in common with those young men whose ideas, before he had met them, he thought he shared. He confined himself more and more to the company of a few friends, Rousseau, Simrock, Friedrich von Beughem, Dieffenbach, the future famous surgeon, and the faithful friend of his childhood, Sethe. " The lyrical half dozen " was the nick-name given to this little group. The bond of union between them was an aspiration towards poetry, with some of them merely a youthful whim, but for others a real vocation.

For Heine the outstanding fact of his stay at Bonn was the growth of the conviction as to his abilities as a poet, which he had already begun to feel when he left Hamburg. But in Bonn he received the first confirmation of this belief from another than himself. He had gone to Bonn with the sole intention of pursuing his legal studies. At first, too, he had conscientiously followed the lectures of the Professors of Law, but the slight appeal which that dry subject had for him was lessened still more by the counter-attraction of the courses in literature and in the history of art, and, above all, by the fascinating personality of August Wilhelm Baron von Schlegel. " With the exception of Napoleon, he was the first great man to enter my life," wrote Heine later. Von Schlegel had been tutor to Madame de Staël's children, and, at the time of his occupation of the Chair of Literature at Bonn, was just over fifty years of age. He had known all the most eminent men of every country, and had become a supreme authority in the field of literature. His refinement and general distinction made a deep impression on the unsuccessful ex-business man from Hamburg. Many years later, when Heine had become a redoubtable opponent of von Schlegel and was writing the epitaph of the Romantic School, he recalled, a little ironically, the unforgettable impression made by this first encounter. " Even to-day I can feel the secret tremor which ran through me when I found myself sitting before him, hearing him speak for the first time. I was wearing a light-coloured redingote, a red cap, and no gloves, and my hair was fair and long. Monsieur A. W. Schlegel wore gloves of shiny leather, he was dressed according to the latest Paris fashion, and had about him the perfume, not only of *eau de mille fleurs*, but of high society. He was elegance personified, and when he spoke of the Lord Chancellor of England he added, ' my friend.' Beside him stood his manservant in the baronial livery, snuffing the silver-mounted candles which stood beside a glass of sugared water on the desk of this marvellous man."

With ill-concealed diffidence Harry Heine plucked up the courage to show his poetic efforts to the great August Wilhelm von Schlegel. The illustrious head of the Romantic School, however, examined the manuscript with the closest attention, and was so agreeably surprised by the originality of the poems that he even took the trouble to correct them for details of style. Heine found the manuscript which was returned to him heavily marked in pencil and with remarks written in the margin. In a letter on the subject, written to a friend, Heine tells of his flattering reception in terms which sound slightly affected : " I am too vain to feel surprised," he wrote ; but his excitement then gets the better of him, and he adds, with youthful candour : " I was mightily proud when Schlegel invited me to go to his house the other day. I chatted with him for hours over the coffee-table."

Thus did the irony of fate lead the father of German romanticism to encourage the creative power of the man who would one day sound the knell of romanticism. Little did August Wilhelm von Schlegel guess that, in helping the student Heine, he was helping to sharpen the instrument which would destroy the brief literary epoch which he himself represented. Nor did he guess that the young man standing half timidly before him was one day to be the herald of a new era in poetry.

For Harry Heine the meeting with Schlegel proved to be the turning-point in his artistic evolution. For the first time his gifts were recognised by such a one as Schlegel, between whom and the humble law student a great social gulf was fixed. For the first time the boy so accustomed to mockery is appreciated at his full value by another than one of his rare but blindly trusting friends. Schlegel, less creative than critical, but an infallible judge, sensed that underneath the clumsy outer form there lay originality which announced a new note in poetry. He helped Heine to rid himself of the classic stammer so readily adopted by minor poets, and set him on the road to simplicity of expression and sincerity of style. He made him undergo the stern discipline of sonnet writing, and even taught him to like its compact form, despite the fact that it was foreign to his temperament. The sonnet figures in Heine's literary output only at this period of his career. It was thanks to Schlegel that Heine became familiar with English poetry, which he began to translate. Like many other young poets of his day he was especially attracted by Byron, with whom he felt such affinity that he later wrote of Byron as " his English cousin."

The gratitude which Heine felt for Schlegel he showed by whole-hearted submission to his master's theories. At that time, although his disaffection with his surroundings was already increasing, he would listen to no criticism of the artistic forms of expression of the moment, and Schlegel's authority in literary matters was above question for him. It was only much later that he dared to acknowledge that Schlegel understood nothing of modern poetry, and that he was only at home in the poetry of the past. At Bonn, Heine was content only to praise the master who had relieved him of those "daggers of doubt," of that worst of poisons, distrust of his own ability.

About this time, and at Schlegel's instigation, he wrote an essay on romanticism, which is nothing more than a repetition of his master's own ideas : the " German Muse " is spoken of as " a fresh young beauty, without affectation " ; and again, the German language is declared to be " our most precious possession, the boundary mark which no neighbour can remove, a clarion of liberty whose ringing tones no tyrant can stifle, an oriflamme in the struggle for the Fatherland."

And yet in this very essay, the language of which is no more his own than are the ideas contained in it, there is one small phrase, hardly a phrase even, rather a remark at the end of a sentence, but which is the echo of a great internal struggle. Writing of the German language, he says that it is the Fatherland " even to those whom stupidity and malice refuse a country."

No more is needed than those few timid words to show that for the Jew Heine a terrible conflict had begun, a fight for that German Fatherland " which stupidity and malice denied him." This fight was to become the chief interest of his life. The struggle began during these months at Bonn, although his sojourn there was relatively the happiest period of his life, and one to which he looked back with longing during the troubled days which came later.

Almost immediately after the defeat of Napoleon there rose a great wave of anti-Semitism in Germany. The economic distress which followed upon the war—all the harder to bear in that it displaced a period of prosperity—pushed the masses to seek somebody on whom to fasten the guilt. And the Jewish money-lender was made the scapegoat, as he always has been made the scapegoat at such periods throughout history. The usual stories were circulated as to their extortionate practices, their cruelties, and their fabulous wealth. As early as 1816 there had been pogroms in several German towns. Excited crowds had surged through the streets pillaging shops and houses, and maltreating every Jew they found. In the end order had been restored by the authorities, but not until the mob had been given three clear days of licence.

The rulers of the country were far from displeased that public discontent should adopt this particular form. They also had an interest in depriving the Jews of their rights as citizens, and thereby procuring for themselves the revenue yielded by the sale of residence permits.

During the deliberations of the Congress of Vienna the Jews had still hoped to preserve the rights which had been accorded to them by the French or by the German princes. The Congress had indeed gone so far as to advise the latter that " the future Federal Diet will have the task of examining to what extent citizens' rights shall be accorded to Jews throughout the territory of the Federation, in return for their acceptance of the obligations of citizenship." This Article 16 of the Statute of the Bund proved, however, to be sufficiently loosely phrased to enable the German princes to ignore it.

Numerous pamphlets and newspaper articles appeared in 1816, fulminating against the emancipation of the Jews. " *Vox populi, vox Dei*—and the voice of the people is not favourable to the Jews," wrote Luden. But the fact that the voice of the people adopted a war-cry which was the signal for all anti-Semitic persecutions in Germany, the famous " Hep-Hep," derived from the initials of the Latin phrase *Hierosolyma Est Perdita*, is proof that the intellectuals were at the bottom of the trouble.

When the Primate Dalberg broke the agreement he had made with the Jews of Frankfurt, to allow them equality of rights against payment of a tax of 440,000 florins, he made his hack-writers explain that Jewish influence was only due to corruption, that they were everywhere the fomenters of social disorder, and that they counted on revolution in order to impose their hegemony on the world. He naturally did not proclaim the fact that in breaking his word to the Jews he had virtually stolen their money.

One of the most formidable theoreticians of anti-Semitism of the day was a Professor Friedrich Rühs of the University of Berlin. His book, *The Jewish Claim to Citizen Rights in Germany*, which appeared in 1815, is an attack upon that claim, supported by a great array of scientific argument. The author admits that he had formerly had humanitarian ideas on the subject, and had inclined towards tolerance for Jewry, but says that, since the sun of Liberty had risen upon the martyred Fatherland, he had begun to search for the causes of Germany's past weaknesses. The conclusion he had come to was that " every nation which desired to establish its own identity and retain its dignity, and which hoped to develop its national character, must exclude and eliminate such foreign elements as are incapable of full assimilation. The Jews are such an element. It would have been better had they never settled among us, or that we had more rigorously prevented their immigration and their propagation. Since they are here it would be cruel to expel them wholesale or to violently oppress them, but it is necessary, first, to establish a fixed ratio between the number of Jews and the number of Germans, and secondly to prevent any further immigration of Jews into the country." Rühs added that Jews should only be allowed to live in Germany on sufferance, but that first of all they must be rendered harmless. He also suggested that the wearing of the mediæval yellow band should be made compulsory for Jews.

The theories put forward by Rühs were moderate, however, as compared with others who wrote at the same time. One of the most violent was J. J. Fries, a Professor of Philosophy and Physics at Heidelberg, who, in 1816, published a pamphlet entitled : *On the Jewish Menace to German Prosperity and the German Character.* "Jewry," he wrote, "is a social disease which owes its rapid spread to money, and is co-existent with misery, tyranny, and taxes." Fries predicted an appalling reign of terror unless the Government intervened quickly to stop the calamity. "The Jewish element has exercised a terrible and demoralising effect both on the upper and the lower classes, wherever it has been allowed to enter. It is essential that this sect should be entirely destroyed, for it is obviously the most dangerous of all the secret or open communities." Throughout his indictment Fries returns again and again to his *Delenda est Carthago* : "Above all, deliver our people from this pest." Like others, he demanded that the immigration of Jews should be forbidden and the emigration encouraged ; that they should be expelled from the country districts and only allowed in towns on certain conditions: but he added: "In the long run all laws which seek to restrict their numbers will prove useless. We should copy the action of the Pharaoh with whose name that of Moses is associated."

Fries could not find words strong enough to express his contempt and hatred for "French tolerance" and the "Franco-Jewish regimes" of the occupation period. The power of the Jews was due to the influence of Napoleon, "a corroding influence at the heart of society." The conception of the "citizen of the world" was attributed to the Jews, and became a chief cause of complaint against them. Cosmopolitanism is Jewish, and cosmopolitanism is the enemy. The Jewish intelligentsia is corrupt, and corrupts the world. The decadence of Christianity is a triumph for this Jewish *élite*, which waits impatiently for the ruin of the nations, a ruin indeed promised to them by their God ; and so on.

This anti-Semitic agitation had all the greater effect in university circles in that the current romanticism was founded on a mystical conception of Catholicism, mediæval and intolerant. Before long, Jewish students were boycotted with all the brutality to be expected of the period. It seemed as though the oppression which they suffered at the hands of a reactionary Government led the students in their turn to become oppressors. To begin with, Jewish students were excluded from the university associations, despite the fact that according to their statutes they should have been open to all.

For the first time Harry Heine began to suffer directly from race prejudice. When anti-Semitic riots had broken out at Hamburg in 1816 he had been absorbed in himself, and, also, he had benefited by his uncle's position. Then it had still been possible to speak with some detachment of the "acute state of tension" which prevailed.

But in 1819 it was different. Heine was grievously shocked by the news which reached him of the pogroms, and by evidence of increasing hostility in intellectual circles. The effect was all the greater since his poetic fancy had set him dreaming of unity with the soul of the people. In consequence he withdrew more and more into himself, even avoiding the company of the "lyrical half-dozen." He went so far as to doubt the friendship of his faithful friend Christian Sethe.

"The life I am leading is as sad and lonely as it could be," wrote Heine in July 1820, at the end of his stay in Bonn. "In present circumstances to seek new friends seems to me both difficult and unwise, my old friends no longer appear to be interested in me."

In this state of wounded feelings, Harry Heine retired to the pretty village of Beul, near Bonn, where he passed the summer. His confidence in his own ability was by then great enough for him to seek to express the bitterness within him in the form of tragic drama, an idea doubtless inspired by Schlegel. Following the custom of the time he chose a picturesque period of the past as the scene to which to transpose the current drama of the Jew as victim of anti-Semitism. He found the analogy he required in the struggle between the Moors and the Christians in Spain. But to this he added his own more intimate drama, the story of his love for Amalie, who remained enthroned in his heart despite the dissipated life he was leading at that time. Thus equipped, Heine settled down to work at the gloomy tragedy of *Almanzor* in his peaceful, smiling village near the Rhine.

Almanzor is a satirical poem and a polemic, rather than a tragedy. The author himself called it a play with a purpose. Some years later, when his tragedies were published, the public quickly perceived the real meaning of this struggle between Christians and Moors. The Catholic Rhineland was under no illusions as to the intentions of the young writer, and the piece aroused such violent anger that his already considerable reputation was greatly increased.

Heine had set out to show in this tragedy the contrast between the Christian doctrine of love and the Christians' methods of conversion, but in the ferment of writing he lost sight of his main theme. The anti-Semitism of the time was inspired by religious and not racial grounds, and its aim was to convert the Jews, to make of them real Germans by forcing them to change their religion and cut themselves off from the main body of Jewry. The satirical descriptions of the Christianised Moors in *Almanzor* are sketches made from life amongst the converted Jews of Hamburg. Heine ridicules their anxiety to become assimilated, and trounces the easy denial of their religion. But his lyrical ardour proves greater than his dramatic gifts and a secondary theme comes to dominate the main idea. The effusive outbursts of Almanzor-Heine swamp the social drama, and his passion for Zuleima-Amalie eclipses the Moor's denunciations of Christianity. The author tried to do too much at a time, and, under the pretext of writing a tragedy, he sought in reality to give full expression to his overcharged feelings. " Into this piece," he wrote, " I have poured the whole of myself, my paradoxes, my wisdom, my love, my hate, and all my folly."

The ardour which he put into this work did not, however, cause him to ignore entirely the world of reality. The remonstrances received from home made him think with anxiety of the future. He realised with a shock that his uncle's allowance was promised only for the minimum period necessary to complete his studies, and that at Bonn he had spent scarcely any time at all on the subject he was supposed to be taking. With difficulty, therefore, and much regret, he decided to leave Bonn and to put himself under the stricter discipline of Göttingen.

On the way from Bonn to Göttingen he made a short stay in Düsseldorf. This was in the autumn of 1820. It was probably in the course of this journey that Heine met the two French prisoners of war who inspired him to write the famous poem, " The Two Grenadiers."

Heine found this visit to the scenes of his childhood tinged with sadness. Hardly any member of his own family still lived in Düsseldorf; the people he met in the streets did not recognise him, nor he them. The houses were newly painted, and the humblest little shop bore the proud announcement " Purveyor to the Court." " Where only the French tongue used to be heard, one now only hears Prussian," he remarked maliciously. Everything was at one and the same time familiar to him and yet strange; to use his own words: " It all had the dead-and-alive air of evergreens in a cemetery."

It was then that he saw the sorry remnants of Napoleon's Grande Armée, which years before he had seen march through Düsseldorf in all its glory, come limping past. They were prisoners of war who had been held in Siberia for several years after the Armistice, and who now were wandering back afoot towards France. " Their nude misery can be seen through their tattered uniforms and in their scarred, weather-beaten faces are deep, suffering eyes. And yet, although mutilated, enfeebled, and often limping, they still walk like soldiers."

To Harry Heine the sudden appearance of these " orphans of glory " was like a cruel revival of the past. How sheltered and how pleasant had been his childhood ! Even so early in his journey through life it seemed to shine in contrast with the present. In those days he had been sure of himself, and the world was full of hope ; and now came stumping past these living symbols of his broken dream.

But if his sensibility was stirred, his artistic talent had ripened to keep pace with it. The emotion roused in him by the sight of the old soldiers became the inspiration of some fine poetry. This ballad must be recognised as more than just the successful result of a fortunate inspiration, it represents another stage reached in Heine's intellectual emancipation. In it he has thrown off all the ultra-nationalism with which he had arrived at Bonn. Events at Bonn had, indeed, done much to rid him of that exaggerated Teutonism " whose whining love for the Fatherland was merely hatred of the foreigner and whose bleating about a faith was lack of reason."

At Göttingen he made still more rapid progress along that road. He found there " the peace of death in all things intellectual." The university was living on its earlier reputation. The character and moral courage of Schlözer had left no trace, and the general tendency of the courses was highly reactionary. The historian Heeren, who later acquired a European reputation for his pragmatic method of teaching history, repeated endlessly to his students that the power and interests of the ruling princes must take precedence over the interests of the people. Heeren considered it a duty to preach hatred of the French, and his colleague Saalfeld raved against Napoleon in such a way that he seemed to proclaim aloud his approaching madness. And yet, despite all this obsession with nationalism, the classes on the history and literature of the Middle Ages, a subject which Professor Friedrich Benecke had been the first to introduce into a university curriculum, were left entirely unattended. " There are nine students following these lectures. I repeat, there are just nine out of thirteen hundred, of whom at least a thousand are German, who can find some glimmer of interest in the way of living and the spiritual legacies of their ancestors." To which Heine remarks : "Germany, land of oaks and dullness."

He found the caste system at Göttingen far more rigorously applied than at Bonn : an impassable wall of prejudice combined with complete indifference concerning all political and intellectual problems. The reaction against Liberalism had been much more far-reaching than at Bonn. "Everyone lives like a hermit," Heine complained, and the same criticism is heard from all his contemporaries at Göttingen. One of them—a student of about the same time, but who was neither a Jew nor so sensitive and unsociable as Heine—has put on record : "One often attended the same lectures for six months without exchanging a word with one's neighbour ; for years we would live in the same house and share the same landing with other students without knowing anything about them, without even meeting them."

So as to mark clearly the distinction between themselves and the plain bourgeois, the princes and other nobility had their own reserved seats at the university, and claimed the same privilege in the town restaurants. Their table talk was confined to chatter about horses, dogs, and women, expressed in the uncouth, clipped slang which served them for language. "Amongst the bourgeoisie, on the other hand, ever since the little town had come to rely entirely upon the students for its living, the average mentality was that mixture of cupidity, servility, and thirst which is the common characteristic of most people who live in towns."

So wrote Treitschke, but Heine himself, later, left an even more scathing description : "It appears that this town was founded at the time of the invasions of the barbarians, and that each German tribe left a sample of itself as pattern. From these samples are descended the Vandals, Frisians, Swabians, Teutons and the rest, each distinguished from the other by the colour of his cap and the bowl of his pipe. These creatures populate the main streets of Göttingen, struggle fiercely with each other on the battlefields of the various inns, and jealously retain the customs of the barbarians, their ancestors."

Heine was filled with disgust by what he saw of these "ancient Teutons," as they called themselves. He heard for himself the interminable discussions on the purity of the German race and its characteristics. He listened to youngsters declaiming endlessly—"with a pedantry as detestable as it was absurd"—on such questions as: "Where does a Germanic being begin, and end?" "In a certain tavern in Göttingen," Heine related later, "I had the opportunity of admiring the precision with which my friends the 'ancient Teutons' prepared the lists of those who would be proscribed by them as soon as they arrived in power. Anyone who was descended, even seven generations back, from a Frenchman, a Jew, or a Slav was to be condemned to exile. Anybody who had ever written anything against Jahn or the absurdities of the old Germans themselves might expect the death penalty, carried out, of course, with the axe and not by that French invention, the guillotine. I remember that on one occasion there was grave debate as to whether or not there should be added to the list the name of a certain Berlin writer who had attacked the physical-culturists in the first volume of his work. The question was, Should they wait for the publication of the last volume, in which the author might put a different construction on his strictures?"

Over and above the behaviour of excited young fools, which Heine called "idealish ruffianism elevated to a system by Herr Jahn," he sensed what he came to see still more clearly later on—the danger of hysterical patriotism. Many years later he compared the effect of this emotion on Frenchmen and on Germans. "The patriotism of the Frenchman warms his heart, and the warmth swells it until his love can enfold, not only his relatives and neighbours, but the whole of France, and finally all civilised countries. The patriotism of the German, on the other hand, makes his heart shrink like leather in the cold, until he loathes all that is foreign, until he abandons all claim to be a citizen of the world or even a European, and desires only to be a German, narrow and limited."

When Heine in later years came to speak of his experiences at Göttingen, he also noted that, although the seekers after the true German soul were only a minority, nevertheless "their fanaticism, carried on with all the fervour of a religion, exceeds in energy the enthusiasm which reason alone can command. In addition they have at their service all the slogans which are most effective with an ignorant people. Words like 'Fatherland,' 'Germany,' 'faith of our ancestors,' etc., will always galvanise the masses more than such words as 'humanity,' 'citizen of the world,' 'spirit of youth,' 'truth.' I mean to say by this that the representatives of the nationalist idea have their roots more deeply sunk in German soil than the representatives of cosmopolitanism, and that we shall always be beaten by them unless we swiftly forestall them—with the help of the guillotine."

But, at Göttingen, Heine had not yet reached intellectual maturity. He was suffering there, as young people of his age do suffer, from the spectacle of a coarse and vulgar barbarism prevailing over the finer strains in human nature. Heine was all the more affected in so far as he no longer had the consolation which he had at Bonn of believing in his own creative power. He hoped to be able to liberate himself from his mental torment by finding artistic expression for it. *Almanzor* was intended to be both his revenge and his justification. But, as the end of his labours approached and the fever of creation began to subside, he whose constant advice to other beginners was, "Be severe with yourself," found his own critical faculty awake. "I have worked at my tragedy with all my powers, sparing neither my heart's blood nor the sweat of my brow, and, now that I am but half an act's length from the end, I realise with horror that the work of which I have thought so much is not only not a good tragedy, but that it does not even deserve to be called tragedy. It is all an artificial thing held up by wires."

There followed a period of complete despair for Heine. As a Jew he received nothing but humiliations ; as a poet his disappointment was all the worse for being self-inflicted. At the same time his love for Amalie drove him to rage in a helpless, hopeless jealousy. So many disappointments were more than such an ardent and hungry nature could bear. He found relief, as he had done at Hamburg, in the easy satisfaction of his senses. The laxity of morals at Göttingen broke down his last scruples. At the period in question, this feudal university had in this respect the worst reputation in Germany.

Harry Heine found himself surrounded by a coarse-living set of youths who boasted loudly and blatantly of their libertinism, and for once he found something in common with his fellow-students. Throughout his life he kept this sort of secret *entente* with the debauched. Later on he wrote :

Selten habt ihr mich verstanden
Selten auch verstand ich euch,
Nur wenn wir im Kot uns fanden
So verstanden wir uns gleich.

" Rarely did you understand me, rarely did I understand you. Only when we find ourselves in the mire do we understand one another at once."

At Göttingen this cynicism was fresh upon him, and he made no attempt to hide it. He did not hesitate to parade with his light-o'-loves on the promenades of the town, to the scandal of the provincial bourgeoisie. An unlucky incident soon caused him to add more trouble to his lot. It appears from the scanty references of his contemporaries that he was one day caught near the town, not only in company which was compromising, but in a situation which was even more so. News of the mischance quickly reached Göttingen and, incidentally, the ears of members of a students' club which Heine had joined as soon as he arrived. It was only a small association of literary aspirants; but its moral tone was, or pretended to be, higher than the others, and Heine was immediately expelled from the association. Although notified, Heine paid little attention to this decision, forgetful alike of the prejudice against him as a Jew, and of his general unpopularity. One day, on appearing unexpectedly at the rooms of the group " as if nothing had happened," he was shown the door with more violence than ceremony. This incident also was taken bitterly to heart, and rankled for years.

If the punishment for his licentiousness had stopped there, he would have had small cause for complaint. Unfortunately his careless living brought him a far more fearsome retribution. Göttingen in those days was not only notorious for the laxity of its morals, it had also an evil reputation in matters of health. A university year-book published about the end of the eighteenth century stated that the number of students in Göttingen suffering from venereal diseases was " enormous." In Heine's day the students spoke quite openly of their experiences. Florincourt, indeed, affirms that " nowhere had he found such open boasting about the contraction of secret diseases as amongst the students of Göttingen."

Heine, too, became afflicted with the malady, which eventually turned his last years into one long martyrdom. He immediately put himself into the hands of a doctor, but the medical science of the day was quite unequal to the task, and Heine's health suffered from that moment onwards.

This unfortunate Göttingen period had yet another blow in store for him. What was at first a small affair, later on put an end to his hopes of a university career. During a discussion in a restaurant, one of Heine's fellow-students gave him the lie. According to the students' code of honour (which Heine later said " deserved a place amongst the *leges barbarorum* ") such an insult delivered in public could only be wiped out in blood. Heine bowed to convention, and sent his seconds to the man, a certain Wilhelm Wiebel. By some indiscretion the news of the projected duel reached the ears of the university authorities, and, since such affairs had been gaining in frequency, a ban was henceforth put upon all duels.

There the matter would have ended, had not Wilhelm Wiebel belonged to one of the feudal students' corps whose notions of honour bordered on the fantastic. Solemnly the corps petitioned the authorities to know, " whether the duel had been called off owing to a reconciliation between the two opponents, or through outside intervention." With the same pompous gravity the Academic Senate replied that intervention had been applied. But the matter had been brought to public notice, and punishment had become necessary. Wiebel was subjected to disciplinary action, and Heine was sent down for a term.

This misfortune worried him all the more because it followed upon a whole series of others. " For three months I have lived in perpetual torment from a variety of causes. I have been pursued by a malignant fate, and now I am to be expelled for half a year for having broken the regulations about duelling." The despair in this letter to a friend was sincere enough, but the same envelope contained a short satirical poem on his expulsion.

So terrified was he of Salomon Heine's anger, and so uneasy about the disappointment he would cause his parents, that at first he did not dare admit to his relations what had occurred. But he was penniless and unable to leave Göttingen. His illness procured him a few days respite in which to pluck up his courage. Then he set forth to join his family in their new home in the little town of Lüneburg, stopping for a few days at Hamburg on the way. " Suddenly I felt as though I had never left the city," he wrote, " and all that I had thought, felt, and experienced in my two years' absence seemed completely wiped from my memory."

His brief stay in Hamburg sufficed to end whatever illusions had survived within him. But he clung passionately to hope of the impossible—and suffered cruelly from the awareness of the certain. " The ravings of all the madhouses have unloosed their folly upon me," he wrote despairingly. The letter is incoherent, packed with bitterness and grief, and with the confession of his love for Amalie which no deception or disappointment serves to kill. It ends with a cynical avowal :

Und wenn das Herz im Leibe ist zerrissen
Zerrissen und zerschnitten und zerstochen—
Dann bleibt uns doch das schöne, gelle Lachen.

" And even when the heart is torn—torn, and cut and stabbed—there still remains for us a strident laugh."

And on this note of "strident laughter" the troubled youth of Harry Heine ends.

CHAPTER IV

THE QUEST FOR IDENTIFICATION

> "How often does the external structure of our life match our true inner existence. In my case, though, the two *never* fit."
>
> (Heine to Immerman, *June 10th, 1823*)

On a fine spring morning in the year 1821, Professor Gubitz received a call from a young man who came to submit some poems to him. Gubitz was well known in Berlin as a wood engraver, a poet, a writer and translator, but above all as the editor of *Gesellschafter*, a popular literary review of the day. His visitor had just arrived in the city and knew nobody. He introduced himself to the editor with the words, " I am entirely unknown to you, but it is by you that I wish to be known." Gubitz looked at the young man, whose name he had not even caught, and answered politely that, if it were possible, he would be happy to be of service.

His visitor's appearance was not prepossessing. Gubitz saw before him a pale, emaciated young man with haggard features, whose clothes hung loosely and who stared about him with screwed-up eyes in the manner of short-sighted people. His strange, wild appearance matched the gloom and feverish fantasy of the " Dream Pictures," a collection of poems, signed " H. Heine," which he was submitting to the editor. It is perhaps to the weird impression he made, and to the air of mystery about him, that Heine owed the success of his visit.

Berlin at that period was a city of contrasts. An insatiable thirst for novelty possessed it, a reaction, no doubt, to the puritanical rationalism of the preceding years. It was a paradise for adventurers of all kinds ; any glib-tongued charlatan and every pedlar of new religion was sure of a vogue. The fashion of the moment was for the sinister and the bizarre, and on the spacious avenues of the city wild-haired poets could be encountered, pacing like ghosts and muttering as they passed. The strange fancies of men like E. T. A. Hoffmann, or the chaotic imaginations of others like Jean-Paul, had created an atmosphere of fiction in the solid bourgeois town, normally so devoted to order and practical affairs.

Beneath the surface, however, the solid spirit of the *Biedermeyer* still reigned, represented by homely habits, modest means, and simple pleasures. The furniture and interior decoration of the *Biedermeyer* were made to last and to enshrine plain comfort and the enchanted circle of family life.

Nevertheless, the *tempo* of the city was quickening even then. Soon the family living-room was to become " the best room," left to sleep coldly under dust-covers all the week, waiting for Sunday's " company." Already Lessing had called Berlin " this galley " and Varnhagen grumbled that " tranquillity and leisured peace are impossible in Berlin ; everything there is a whirl of activity and a mad rush of work."

Berlin from the very beginning has been a city hungry for novelty, yet a slave to appearances, as if engaged in an eternal search for its own character. For more than a century its critics have remarked that the loaded tables and ostentatious display of its receptions are made up for by the everyday dish of potatoes and the thinly spread butter of ordinary occasions. The lady of the house appears abroad in silk and furbelows, but at home she wears the eternal cotton apron ; her husband bursts forth on Sundays in the newest clothes, but more often than not he spends his evenings at home in a shabby dressing-gown. For more than a century, too, visitors to Berlin have asked how its inhabitants can find the money for all the outbursts of good living which even the middle classes seem to enjoy. For, instead of living according to their means, each apes the standard of his richer neighbour, as if determined to reach the standard of the class to which he aspires.

This vice of imitation, the weakness most characteristic of Berlin, also affects the intellectuals. Sensations must be enjoyed in common ; ideas must be shared with a group of others ; everything that is done must be done collectively. And this makes it necessary to know all that is going on, and to hear all that is being said. To this end reference-books are devoured, and the latest reviews and periodicals scanned for all the gossip. An author who is fashionable is for a time besieged with attention ; the last actress to attract notice becomes the cynosure of all the town.

In 1821 this craze for novelty could only find expression in the fields of art and society. In the political world there reigned the silence of the grave ; a network of spies and the barbed wire of censorship created a tyranny which effectively stifled all freedom of opinion in that direction. In addition, Berlin was a new town, totally lacking in tradition or atmosphere, a parvenu amongst cities and therefore an ideal sounding-board for new and noisy catchwords. " Berlin is not a city," mocked Heine later on ; " it is just a place where a crowd of people have got together, amongst them many intelligent folk to whom the town itself means less than nothing ; those are the people who make the intellectual life of Berlin."

In point of fact, this intellectual life of Berlin in the period between the end of Frederick the Great's reign and the wars of liberation had been formed by two foreign elements, the French emigrants and the emancipated Jews. The Jewish colony in Berlin had only been freed from the ghetto for one generation, and owed its importance, according to Mirabeau, to one man—Moses Mendelssohn. Its influence was exercised above all through the literary *salons* of its richer members—women such as Henriette Herz, whom the Berliners, seeking flattering analogies, called their Madame Récamier ; and Rahel von Varnhagen, whom they called their Madame de Staël. These were the women who grouped around themselves the intellectual and fashionable *élite*. Their husbands, especially the Jewish husbands, were rarely seen in the literary *salons*. " To meet the best society without ceremony, one must be introduced to the *salons* of the Jews," wrote the pastor Schleiermacher.

Literary reputations were made in those drawing-rooms, new ideas were circulated and friendships formed which often bridged the normal chasms of society. Writers and poets like Adalbert de Chamisso and the Baron de la Motte Fouqué, both of them descended from French emigrants, rubbed shoulders with scientists like Humboldt and savants such as Fichte and theologians like Schleiermacher, or with diplomats like Gentz—whose anti-Semitism did not prevent his becoming the firm friend of Rahel Levin, later the wife of August von Varnhagen. Many members of the nobility were regular *habitués* in the *salons*, even some of royal blood such as Prince Augustus and the handsome but unfortunate Prince Louis Ferdinand. The Jews were not only wealthy; they were also the most cultured element of the community. They wanted to enter high society, and they turned to the highest chiefly because they found amongst that *élite*, which had mostly been educated in the ideas of the French encyclopædists, a lack of prejudice which still existed amongst the bourgeoisie. The aristocracy, wrote Carl Hillebrand, "needed no second invitation." After the defeat of the French, there came a sharp reaction against the Jewish *bureaux d'esprit*, and German Christian sects clamoured for the exclusion of Jews, Frenchmen, and Philistines from society. But the influence of these *salons* remained so strong, and the friendships they had engendered proved so firm, that even the very inspirers of the German-Christian movement, such as the Arnims and the Brentanos, were obliged to surrender, and themselves to seek admission to the only circles which the intellectual *élite* frequented.

Heine found the doors of these *salons* wide open before him. His first poems were published in the *Gesellschafter*, and a collection of them appeared in book form at the end of 1821. They were acclaimed by a society avid for all new forms of expression. Fame had come to him at a stroke. Heine, like Byron, could boast that he had awakened one morning to find himself famous. His verse appealed, however, to a far bigger world than that of letters and society. In plain, intelligible language they told of sufferings familiar to all. Everyone found in them the reflection of his love and the story of his own desires and frustrations. The music of his words sank into the memory, and the easy, familiar tone, if it called forth the sneers of the pedants, awoke in the wider public the conviction that only a really great poet could use such words so successfully. That, at least, is the opinion of one critic of the collected works, who wrote: "Since Buerger we have had no German poet who is so completely successful as Herr Heine. . . . If the 'Two Grenadiers' had been written in French it would have become a popular French song. . . ." Contemporary criticism also realised the modernity of Heine, the need for passionate self-search and the confession of intimate weaknesses so as to find in them what is true of all men. "Our literature has never possessed a poet who so boldly exposes his own subjective feelings and the depths of his own personality with such astonishing lack of self-consciousness," wrote the critic of the *Rheinisch-Westfälischer Anzeiger*. The same critic emphasised another modern trait in Heine: the man whom he analyses is the man-in-the-street; "It is ordinary humanity, and nothing else, which lives in these verses . . . in short, Heine is a poet of the Third Estate."

Nevertheless, some exceptions to the general enthusiasm there were from the beginning, prompted rather by suspicion than by anything actually found in the poems. "Nature has chosen him for her favourite, has heaped upon him all her gifts in order to make of him one of the greatest poets of Germany. It depends upon himself whether he will become this—or whether he is to be a will-o'-the-wisp or a poisonous plant, harmful to his country."

For weeks Heine had lived in that state of agonised anticipation known only to writers. Day after day he had paced the pavement in front of the book-shop where his volume of poems was shown in the window. He became his own advertising agent, and missed no opportunity of reminding both personal friends and literary critics of his work. But his success, when it came, surpassed the expectations aroused in him by the compliments he had solicited, for, as is usual in such circumstances, his friends fought shy of compromising themselves by too great a show of enthusiasm. Once the book had appeared, however, Heine found his world at his feet ; the literary *salons* vied with each other in welcoming the new lion of the day ; women acclaimed him as the German Byron; old friends hastened to remind him of ties they had previously forgotten, new ones sought him out. Poets already famous, such as de la Motte Fouqué, dedicated their verse to him, and at once a crowd of minor poets flattered him by imitating his style. Even before his volume was published, Heine found himself obliged to deny the authorship of several poems which were attributed to him. Such an amazing success, such a triumphant justification of his existence, transformed the world for him and made it a place teeming with joy and interest. He found himself installed in the heart of the intellectual *élite* of his time, dull care fell away, memories of his unhappy youth faded, and a new chapter opened before him.

But the contrast between outward appearances and his inner life existed nevertheless. Outwardly Heine was much like all the other young fops who sauntered along the spacious Unter den Linden, gaily dressed in their coloured vests and Bolivar hats, and winking at the pretty girls they passed. He frequented the fashionable restaurants and cafés, the opera, the masked balls, the Jewish *salons*, and the receptions held by the aristocratic world. He mingled with the crowd which cheered royalty as it passed and, like the crowd, acclaimed the beauty of the Princess Alexandrina. Judging by the column he wrote for a Rhineland paper, he seems to have brought even his opinions into harmony with the official view. He admired the actresses who were all the rage and the composers with the biggest following. Whatever was, was right, even down to the handsome Prussian officers who strutted by in the streets. Only very occasionally did the turn of a phrase reveal the irony within him—such quips, for example, as : " This fellow is not one of those who invented powder, but one of those who use it ; he is a military man."

Like many other young men of his time, he attended the university merely because to do so was the official reason for his being in Berlin. But he was more often to be found hearing Hegel expound philosophy, or Bopp Sanscrit, than at the courses in law given by the reactionaries Schmalz or Savigny. The number of terms for which his uncle had agreed to pay were fast drawing to an end, but he consoled himself with the hope that Salomon Heine would prove indulgent now that his nephew was a celebrity. His relations with his uncle had been somewhat improved by the good offices of Professor Gubitz. When Salomon Heine appeared in Berlin during the spring of 1822, he was so enraged by his nephew's obvious lack of interest in his career that he threatened to cut off all supplies of money. But Professor Gubitz had pleaded that there were extenuating circumstances for the poet, and he used with the uncle all the respect which he felt was due to the wealthy Hamburg banker. Harry should not be judged by ordinary standards : " Such an uncle cannot abandon such a nephew." To which Salomon Heine replied that he had no desire to abandon him, but that he " ought to learn the value of money, each according to his profession." But there was a note of astonishment perceptible in the remark he made to one of his Berlin friends : " This gentleman professes to think it may be a question of genius. Well, I would like to believe it."

Meantime Harry was being reproached by someone else for wasting his time and his gifts, and by one who had far more influence on him than his uncle. This other critic, Rahel von Varnhagen, was thinking solely of his work and not at all about his career. She wanted Harry to be *wesentlich*, to plunge beneath the surface and seek for deeper things within himself.

Rahel Levin was one of those remarkable women who seem to be born to serve as the guiding star for exceptional minds, and, without being in the slightest degree creative themselves, to possess the power of inspiring the best in them. Born in 1771, the daughter of a Jewish jeweller, she had grown up amid the clash of two centuries and in an environment which received the full impact of the new currents of ideas, the arrival in power of the middle class, the liberation of the Jews from the ghetto, and the relative emancipation of women. She herself shared in the passion of these great fights ; she could even claim to have been an important factor in the victories, simply by being what she was—an inspiration. She was entirely of her time, and one could not imagine her existing at any other period. Her great personality far surpassed the average of either her sex or her race ; she was, in fact, truly representative of herself alone, Rahel Levin—that is to say, of the highest point to which a member of the middle class, a Jewess and a woman of that period, could evolve.

Even as a girl, living in what was little more than a garret, she had attracted the most eminent men of her time to the literary gatherings she had been wont to hold there. The influence she exercised is the more amazing in that she possessed neither the startling beauty of Henriette Herz nor the advantage of a great name, like Mendelssohn's daughters, nor even the wealth of the other women who founded the *salons* of the period. Small and delicate, in her young days she was even lacking in physical charm. She had a long, thin nose set in an oval face, and a high forehead crowned with thick black curls. An obstinate chin did not help to relieve these somewhat unprepossessing features. But in her large dark eyes there dwelt a gaze of which Varnhagen had said, when he first met her, that " one did not know if it gave more or took more." Every thought that passed through her mind was reflected in her expressive features, at one moment shining with a strange beauty and passionately earnest, the next transformed into a mask of severity and tense with determination, or again changing suddenly to a smile of such rare sympathy that it drove all hardness or sadness from her countenance. It was, above all, her voice which enchanted those who met her—a warm, deep voice, with a wide range of tone, which penetrated farther and affected her hearers more even than her words. She understood everything and everybody with a sovereign intuition, and in that lay her genius. "Rahel does not reason about a subject," said Goethe, " she possesses it."

Such insight comes only from inexorable self-knowledge. Rahel had learnt to form her opinions of men and events by first conducting the most searching examination of her own character. She believed that nobody could claim to possess personality who had not the courage to be ruthless with himself. A woman so constructed was inevitably condemned to suffer all her life from the disparity between her feelings and her clairvoyance. Throughout her active and successful career comes the plaintive refrain, " I have never had any luck in life."

But she was big enough to forget self, and she found opportunity of satisfying her love of greatness and to efface herself triumphantly. She gave herself up to the genius of Goethe. The fact that Goethe became recognised during his lifetime as the greatest mind which Germany had ever produced was in no small degree due to the tireless efforts of the Jewish jeweller's daughter of Berlin. Rahel was forty years old before she married Varnhagen, but even after her marriage she continued to be the apostle of this new religion and to preach Goethe to the intellectuals by whom she was surrounded, above all to the younger generation.

When Heine met her she was already old and infirm. Her drooping chin and bent shoulders gave her the appearance " of an old fairy, not to say a witch," to quote Grillparzer. But she had lost neither her tenacity of purpose nor her spiritual charm, and she thrilled as ever to the exceptional. She completely enslaved the young man of twenty-four, and held him as though spellbound. " I should like to have engraved on my collar the words, 'I belong to Madame Varnhagen,' " he wrote. From the time of his first meeting with her he published nothing without first submitting it to her judgment, and she, on her side, spared him neither encouragement nor criticism. She knew instinctively that

Heine's extraordinary gifts made it possible to ask much of him.

With her infallible intuition Rahel saw at once all that was " exceptional and refined " in Heine. " He understood me, and I often realised, when others did not understand, what won him over to me and why he accepted me as his mentor."

Meantime a friendship sprang up between Heine and Varnhagen which proved unusually firm under the test of time and passing differences. Varnhagen was a living paradox. He was so proud of his aristocratic origin that he added a " von " to his name which became sharply contested. On the other hand, he did not hesitate to marry a Jewess. He was deeply attached to his diplomatic career, and yet, when stationed at Karlsruhe, he quixotically sacrificed it by espousing the liberal cause. After losing his post he worked assiduously to ingratiate himself again with the authorities, but at the same time he kept up his connections with the progressives, to whom his house was always open.

Physically Varnhagen was of distinguished appearance, with soft, ill-defined features and piercing blue eyes shining through glasses. He had a small vain mouth, the lower part of his body was too short, but his carriage was erect. His voice was high-pitched and sometimes sharp. He was always to be seen with a note-book in his hand, peering into his own drawing-room to see those with whom Rahel spoke alone. Then he would draw them aside and ask what she had said to them. Under his stiff and formal manner he was known to be avid for scandal and a repository for all the gossip of the town. Though for years without a profession, he was as busy as a Chief of Staff, scanning all the papers, reading all the new books, piling up notes on people and events, and compiling whole volumes of memoirs.

And yet, after a devoted married life with Rahel, he became engaged soon after his wife's death to the beautiful Marianne Saaling. His contemporaries found him irritating. " His company is almost intolerable for other men," said Chamisso, who was exasperated by his vanity and his constant disparagement of others ; and Savigny declared bluntly, "Happily there are few men like him, for if there were, life would be considerably less agreeable." Nevertheless, one day, late in his life, Varnhagen was to come out in his true colours. After the revolution of 1848 he sided openly with the radicals.

Heine alone seems to have understood the fund of audacity which lay hidden behind his curious bearing. "Varnhagen an aristocrat?" he said. "Believe me, it is purely a matter of circumstances. If the opportunity presented itself, Varnhagen would be a perfect Robespierre." His friendship with the Varnhagens was the great event of Heine's life in Berlin. Rahel's *salon* also held an attraction for him other than the master and mistress of the house, namely the wife of Ludwig Levin, Rahel's brother, known as a dramatist under the name of Ludwig Robert. Heine's admiration for Friederike Robert, "most beautiful of women," was so obvious that in literary circles Friederike was thought to be the young poet's muse. The love-lorn Heine wrote that she combined the mystery of the past with the charm of the present. But Börne, who was not attracted by her, said spitefully that "she thinks only of showing off her good looks; she does so successfully, but she has no soul." Her beauty, at least, was not exaggerated. She had a small and well-poised head, a perfectly oval face framed in coils of soft black hair, and a high forehead. Her arched brows seemed to contrast with the calm expression of her almond eyes, but formed alliance with "that most ravishing of smiles" which played round the corners of her tiny mouth.

Friederike Robert had reached the calm of married life after a hectic and disastrous liaison with a wandering Italian theatre director. She had no desire to disturb her new-found tranquillity by any affair with a young poet. She let him pay court to her, listened patiently to his confessions and his tirades, accepted graciously with her "ravishing smile" the homage of his poetry, but she had learnt wisdom and controlled herself. Börne gave a cynical explanation even of this virtue: "She is too indolent to be unfaithful to her husband," he said.

To Friederike Robert, Heine dedicated several of his poems. His love for her was a sort of pagan cult of beauty. The same appears to account for his attachment to a young Polish nobleman, Count Eugène de Breza, who was Heine's inseparable companion during his first months in Berlin. The Polish student possessed the beauty of a Greek god, so radiantly perfect that it induced belief in a corresponding perfection of character. Gay, careless, and witty, he seemed equally composed of a desire to please and a need to be admired. Years later Heine wrote : " I had a Polish friend for whom I would give my life even to-day, though the fellow was not worth two sous. He had venereal disease and no principles, but in his voice, if he was only asking ' What ? ' there was such a tone that at the thought of it even now I scarcely know whether to laugh or cry." In Berlin, however, Heine had not yet discovered " the little yellow stone of falsity " in his friend, and when Eugène de Breza, who had proved too attractive to the Duchess of Cumberland, was asked by the authorities to leave Berlin and to trouble the peace of aristocratic homes no more, Heine lamented the departure of " this most likeable of mortals " and " most gracious of friends." " He was the only man with whom I was never bored," he added.

During the summer of 1823 he paid a visit to Breza on his estates near Gnesen. There he met a young Jewess, still almost a child, who seems to have inspired one of his most popular poems :

Du bist wie eine Blume
So hold und schön und rein.

" You are like a flower, so dear, so lovely, and so pure."

" I went there," he wrote on his return, " to seek those pure and healthy natures which I know so well how to recognise, because the impure and the unhealthy are so familiar to me."

The impure and the unhealthy did indeed continue to attract him. He carried on at the same time his passionate adoration for Friederike Robert, his flirtations with chaste and stately baronesses, and his adventures with Berlin girls, whom he would beg not to recognise him when they passed him in the Linden. He would go straight from his society tea-parties to riotous bohemian company which had nothing in common with the literary *salons*. Almost every evening Heine was to be found in the cellar tavern of Lutter and Wegner, where a noisy crowd gathered nightly " for what the good citizens of Berlin call orgies." As a matter of fact, nothing more was to be found there than thick clouds of smoke, plenty of cheap liquor, and a great deal of noise and animation. The place was the haunt of second-rate young poets, of young men who talked much and did nothing, and of failures of all kinds. The centre of attraction was the great actor, Ludwig Devrient, who came on after the play was over in the theatre near by. Devrient would sit rolling his great eyes and making his deep voice reverberate from the vaulted roof, until drunkenness sent him to sleep. From time to time he would be joined by some older companion in drunkenness ; E. T. A. Hoffmann, perhaps, would tear himself from his sick-bed and stagger to the cellar, a wreck of a man, with haggard face, feverish colour, and wandering gaze.

Dietrich Grabbe, too, would sometimes be there—" a drunken Shakespeare," as Heine called him. Grabbe was a lusty peasant, possessed by a sort of creative demon, who sought to drown in alcohol the memory of horrible privations. Heine's delicate perception recognised his worth under the rough, chaotic exterior of his dramas. When Gubitz showed him a manuscript of Grabbe's which he said was incoherent and impossible to use, Heine replied : " You are wrong, my friend ; he is not a madman ; he is a genius." He brought Grabbe's tragedy to the notice of Rahel, but she returned it in the middle of the night, saying that she would get no sleep if she knew such a work was under her roof.

Despite Heine's efforts to help him, Grabbe bore a grudge against him, as he did against all who had succeeded and who no longer suffered from abject want, or pawned their mother's silver to buy a glass of wine. One evening Heine was sitting before the glass which he scarcely sipped, silent as usual amidst the tumult, well clothed, well fed, listening with his superior smile to the flood of talk and crazy projects. Suddenly Grabbe leapt up and seized the poet's thin body in his great coarse hands, shaking him furiously and shouting that his poetry had no body to it, that he was an impotent weakling and for that reason what he wrote was sickly sentiment. Bawling out that Heine was a dirty Jew, he threw him brutally out of the door, shouting insults after him.

Curiously enough, although Heine all his life kept strict account of the grudges he owed, in this case he forgave and forgot the incident. The reason was that he understood the other's disgust, and that he shared his rebellion to a degree which the peasant Grabbe was incapable even of imagining.

Whilst his life as a successful poet seemed to be passed in jollity and comfort, below the surface his grief grew ever deeper. On the one hand he possessed the realisation of his dreams, on the other recognition of his final defeat. His last visit to Hamburg had shown him, once and for all, that Amalie was lost to him. Possibly the blow was made the harder because his success in Berlin had unconsciously revived his hope. In any case, the news of her marriage with a certain John Friedlaender of Königsberg, which took place in August 1821, unloosed in him a flood of torment. Jealousy and bitter heart-burning mingled with pity for the woman who knew no better than to tie herself to a man for whom she did not care in order to forget another to whom she was devoted :

Ich grolle nicht und wenn des Herz auch bricht,
Ewig verlorenes Lieb ! ich grolle nicht.
Wie du auch strahlst in Diamantenpracht
Es fällt kein Strahl in deines Herzens Nacht.

"I bear no grudge, even if my heart should break—love lost for ever. Though shining bright with diamonds, no beam can penetrate thy bosom's night."

Little did Heine think, when he wrote " Ich grolle nicht," that it, and so many others of his poems to Amalie in the " Book of Songs," would be repeated by generations of young men crossed in love ; that it would be set to music a hundred times, sung by girls who had never known love and by old women recalling the dreams of their youth. The words, which were so new and so sincere when Heine wrote them, were destined to become hackneyed by repetition, frayed with much use, and worn smooth like coins by passing through many hands.

Nevertheless, Heine was not content, during those first months of Amalie's marriage, merely to " make little songs of his great suffering." His distress was great enough to demand a fuller and more violent expression. For the second and last time in his life he attempted drama. He plunged into the work in a state of almost hysterical excitement. The man who never improvised, who could not write even a quatrain without revising it a dozen times, sat down and dashed off the long dramatic poem " William Ratcliff " in three days. He felt that he was writing under supernatural guidance, and claimed to hear " the beating of great wings about his head." This conviction of inspiration long deceived him as to the value of the work ; the emotion he felt surged in himself but did not live in the drama he produced. The chief characters were artificial and lifeless ; only when read in conjunction with Heine's personal story did they assume some semblance of reality.

This artificial tragedy, stuffed full of ideas and phrases garnered from English and other literature, was the least original of all his work, even of his younger days. He said himself later on that it was "the chief confession" of his youth. But it served to release him from the intensity of his passion for Amalie. Afterwards there remained only " a feminine shadow dwelling in my poems," and an incurable regret which haunted him almost for the rest of his life.

But this failure had also the effect of destroying in him for ever the faculty of confidence in himself. Henceforth he became so prepared for misfortune, so more than ready to meet deception half way, that even at moments when life seemed to pour upon him the realisation of his most ardent desires he could only think of possible disasters.

Anyone else, even an older man of ripe experience, would have been carried away by success such as his when his volume of poems was published. But Heine, listening to the praise which swept in upon him from all sides, could think only of the day when admiration would turn to abuse.

Only a few months after he became famous he wrote : " For long I have foreseen the time when an exaggerated enthusiasm for my person would be reduced to ashes, and to ashes cooled by rain whose residue is mud. . . . I await that moment now, and I shall see without bitterness those who cheered me to the skies, change tune and drag me through that mud."

When his old friend Rousseau dedicated to him a series of sonnets glowing with praise, Heine, out of gratitude, wrote an anonymous article on the poems of Rousseau. But he could not resist adding a personal note : " The head of Heine is so encircled with the halo of his poems that M. Rousseau could well afford the pleasure of throwing at this self-crowned head a few small pellets of mud ; it would be pity if he does not do so ; it would also be contrary both to custom and to the very essence of human nature." And, again, when Baron de la Motte Fouqué expressed his admiration in a poem, Heine's first reaction was to say, " He will be sorry for having written these verses on the day he sees my genealogical tree."

There was the rub ! It was his position as a Jew which wounded him most deeply. Across the coloured thread of his life in Berlin there comes always, in various hurtful forms, the reminder of his racial origin. He found it expressed most brutally in his university life. " The students took it upon themselves to behave like modern Templars," said Treitschke ; " they displayed their hatred of the Jews with a ferocity which strongly recalled the times of the Crusades."

But anti-Semitism pursued him even in his love-affairs.

One day, in some shady corner of the Tiergarten, he embraced a young noblewoman who was unaware of his origin. Even as he kissed her, the woman whispered how she loathed his people. This incident troubled him for a long time, until he rid himself of it by writing the satirical poem, " Donna Clara," based on the occurrence.

His state of melancholy was increased by the effects of his recent malady. He was troubled by constant headaches, a form of torment from which he suffered all his life and which he likened to drops of boiling lead running through his brain. His nerves were on edge, and the slightest noise, even in an adjacent room, reduced him to frenzy. His face began to assume the expression of one who was in constant pain. For hours he lay stretched at full length on the sofa in his room, nursing his aching head in his hands, with eyes half shut, querulous and shivering ; whilst around him his friends laughed at his " imaginary symptoms."

" Isolated and ill, a prey to my enemies, incapable of any enjoyment in life, such is my existence here," he wrote to his confidant, Sethe. His attitude of distrust increased until it came to border on persecution mania. " I know for certain that a group has been formed here for the purpose of driving me mad by calumny." He talked of Berlin as " a nest of falsehood," and saw himself surrounded by enemies and traitors. He had confidence only in Rahel and her husband. " During the day I am a prey to increasing suspicion. I hear my name pronounced everywhere, and always with sardonic laughter. . . . At night I am unable to sleep ; I see as in a dream my so-called friends exchanging stories about me, and passing little bits of paper from one to another." These suspicions may have had some basis in fact ; it appears that his enemies from Bonn and Göttingen really had spread unpleasant rumours of his life in those towns, for he adds : " These miserable cads have done their best to poison the air of Berlin for me."

One note is struck again and again throughout his letters, recalling the subject which was always in his mind. " I am not a German, see Rühs, Fries, and others." The vehemence with which he saw himself denied the right of being German, though it came at a moment when the critics were acclaiming him as a great German poet, and when he himself felt capable of enriching the poetry of his country with work of permanent value, aroused in him revolt and the bitter hatred which comes from exasperation.

" We can be friends no more. But do not think that I have anything against you personally, my dear Christian. When I write that we can no longer be friends, it is because I have always been honest and sincere with you, and I would not begin now to deceive you. Everything that is German disgusts me, and you, alas, are German. All that is German has the effect of the nux vomica upon me. The German language itself offends my ears. My own poems repulse me when I remember that they are written in German. I dislike writing even these lines, for the German characters irritate my nerves." Then he continues in French : " Never would I have believed that these brutes called Germans were a race at once so boring and so filled with malice. As soon as my health is better I shall leave Germany ; I shall go to Arabia ; there I will lead the pastoral life ; I will be a man in the fullest sense of the word ; I shall live amongst the species of camels which are not students ; I shall write beautiful verse in Arabic like Morlaccat and will sit upon the sacred rock where Mojnun sat and sighed for Leila. . . ."

Other young Jews of this period, who, like Heine, were subjected to constant humiliation, and who also wished to be assimilated by Germany, sought to excuse themselves for their origin by renouncing it more or less openly. Or, like those whites of North America who have a touch of negro blood, they tried to escape attention. But Heine's pride forbade him to repudiate what was an integral part of his being. His dignity as a man drove him rather to seek refuge in the very heart of persecuted Jewry. The reaction was natural enough in a young man of his temperament, which, for all his stormy personality, made it impossible to exist alone surrounded by indifference or hatred. He had to attach himself to some cause, to join some active group and thus either return to a common past or march with others towards a common future. " My attachment to Judaism has its roots solely in a profound antipathy to Christianity," he explained later. " I, who have no use for any dogmatic religion, shall perhaps one day become converted to the most orthodox rabbinism, because I consider it a good antidote."

In actual fact, his progress back to Judaism was very difficult for him, because since early childhood he had had no contact with religion, and had even lost the instinctive sentiment of racial solidarity. Heine came to Judaism almost as a convert, lacking entirely the memory of a spiritual or moral bond with the community. He had to start from the very beginning and grope in the depths of his being before he could find in himself the broken threads which should unite him with Jewry.

Chance, however, brought him in contact with a group of young people who were in the same position as himself and who shared the same aspirations. In 1819, the year in which the anti-Semitic troubles broke out in Germany, the jurist Edward Gans, with Leopold Zuntz and others, founded in Berlin an " Association for Judaic Culture and Science." Their aims were twofold : to defend their co-religionists and to work for their emancipation. These men were also engaged in exploring the past for the purpose of creating a spiritual and moral unity, and with a view to clearing away the obstructions due to the ignorant superstition of the Jewish masses, to the intolerance of the orthodox rabbis and the Byzantinism of Talmudic dialectics.

They were interested above all in preparing the future, however. They fought against the fundamentals of anti-Semitic prejudice, against the ghetto mentality and scholastic interpretations of religion. By the scientific study of their history they tried to bring the Jews to recognise the true mission of their race and to develop in Jewish youth a European conscience.

Within a few months of writing the letter to Sethe quoted above, Heine became an active member of this association.

He took its activities very seriously, went regularly to its meetings, took part in the debates, and drew up reports. He showed himself of great value in the school attached to the association, where young Jews, especially those from the east who had escaped from the rabbinical colleges, were taught to understand the Europe in which they were living. Heine gave lessons in French and German, and also taught German history. Before these young people of his own race, who would not mock at his enthusiasm, he gave his romantic fancy free rein in expounding the great past of his country.

This work brought him into contact with Gans, a man with a magnificent head like that of a Greek thinker ; with the philosopher Lazarus Bendavid, a disciple of Kant ; and with the orientalist Ludwig Marcus, " the little man with the great soul." But above all he won the friendship of Moses Moser, a friendship which lasted throughout his life and became a model of devotion, patience, and generosity.

Moser was a round-shouldered little man with prominent eyes and a high, square forehead, made more noticeable by his crisp black curly hair. His eyelids were swollen and red from working at night, and his firm, strong mouth was thick-lipped and Jewish. But his outwardly unprepossessing appearance was relieved, and even made attractive, by his expression of kindliness and understanding. By profession he was an employee of the Friedlaender Bank, but in his spare time he was a mathematician and astronomer, a student of Sanscrit and of Hindu literature, and a follower of Hegel's lectures. He was as proficient in modern as in ancient languages, and could read Plato and Tacitus in the original with the same facility as Dante and Shakespeare. And yet with all this learning he was no book-worm, but a man of action, practical and resourceful, whose advice was always worth having and who was always ready to assist his neighbours. " An epilogue to Nathan the Wise," said Heine of his "arch-friend " Moser, and he wrote later that he " fought and suffered like an unknown martyr. His name remains unknown, and one may search in vain for him in the lists of those who sacrificed themselves for humanity."

For years Heine had resort to Moser in all his greatest difficulties, and his call for help never fell on deaf ears. Throughout his troubled existence his friendship with the bank clerk Moses Moser was for him an encouragement and a sanctuary. Incidentally, this friendship was the only positive result of his work for the association, which, begun with so much enthusiasm and hope, ended only in fresh disappointment.

The first lesson which Heine learnt there was that the famous "Jewish solidarity" was a myth. The emancipated Jews feared the uneducated multitude which pressed upon them from below. Those who had succeeded felt their position menaced by the arrival of newcomers, who reminded them all too forcibly of their own origin. They declined any responsibility for their co-religionists, they had no desire to be drawn into struggles which meant identifying themselves with the whole race, and they eased their consciences by subscribing to philanthropic works. The mentality which their position as members of a tolerated section of society had developed in them led them to be prudent and timorous. Their motto was to do nothing which might concentrate attention on themselves, but rather to surmount unnoticed, one by one, the tremendous barriers which separated their race from the rest of the world. "The Association for Judaic Culture and Science" soon found itself confronted by serious material difficulties, because the rich Jews refused to give any help. Gans wrote in his report, "The only link which unites the Jews is that of fear; the only higher interest for which they are willing to part with some portion of their worldly goods is that of charity."

When the association finally became obliged to abandon its work through lack of funds, Zuntz issued a scathing indictment of his co-religionists: "The Jews and the Judaism which we tried to reconstruct are divided amongst themselves, an easy prey for barbarians, fools, and usurers. For a long time to come we shall see this people as it is to-day, adrift and without discipline or principles, turning to Christianity because they have nothing else to turn to ; one section still sunk in the squalor of past ages, despised by Europe, another rustling papers in minor Government offices, rich or bankrupt, persecuted or tolerated in turn." Once more Heine found closed to him a road down which he had plunged full of eagerness and illusion. But, although he shared the same bitter disappointment as his companions, he at least drew from it other conclusions than some of them. Edward Gans declared that " since there is such stupidity and indolence amongst the Jews, since ineptitude and improvidence are so widespread amongst them, it is not worth while to bother with such a pack." He gave up bothering forthwith, and devoted his attention to carving his own career. But, in spite of Hardenberg's interest in him, he was unable to obtain a professorship at the university. He was met by the flat refusal of the King, who demanded that he should first adopt Christianity. Such a condition was asking a lot from such an ardent defender of Judaism, and Gans left the country to try his luck first in France and then in England. He even thought of emigrating to America. After a series of vain attempts abroad he returned to Berlin, however, where he finally obtained the coveted Chair—at the price of conversion.

Heine was indignant at the " treachery " of Gans, for " it is the time-honoured duty of a captain to be the last to quit the sinking ship. Gans, though, has been the first to save his skin." He sent him a satirical poem ending with the lines:

Gestern noch ein Held gewesen
Ist man heute schon ein Schurke.

" A hero only yesterday, but to-day a rascal."

Heine's own conclusion to this chapter of his life was different. " I shall never cease to bestir myself on behalf of the rights of Jews to equal citizenship, and when troublous times come, as I feel sure they will come, the German mob will hear my voice resound from their drinking-halls to their palaces."

This new disappointment served only to confirm an impression which had already awoken within him before he launched himself into the blind alley of his attempt to help the Jews emancipate themselves. He realised that failure was inevitable, because it was impossible to unite the discordant elements of Judaism. He realised, too, that social factors are more powerful than either religious bonds or racial solidarity. The gulf which separates the possessing classes from the disinherited masses is too deep to be bridged by worship of a common God or the hurt of a common wrong. Heine saw the class struggle carried on even in the heart of Judaism, and he knew then that the emancipation of the Jews could only succeed within the framework of a greater social emancipation.

He had already given evidence of recognising the terrible scourge of social injustice in his poem "Ratcliff." It is curious that the subject should have struck him at that early stage, when he himself was so absorbed in the drama of his own affairs and when, too, the literary currents of the day all tended towards an exaggerated subjectivism, and public opinion was still indifferent to social problems.

One of the characters in the poem in question is made to say that all humanity is "divided into two nations, engaged in fierce struggle ; one the satiated and the other the starving." The spirit of social rebellion is expressed through the mouth of Ratcliff :

und einen Mann ergreift der Zorn,
Wenn er betrachtet wie die Pfennigseelen,
Die Buben, oft im Überflusse schwelgen,
In Samt und Seide schimmern, Austern schlürfen . . .
In goldnen Wagen durch die Strassen rasseln,
Und stolz herabsehn auf den Hungerleider,
Der, mit dem letzten Hemde unterm Arm,
Langsam und seufzend nach dem Leihhaus wandert. . . .
O seht mir doch die klugen, satten Leute,
Wie sie mit einem Walle von Gesetzen
Sich wohlverwahret gegen allen Andrang. . . .
Weh dem, der diesen Wall durchbricht !

Bereit sind Richter, Henker, Stricke, Galgen,
Je nun, manchmal gibt's Leut' die es nicht scheuen.

" A man is seized by anger when he sees how paltry souls wallow in abundance and shine in velvet and silk and gorge on oysters . . . and rattle through the streets in gilded carriages and look down proudly on the hungry man who, carrying his last shirt on his arm, wanders slowly and sighing to the pawnshop. . . . See these clever, well-fed people, and how they have protected themselves against the throng with a bulwark of laws. . . . Woe to him who breaks through this bulwark ! Judges, executioners, ropes, and gallows are ready—and yet sometimes there are men who dare to do it ! "

Many years later, when this work had come to mean no more to him than a faded chapter of his own youth, Heine turned with pleasure to the poem on account of this early awakening of his social conscience. " In ' Ratcliff,' " he wrote towards the end of his life, " the burning question of the daily broth is asked, the broth into which so many bad cooks now dip their spoons and which boils ever more fiercely every day."

It was not mere chance that Heine from that moment mingled this great question with the expression of his most intimate sufferings. A settled impulse already urged him to do so, and his experiences with the association transformed the impulse into deep conviction. Thus, in toiling painfully to find his own place in life, Heine came to find himself one of a great army of oppressed. Henceforth his own struggle became for him identified with the struggle of the dispossessed. He came consciously to detach himself from the existing order ; between himself and the class into which he was born he felt that an abyss was forming. Writing to his sister's *fiancé* towards the end of his stay in Berlin, he said : " I find it quite natural that a man in comfortable circumstances, and happily engaged to boot, should shrink from the idea of the overthrow of society, and that he should rather be concerned for his own security and that of Europe. But for me quite other factors are in play. Besides, I find myself curiously disposed, when I come across an item in the paper to the effect that several people have died of cold in the streets of London, or of hunger in the streets of Naples——"

The result of Heine's sojourn in Berlin was the awakening of a social conscience.

CHAPTER V

THE BIRD OF PASSAGE

Es treibt dich fort von Ort zu Ort Du weisst nicht mal warum.
("In der Fremde")

HEINE LEFT BERLIN to become a wanderer on the face of the earth. For years unrest drove him from place to place, at home nowhere, seeking he knew not what. Someone who met him on one of his journeys likened him to Goethe's "bird of passage." Sleeping one night in a village inn, the next in a mansion, to-day in furnished rooms, to-morrow in his parents' house, wherever he went he seemed like a traveller who had stepped from the coach the day before and had passed a wretched night in the local hostelry.

His first halting-place was Lüneburg, the peaceful little town surrounded by heath, to which his family had retreated after the collapse of their business venture. Salomon Heine himself had chosen the place as a retreat for his brother. It had been a great day in the life of Lüneburg when the famous banker from Hamburg had driven up in his coach and four to seek quarters for his relatives. But, in spite of this sensational beginning, the little place remained characteristically hostile to the newcomers. "As soon as I set foot in Lüneburg," Heine wrote, "I became aware of the anti-Semitism which prevails here and I resolved to live the life of a hermit." His relations also kept to the family circle, for the other Jews in the place consisted solely of "pedlars and beggars." The financial straits in which the Heine family found themselves enhanced their social isolation.

"This is the home of boredom," Heine cried as soon as he had arrived; and to the lack of interest elsewhere was added a somewhat strained relationship with his own people. Coming straight from two years of fame in Berlin, Heine no longer felt himself to be the eternal prodigal who returns home to be petted and comforted. On the contrary, he felt that his success gave him a certain right to the admiration of his family, and he was offended at being treated with the same commiseration as before. " There are people," he wrote later on, " who think they know all about the bird, because they saw the egg from which it was hatched."

Betty Heine frankly considered his literary work to be a waste of his time and talent, and an obstacle to his business career, which she still thought should be his chief aim in life. She had read his poems, but, according to Heine, " without thinking much of them." Even his Sister Lotte, to whom he was devoted, " seemed only to tolerate them," as he wrote with bitterness. That hurt him most of all, for there was a strong resemblance between his sister and himself : " We understand each other so well," he once wrote ; " we two alone are sensible, the rest of the world is mad."

As for Samson Heine, he had never read a single line of his son's verse, but then he had no need to do so, for he believed blindly in his genius without knowing anything about it ; he devoured every article about him, and lamented if others were praised, for there would be less glory left for Harry. He thought that competition prevailed in literature as in commerce, and that the market for praise was limited. He would not allow Goethe to be spoken of highly in his presence, for, if everybody admired Goethe, how could his Harry continue in business ? He carried jealousy of his son's fame to such inordinate lengths that he would not have Goethe's books in his house—his children found themselves obliged to stick the harmless name of Schultz on the backs of Goethe's works !

In the evening of his days poor Samson Heine was oppressed by the thought that nothing he had ever attempted had been a success. He was saddened rather than embittered by the realisation. Mutely he wondered why misfortune should have so dogged the steps of one who had always wished well to others and had been so liked by everyone.

Now the last hopes of the old man, whose life had been so full of dreams, were centred on his eldest son—from his son would come the miracle which he himself would never now perform. But he felt no need to study the boy's work in order to lose himself in dreams about his future. Perhaps he instinctively felt that with his simple mind and humble education he would in any case understand little of this new form of poetry. Perhaps he even feared to feel himself too much a stranger in his son's strange world, and thereby to suffer more.

Harry, however, was still too young to understand this in his father. To him, his whole family, including his father, was indifferent to his genius, and the fact irritated him. "My brothers understand nothing of my work," he wrote again. Gustav, the younger of his two brothers, was brimming with self-assurance and already displayed the cocksure tone which never failed to exasperate his brother throughout his life. He was a bumptious, irrepressible young fellow, of inexhaustible and platitudinous eloquence, and, in addition he enjoyed boisterous good health to what seemed an excessive degree in such cramped quarters.

"Gustav is very well—too well almost," wrote Harry irritably. There was a facial resemblance between the two brothers which did nothing to alleviate their effect upon each other. Watching the sly look of his eyes, the long nose, and his insolent gestures, and listening to the facile irony which fell from his lips, Harry felt himself to be followed about by his own caricature. Gustav was easily interested and as quickly tired of things. He made hasty promises which he never kept, became filled with enthusiasm, and promptly retreated at the first sign of difficulty. All this to Harry was like watching his own image in a distorting mirror, and, no doubt, that alone sufficed to explain the antipathy which he always felt for Gustav.

Maximilian, the other brother, was in such strange contrast to his eldest brother that one might almost believe that he had done it on purpose. He was a quiet studious youth, slow and deliberate, persevering and kindly in a passive way, physically unattractive, and much less gifted than either of his brothers. But he was so conscious of the advantage given to him by his capacity for steady work and his common sense that he soon came to develop a pride in his own mediocrity. He was the man in the street in person, who, because he was so normal, felt a sense of superiority over his more talented fellow-creatures. At the period in question he was passing through a precocious phase of pedantry, and one day when he, a mere schoolboy, discovered a flaw in a hexameter written by his poet brother, he made such play with his little triumph that Heine became for ever disgusted with that form of verse

In the calm of this country life which left more time for introspection, Harry became even more aware of his own contradictory temperament than he had been in the hurly-burly of existence elsewhere. His acute sensibility constantly drove him from one extreme to the other : one day he would be full of comprehension for others and spend himself in affection, on the morrow he would be guarded and taciturn. With no distraction from the outer world to provide a brake for his imagination, he came to feel that his instability was an incurable weakness. " My spirit is as elastic as rubber, often it expands as if it would contain the infinite ; but often, too, it shrinks to miniature proportions." He felt himself essentially modern and yet at the same time to be in sad contrast with his times. The dwindling romantic in him had not destroyed the belief that all life is one. Instinctively Heine came to long to get away ; he thought to escape from himself by fleeing the places where he suffered most.

His heart was set on a trip to Paris. He wanted to cut himself off entirely from what lay behind him and to seek to build anew in fresh surroundings. " But my whole life is limited by this fatal money business." He was obliged to obtain first the consent and then the financial aid of his uncle. In June the whole family assembled at the Zollernspiecker for the ceremony of Lotte's marriage with the Hamburg business man, Moritz Embden. The bridegroom was a nice enough fellow, reliable and practical, hiding a considerate nature under a somewhat awkward manner. He was a good partner for the delicate, sensible young girl, of whom her brother said affectionately: "My darling Lotte is all composed of music, measure, and harmony." The Hamburg branch of the family turned up in force at the ceremony—Uncle Heinrich (to whom Harry was particularly attached), Uncle Salomon, with his wife, his son, and his daughters. The only missing member was Amalie Friedlaender, who had just brought a son into the world. The most friendly atmosphere reigned at this family reunion, and social distinctions were effaced by the warmth of memories shared in common. Even Uncle Salomon was in high good humour and greeted Harry with cordiality, a fact which did not prevent his nephew from remarking maliciously that wild animals are always most domesticated at feeding-time.

On this occasion Harry met again his cousin Therese, the younger of Salomon's daughters. She was then sixteen, and he had not seen her for four years. At once he was struck by her resemblance to Amalie:

Die Kleine gleicht der Geliebten,
Besonders wenn sie lacht;
Sie hat dieselben Augen
Die mich so elend gemacht.

"The little one resembles the beloved, especially when she laughs. She has the same eyes that made me so miserable."

Once again the hateful past is revived and takes possession of him in another form, but with the same disastrous effects.

"The old passion breaks out again in me; I am in the toils of an evil genius," he wrote a few days after his sister's marriage. He had gone to Hamburg with the intention of speaking to his uncle about his projected journey, but had arrived to find that Salomon had just left the city. "The magic of the place had a terrible effect upon me." He spent the stifling days of July in Hamburg, battling vainly with himself. He realised only too well what "this new folly, grafted on the old " must mean for him, and he was shaken with impotent rage at his own weakness. At night he wandered endlessly through the streets of the city, where the past rose up to haunt and terrify him, until he cried, " I long only for eternal oblivion."

And yet, in the solitude of Lüneburg, he had planned this visit to Hamburg as a triumphant return to the scene of his earlier defeat. He had begged Varnhagen and de la Motte Fouqué to give him letters of introduction, for he wanted to shine as the successful poet in the spot where he had been known only as the banker Heine's poor relation.

But this fresh turmoil into which he had been thrown destroyed his hopes and upset all his fine calculations. He was so on edge that when by chance he ran into Varnhagen, the two friends quarrelled violently over a trifle. " It happened at a moment when I was beside myself—when the least lack of sympathy, a word, a look, a gesture even, struck me as if to cause an incurable wound."

Finally he fled from Hamburg, " the place where I am afflicted by the torments of the damned and for which I pine nevertheless—at once my Elysium and my Tartarus." One night, at the height of a raging gale, he embarked for Heligoland. The boat never reached the island ; all night long it ran before the storm, buffeted by the waves, with water sweeping over the decks. The little vessel was in great danger, but Heine, wet through and clinging to the railing of the upper deck, was excited by the crash of the water and the shrieking of the wind through the rigging, which drowned the shouting of the sailors and the moaning of the other passengers. This night of terror was his first encounter with the passion of his life, the sea. He spent the next six weeks at Ritzebüttel and learnt for the first time to recognise the ocean as the great healer of mind and body.

But he indulged also in his other " customary remedy, which consists in extracting from my tortured body all the joy of living of which it is capable." During his short stay he spent thirty louis d'or, which, with characteristic improvidence, he drew from his uncle's allowance for the following month. This time Salomon Heine was seriously angry. There was a violent scene, the outcome of which was that the allowance would only be continued on condition that Harry promised to go on with his reading for the law, and take his examinations the following year. He could do no other than accept the ultimatum, and he returned immediately to Lüneburg to immerse himself in his legal studies.

The autumn of 1823 was passed thus in serious methodical work. At the same time, however, he began to busy himself with the idea of writing a novel. His experience with the Association for Judaic Science and Culture had left in him a profound interest in his race. He decided to attempt in writing what he had been unable to accomplish in the field of action. He would write the apology of the martyred Jewish race. In *Rabbi von Bacherach* he sought to record the thousand years of persecution, tracing the present-day anti-Semitism back to its roots in the mediæval past.

He began to vary his study of the dry tomes of jurisprudence by reading the history of the Jews in the Middle Ages. But the face of Therese Heine appeared to him constantly above the books which littered his table. And as he worked there came to him words of music which have become immortal. All through those grey days of the northern winter, songs were born which drove out the dislike he felt for a form of study so repugnant to his nature. From this period came some of the sweetest lyrical verse which the German tongue had known since Walther von der Vogelweide. It was at Lüneburg that Heine wrote the poem " The Fisherman's Daughter " : " My heart is like the ocean, it storms and ebbs and flows " :

Mein Herz gleicht ganz dem Meere,
Hat Sturm und Ebb' und Flut ;

and the lines which became the favourite poem of the unhappy Empress Elizabeth : " What is the lonely tear doing, that only darkens the sight " :

Was will die einsame Träne'
Sie trübt mir ja den Blick.

There, too, he wrote the famous ballad of the Lorelei. He borrowed the theme of the mermaid of the Rhine from the work of a forgotten poet of no particular distinction, Count Loeben. He treated it with such simplicity that it became one of the most popular of German airs. Instead of employing a legend to make a poem, he wrote a poem which created a legend. Heine the Jew was so near to the heart of the German people that this figment of his imagination seemed to them a genuine evocation of the German past. Henceforth generations of travellers, as they sailed down the Rhine, would look and wonder at the Lorelei rock, for naturally a particular rock was soon discovered as the one-time abode of the mermaid.

Before many years were past the legend had become a tradition. Learned people even professed to have discovered the existence of a Lorelei cult amongst the prehistoric tribes that had lived along the Rhine. A committee was formed to erect a temple in honour of the river deity on the rock, so that her memory might be commemorated for ever. The rock is still pointed out with pride, but the temple was never built, for other learned but rather more conscientious persons proved that the " Lorelei legend " was no older than the third decade of the nineteenth century. It had been born in the fertile mind of Harry Heine, in whose humble work-room overlooking the market-place of Lüneburg " the golden treasure of her hair " had first seen the light of day.

Heine gave the series of poems, most of which dated from this period, the title of *The Home-coming*. It was descriptive as much of his return to his old passion as of his return to the humble abode of his parents. Nevertheless the joys and sorrows of this new springtime of love were attenuated by the recollection that it had all happened to him before.

Glaub' nicht, dass ich mich erschiesse,
Wie schlimm auch die Sachen stehen.
Das alles meine Süsse,
Ist mir schon einmal geschehen.

" Do not believe that I shall shoot myself. Bad as things are, it has all happened once before, my dear."

In January 1824, Heine left Lüneburg in order to return to finish his studies at Göttingen. One of the most marked characteristics of this period of wandering was that he approached each fresh halting-place with disgust, that he quarrelled constantly with his companions, but that, when the time came to leave, he was filled with regret, and found any excuse good enough for postponing his farewells.

In Göttingen unpleasant memories of his first stay rose to greet him. But Heine, the successful poet, is no longer the student striving in vain to be like others. On his first visit he had complained bitterly about the mediocrity of his companions, now he cultivates that mediocrity as a safeguard against himself. "I have chosen a set of the most imbecile creatures conceivable with whom to drink. As soon as I leave my work they crowd around me, so that no rational thought can enter my mind." He refused to be considered a professional poet: "I abuse anybody who speaks to me of Ratcliff." But he gladly allowed himself to be fêted, as *primus inter pares*, by a whole phalanx of young literary aspirants, and they soon succeeded in rousing him to take an interest in life. Heine was much more dependent on others than he cared to believe; he could not feel happy without the approbation even of those whom he despised. Until then he had never known careless gaiety with men of his own age, and thus it came about that in Göttingen, where he had spent some of the worst hours of his life, he began to enjoy a belated period of youth.

Unhappily it came too late to melt the crust of suspicion which was the worst scar left on him by his life of solitude. He was merely enjoying a relatively calm and happy stage before he resumed his wandering life of misery.

His restlessness had not really left him. At Göttingen it was betrayed by his incessant changing of quarters. He moved from one set of rooms to another—from the town to the outskirts, and from the outskirts back again to town. This curious habit stayed with him as long as his health enabled him to move with ease. Never for any length of time could he be satisfied with the same view from his window or the same faces around him. This characteristic is all the more remarkable in that he was completely indifferent to the details of his abode—he felt no necessity for feeling that any one place was his home. Wherever he lived, trunks stood about the place half unpacked, table and chairs groaned under a mass of books and papers, clothes lay about anywhere in disorder, and the whole was invariably covered with a thick layer of dust, which he strictly forbade the servants to sweep away. He himself usually slept in the middle of all this litter, on a bed which he had dragged from the alcove into the "best room." There he would lie, glancing indifferently through half-shut eyes at all the muddle. "Only the brush of a Teniers could do justice to the state of disorder in Heine's rooms," wrote one who knew them. But Heine shrugged his shoulders; he was scrupulously clean in his own person, but cared nothing at all for the condition of things around him.

"There are few who worry inwardly so cruelly, and so silently as Heine," observed one of his friends; "few whose inner life is less to be judged by outward appearances than his." But, when he did emerge from his long meditations, he refreshed himself by indulgence in deliberately simple forms of amusement. "He surrounds himself with the most atrocious fools," grumbled one friend. "He has an incomprehensible habit of mystifying folk," said another. He took pleasure in practical jokes, and usually chose staid, respectable persons as his victims. When his pranks were laughed at, or his witticisms were repeated from mouth to mouth, he was delighted. Those who knew him better were astonished at the contrast between this malicious humour and the wealth of sincerity and kindness in him. One of the more intelligent of his companions, who seems to have studied Heine minutely, exclaimed, almost with surprise, that he was "a great genius, but at the same time not at all swollen-headed."

We find Heine, as he appeared to his contemporaries at Göttingen, in a poem by Philip Spitta, a future writer of pious lyrical verse. "One day the Devil went forth into the world. At length he came upon a hut covered in flowers where Love dwelt, but it was a sick Love tended by Angels. The Devil took up his station by Love's side, and henceforth passers-by heard his sinister laughter mingling with the angelic voice, and saw his infernal visage framed in heavenly roses." "The portrait is very like me," Heine is said to have remarked, and, according to those who were present, there were tears in his eyes when he spoke.

At this period he was much occupied by the problem of the eternal struggle between good and evil in the human soul. "Each of us should write his own *Faust*," he said one day. He wanted to try his hand at the rash project, but his Mephistopheles would be the opposite of Goethe's; and would be the chief theme and principal actor in the drama. He spoke much of his plan, and even expounded it in detail to a friend, who became suspicious at Heine's readiness to discuss the subject, knowing that he, like all truly original workers, guarded jealously from the public gaze the intimate processes of his invention. This friend noted in his diary that the poet Heine probably only talked so much about his *Faust* because he had no serious intention of undertaking it.

Nevertheless Heine continued to speak of it; he even mentioned it to the one person above all others to whom he should not have broached the subject, since it could only irritate him—to Goethe himself.

In the autumn of 1824, Heine set out alone to walk in the Harz mountains. It was one of the first excursions into the German countryside that found a place in German literature. His experiences were published under the title *Reisebilder*. The name, like the idea itself, was new in Germany, though both have since been repeated and imitated again and again. At the end of his tramp he arrived at Weimar, and, on the first of October, begged an audience with His Excellency, Wolfgang von Goethe: "I do not wish to thrust myself upon you; I want only to kiss your hand and leave." There was a certain shyness about his manner of presenting himself to the great man, to whom he bore letters of introduction from Varnhagen and another friend. Humbly he added:

" I also am a poet," a fact which it seemed necessary to mention, for, although Germany already rang with his praises, the Olympian of Weimar did not seem to have noticed it. Heine had sent him a copy of his first volume of poems, as also of the second which contained the tragedies. At the same time he had addressed to him a letter full of the most respectful admiration. But Goethe, usually so punctilious in such matters, had not even sent an acknowledgment.

At last, with clothes worn and torn from weeks of cross-country rambling, with a beating heart, and his throat contracted with emotion, the young man stepped across the threshold of the house on the Frauenplan at Weimar. His customary self-assurance had vanished. He felt no more than a shy and awkward student standing before a great master, from whom he awaited the decisive word which might change his whole career. His first impression was one almost of fear. A recent illness had clearly left its effects on Goethe. The great head, in its halo of silver hair, was still erect and impressive, but his face was furrowed with deep hollows, his skin was yellow like parchment, and criss-crossed with wrinkles, and his toothless mouth quivered unceasingly. Only the large dark eyes still shone with their old calm. They turned upon the young man, as he entered, a piercing, incisive gaze, which seemed to search into every corner of his being, and yet so distant that it seemed their owner could scarce have noted what he saw. Heine found, to his surprise, that he was not, after all, unknown to the great poet. Goethe's memory was prodigious ; he even remembered that friends had spoken of Heine's ill health ; he asked after it with a kindly smile, as if glad to find it better than he had expected. But his interest in the intellectual activities of his guest seemed considerably less. He did not appear to realise the agony in which Heine awaited a word from him about his work. Full of benevolence towards the young man who had been so warmly commended to him by such friends as the Varnhagen, the grand old man appeared to have nothing to say to Heine as a poet. No doubt, with an appropriate word, Heine could have broken down the wall of silence behind which Goethe dwelt increasingly at that period of his life, but he was disconcerted by the impenetrable gaze.

" During long winter nights I had rehearsed to myself the brilliant, profound, and witty things I would say to Goethe, if ever I met him." But when the moment came they had all gone from his head ; he found himself babbling platitudes while his mind groped desperately after those vanished marvels. He talked of his journey, and Goethe smilingly remarked upon the excellence of the plums that grew along the road between Jena and Weimar. Possibly the old man suddenly realised the distress hidden under these banalities, for he asked, without warning, on what particular work Heine was then engaged. It was the long-awaited moment, the turning point of his career. Now he could pour out his confession, submit to Goethe's judgment all his moral hesitation, the uncertainties of his thought, and the caprice of his inspiration. But, alas, his embarrassment could not be overcome ; the separate currents of his thoughts and his words would not unite ; despite himself, he blurted out in answer, " A *Faust*."

Instantly the old man became frozen stiffly. He himself was still working at the masterpiece of his life, which in his diary he called " his chief affair." He was then engaged, with a final effort, in summoning all the wisdom of his maturity in order to put the finishing touches to it before the end, which he felt approaching, overwhelmed him. And now this young man before him, the very type, evidently, of that discontented, incoherent, and unblushing youth which Goethe in his old age found so hard to tolerate —this young man dared to speak of attempting the mighty problem which he, Goethe, had not succeeded in mastering !

In the frigid voice of the diplomat, Goethe changed the conversation to another subject. " You have no other business at Weimar, Herr Heine ? " Heine's pride rose in revolt ; it was too late, in any case, to take back the unhappy word. " When I pass from the door of Your Excellency, my business at Weimar will be terminated," he answered. And Goethe noted simply in his diary : " 2nd October. Heine of Göttingen."

This lost opportunity rankled long in Heine's breast, and the recollection of it came back to him again and again as that of a shameful defeat. He tried to console himself by pretending that Goethe was afraid of his original and independent mind, and that he only cared to foster the talent of writers of little importance : " To be praised by Goethe has become almost a symbol of mediocrity." Only later did he realise the real reason for the unhappy incident. " Goethe and I have heterogeneous natures ; it is inevitable that we should antagonise each other." It pleased him to see in the contrast between them the materialisation of the clash between two literary epochs. " The principle of Goethe's time, which was the idea of art in itself, is disappearing ; a new era is dawning, bringing with it a new principle." Heine said later of Goethe that he was " the great genius who stood aloof from his age."

He felt that he himself occupied so advanced an outpost in this new era that he became haunted by his lonely position. Consumed as he was by the need for encouragement and support, he scanned the horizon desperately for kinship. He found a companion in Karl Immermann, Judge of the District Court of Magdeburg and a dramatist and poet, with whom he had been in correspondence for two years or so. The acquaintance had begun when Immermann sent Heine a word of encouragement after the publication of his first poems. He also published a friendly criticism of them, which had sufficed to draw from Heine, tortured by his lack of self-confidence, a stream of declarations of gratitude and fidelity. As soon as he learned that Immermann had expressed himself strongly concerning the narrow spirit of the university associations, he wrote to him exulting : " Forward, then, to the fight against social injustice, against the imbecility which reigns supreme, against evil ! If you will be my brother-in-arms in this most holy cause, I give you my hand."

He spared no pains to be useful to Immermann by introducing him to publishers; he showered him with compliments, and gave him the benefit of his clear judgment. All the innate bounty of his nature was expressed, almost naïvely, in Heine's relations with Immermann. Not until two years after he had launched his first appeal to him did he make Immermann's personal acquaintance, just as he was setting out on his wanderings in the Harz. It was the only time the two poets actually met, but they remained united throughout their lives, fighting the same enemies, helping each other constantly—friends despite all the differences of origin, talent, and methods of work which distinguished them. Gratitude and fidelity alone did not suffice to explain this friendship; involuntarily Heine once let out the secret: "It is so terrible to be quite alone."

It was a good period in his life. Fear of solitude led him to adapt himself to his age and to his fellow-creatures, and a more sympathetic environment tended to make the adaptation easier. There was less hostility around him; he began to expand, and to find in himself the high spirits natural to his years.

In an atmosphere in which hatred of the Jews was less marked, Heine came to reconsider his detestation of all that was German. In Lüneburg he had made one friend, a man named Christiani, and to him he wrote what seemed a confession wrung from him after much heart-searching. "You write that it will cost me much to rid myself completely of my German nature. . . . I know that I am the most German of animals; I know only too well that the German atmosphere is for me what water is to a fish, and that I cannot escape from this, to me, vital element. . . . At bottom I love everything German more than anything else in the world. In my breast are the records of German sentiment; my two books themselves are archives of German song." He spoke of the anger which had cut across his love for Germany—"this anger provoked for good reason." His rebellion against Germany appeared to him then as a mere youthful escapade, a stage in his evolution, which was now over. In point of fact, he was more ready to make concessions because of his love for Therese, just as he had been because of his love for Amalie during adolescence.

At Göttingen he pursued his legal studies as he had never done before. It was far from being an easy task for him : " What ordinary people understand easily enough, I can only get into my head with the greatest difficulty." Throughout his letters there recurs the constant complaint : " Jurisprudence worries me to death." But his efforts were sustained by the determination to make himself independent of his uncle once and for all. " I want to eat my dinner in the scales of Themis, and not in my uncle's cup of pity. I am not big enough to endure the humiliation."

But he knew that even if, after much labour, he succeeded in obtaining his degree, his career would always be hampered by the fact that he was a Jew. Conscious as he also was of his slight aptitude for the legal profession, he concluded that even if he set up as a lawyer he would not be sure of earning his living. He therefore based his hopes rather on becoming a civil servant, and asked his friends to find out what his chances were. But he discovered that even the smallest administrative post was closed to him so long as he remained unconverted. Disposed as he then was to make any concession, he began seriously to consider the hardest concession of all. In Berlin he had been indignant at the " treachery " of Gans, yet during his stay at Lüneburg his parents—even the fervent Jew, Samson Heine—had already begun to discuss the possibility of his conversion. " None of the family are against it, except myself," he wrote bitterly. And at Göttingen, where he felt his own opposition weakening, he uttered what seems a cry of despair : " I have not the strength to hear myself called ' dirty Jew.' " At length, and after much hesitation, he made his decision : " Baptised, and doctor in law, I shall return to Hamburg."

In April 1825 he felt himself ready to take the examination. For some months his health had been getting steadily worse ; his headaches had returned and were as severe as ever, and he was again under constant treatment by his old doctor. His nerves were shaken by fear of failure. In his request to be admitted for examination, he pleaded the state of his health as an extenuating circumstance. " The headaches from which I have suffered unremittingly for two years have been a great hindrance to my work, and are responsible for the fact that my knowledge is not as great as my perseverance and my zeal would warrant."

His nervous condition increased when he heard that Professor Hugo had been nominated doyen of the Faculty, for he suspected him of being the friend of his worst enemies. But during the examination this dreaded doyen celebrated Heine's promotion in a magnificent speech in Latin. To his immense surprise, Heine heard the man, whom his persecution mania had led him to believe to be his adversary, laud his poems to the skies, and declare that, " according to universal opinion, they are of a quality to be classed with those of Goethe." The Professor added that " Goethe also had earlier expressed himself more completely as a poet than as a jurist." Intoxicated with joy Heine exclaimed that " Hugo is one of the great men of the century ! "

It seemed as if Heine's second stay at Göttingen was going to terminate on a note of triumph. Professor Hugo was again most flattering in the course of a dinner which he gave. Salomon Heine also passed through Göttingen, and behaved most affably towards his nephew. But the second part of the programme remained to be fulfilled. It tormented him, and his joy in all the rest was spoilt.

His baptism took place in the strictest privacy, at Heiligenstadt near Göttingen, on June 28th, 1825. He submitted to the long catechism, which was obligatory before baptism, in the small and poorly furnished study of Pastor Grimm. He was not content merely to recite answers he had learnt by heart ; as a child he had attended the religious classes of his Catholic school, and all his life he had been interested in Christianity as a philosophy. He astonished the two clergymen by the gravity of his replies and by the lucidity of his questions. After the baptism, Heine was asked to stay to lunch. No doubt Pastor Grimm thought, in view of Heine's reputation, that his own monotonous existence would be enlivened by a memorable interview. But the neophyte became rapt in silence, and hardly replied even to the questions which were put to him. The two clergymen understood what this silence meant, and they exchanged looks almost of compassion at the signs of the internal struggle which flitted across the face of the young man. It was not a question of the Jew, Heine, revolting against his new faith, for he had long been without religion, it was the man in him rebelling against the concession to his personal interests which had brought him there, and suffering, too, at having deserted the community to which he belonged.

What he himself called his cowardice long weighed upon him. He never attempted to colour his conversion with any other motive than of expediency. "I should regret deeply if my baptism could appear in any favourable light," he wrote to Moses Moser with his usual bluntness, and he added : "I assure you that, if the law had permitted me to steal silver spoons, I should never have become converted." Later he said, using the form of paradox which can conceal so much bitterness : "That I have become a Christian is the fault of those Saxons who passed without warning to the service of the enemy at the Battle of Leipzig. Or it is the fault of Napoleon, who, after all, had no need to go chasing off to Russia, or perhaps of his teacher of geography at Brienne, who omitted to tell him that it is very cold in Moscow in winter-time?"

Several months later, he wrote from "the accursed town of Hamburg" to his friend Moser : "As I am temporarily without funds I will give you an entirely original Christmas present—the promise that I will not kill myself immediately." On leaving Göttingen he had taken a considerable trip before returning to Hamburg. He had passed the summer at Norderney, where the sea, which had moved him so deeply on his first encounter with it, had given him that capacity for feeling at one with nature which until then he had lacked.

Hitherto the countryside had been for this romantic poet

no more than a background for his personal drama, an accompaniment to his own feelings. In spite of the large place which nature had occupied in his poetry, it had played no greater part than that of the silent confidant of his own sufferings. The flowers invoked as witnesses to his passion were flowers which had never bloomed ; the songs of birds which echoed through his verse were songs which had never really filled his ears. Even when he went afoot into the mountains to catch the sound of their breathing, he retained, amid the silence of the open spaces, the attitude of one who hears only himself.

But, for some strange reason, this landlubber, who saw the sea for the first time when he was full-grown, suddenly discovered it to be his spiritual home. The sea was a revelation of nature to him, and its effect upon him was so great that it swept away all trace of the conventional imagery which he had hitherto employed. In the poems he wrote whilst still under the first impression of it, human destiny appears as governed by the elemental power of nature. Heine himself realised the change : " These poems are amongst the most individual things I have ever written."

Much later, when he had become acclaimed by critics and public opinion alike as " the poet of the sea *par excellence*," he recalled the obstacles against which he had had to fight in the beginning. " It was an exceedingly difficult task, for who, in Germany in those days, knew the sea ? To-day everybody knows it. But to describe the ocean at that time was to describe something of which the general public was completely ignorant. And to tackle the unknown is always difficult."

The latter part of this summer of 1825, spent at the seaside, was for Heine all golden with sunshine and the joy of creation, enlivened by a pretty creature who "flattered his vanity." On his return to Hamburg, he felt that he had at last made his peace with himself and with the world around him. " Maybe," he wrote to Sethe, " I shall soon be able to announce that I have set up as a lawyer in Hamburg, that I have married and settled down, and am writing a great deal." That at least was then his programme for the future. He made ready to play the part of a young man established in middle-class society. His old friends who met him in the street were astonished to see the change both in his appearance and his behaviour. " He was no longer a man who had withdrawn into himself," one of his cousins remarked. " His manner was easier and less affected, he had become a man of the world, more even, a distinguished gentleman, aloof and self-controlled." This was precisely the impression which Dr. Heinrich Heine wished to make.

A short time afterwards, nothing remained of this programme. He himself was never able to explain why the plan of opening a lawyer's office in Hamburg came to nothing. " I have other things in my head, or rather in my heart, and have no desire to worry about the reasons for my actions." The principal reason was, however, the " civil war " which again raged within him. Therese Heine was perhaps more susceptible to the charms of the distinguished gentleman than her sister Amalie had been to the passion of the effusive but awkward adolescent. Therese may well have remembered the courtship with regret later on, for she does not appear to have been happy in her marriage. But the girl's sympathy for him could not stand against the atmosphere of hostility which surrounded Heine in the house of his uncle, nor against the intrigues of her brother-in-law, Moritz Oppenheimer, " whose smile suffices to undermine the esteem which others might have for me "—as Heine wrote. Above all she could not withstand the profound contempt which Salomon himself betrayed towards his nephew.

Heine, who in the autumn still thought that he would soon be able to announce his marriage, came to realise before long that this " new springtime of his heart " was yet another cruel illusion. " He who loves once, and only once, is a God ; but he who suffers twice from an unhappy love is a fool. Fool that I am, I love again without the recompense of love ! "

More and more did he lose the self-assurance with which he had come to Hamburg. He began to realise that his conversion had been more detrimental than useful to him. " I am detested now by both Jews and Christians ; I deeply regret my baptism." Something very like a superstitious fear of the vengeance of an offended Jehovah took possession of him as he lamented : " Since that moment I have gone from misfortune to misfortune."

Imperceptibly his earlier state of mind returned ; he became again a prey to persecution mania and his own obstinacy. His hand-to-mouth manner of existence and his fatal habit of postponing decisions and shunning responsibility became a justification of all that his enemies said against him. His brother-in-law, Moritz Embden, sought to persuade him to give up a way of living which brought him into such doubtful company. Full of goodwill, he intervened with Salomon Heine, but only succeeded in rousing the banker to a state of blind fury. When Lotte also pleaded with her brother in support of her husband's common-sense appeals, Heine exclaimed melodramatically, with the exaggeration of one who knows himself to be in the wrong : " These days I have lost even my sister."

Inevitably his old hatred for Hamburg returned, with the same violence as before, and also the same incapacity to escape from it. He repeated the things he had said of it ten years earlier : " Hamburg is nothing but a counting-house by day and a bawdy-house by night." He wrote nothing, and nothing of his was published for a long time. " They think I am a light that has been extinguished," he said. For over a year his *Travels in the Harz* had been lying with a Berlin publisher, unaccepted.

It was at this moment that Heine met a man who was destined to play a decisive part in his life—the publisher Julius Campe.

He went one day into the bookshop of Hoffmann & Campe to ask for a copy of his tragedies. Campe himself handed it to him, and with it, like a good salesman, Heine's first volume of collected poems, which he warmly recommended. " No, thank you, *mein Herr*," his visitor interrupted, " I do not like them ; in fact I despise them." Julius Campe shot a glance at his customer, whose identity he perhaps already guessed, for he exclaimed, in his loud-voiced jovial manner : " What ? You despise them. Why, sir, if that is so, you will have to deal with me ! " " Indeed, sir," replied the flattered author, " I know them better than you can do, for it was I who wrote them." Julius Campe had a great talent for seizing opportunities ; he laughed now, one of his most hearty laughs : " Well, well, my dear doctor, if ever you write anything so worthless again, and have no better publisher at hand, I should be honoured to have the name of my firm appear upon the jacket."

" Be very careful," answered Heine. " I may take you at your word." And he remembered how his Berlin publisher had only recently refused to pay him two louis d'or for sixteen pages of his *Travels in the Harz*, and that Brockhaus had shown no interest at all in his new work. The day after this conversation Heine sold to Campe a volume called *Reisebilder* for the price of fifty louis d'or—a price which the Berlin firm had found too high. " From that moment Heine visited me daily in my office, and we became close friends," said Campe, in his account of his first meeting with Heine.

It was a strange friendship which was formed that day between the Hamburg publisher and his author. Rarely have two such totally different characters been bound together by such a long collaboration, which lasted, indeed, until the death of Heine.

Julius Campe, older than Heine by five years, was predestined to become a publisher: his two elder brothers were both either proprietors or co-proprietors of bookshops and publishing houses. He may be said to have grown up amongst bookshelves, and at an early age had entered the firm of Hoffmann of Hamburg, which his brother August managed with his father-in-law. He had then gone as a voluntary helper to his brother Friedrich's shop in Nuremberg, and had finally completed his education with a Berlin firm. Physically he looked more like a man from the country than one who was shut up all day amongst books. He had, in fact, not been so shut up all his life, for, during the Wars of Liberation, he had enlisted in the Lützow Brigade, where he had been present at the tragic death and funeral of the war-poet, Theodor Körner. Later he had paid a visit to Italy, the only artistic memory which illumined his business-like heart. By the time he returned to Hamburg, in 1823, to take over the management of the firm of Hoffmann & Campe, the ex-salesman had become a man as devoid of culture as he was of literary preferences. But, however indifferent he may have been to their contents, he had a *flair* almost amounting to genius for recognising the commercial value of a book. His shrewd and eager eyes had for years been accustomed to study the reactions of customers, and he had made it his business to probe the secrets of those mysterious laws which govern the success or failure of literary works. He trusted blindly to his own instinct in such matters. It was perhaps just because he had no personal preferences that he was able to launch out boldly as the protector of an unknown author or of a disputed book. He even preferred unknown authors to those already established in public favour. There was in him something of the explorer possessed with a passion for discovering virgin territory. His liking for taking chances enabled him to find satisfaction in a profession which otherwise would have seemed dull and unexciting to such an energetic man. For him it was a life of perpetual adventure. He explained his preference for young authors by saying that he did not want to grow old : " I do not want to remain behind the times . . . the future belongs to youth, and so long as I bind myself to them I feel sure of remaining faithful to the idea of progress."

This taste for the new, however, was combined with a hard head in business matters, and his courage was tempered by a prudence which sometimes came very near to avarice. Behind his genial air and his jovial, healthy smile there was concealed the cunning of a peasant, deaf to all appeals of sentiment. When Julius Campe negotiated a contract with an author, he knew in advance that he would be the gainer from the deal. His method in such matters was that of the horse-trader—depreciation of the object to be purchased, pretence of indifference. Only when the business was finally concluded did he appear again as the honest man, the faithful friend and good companion. He affected to be unable to understand how an author could complain of the benefits he received from a publisher so prodigal of his courage and his energy on his behalf.

Campe's infallible *flair* showed him at once the interest of Heine's work, and he did not hesitate a moment to buy the book offered to him. A year later, grumbling because he disliked poetry, he bought the first and following editions of the *Buch der Lieder* for the same price of fifty louis d'or.

He was equally quick in summing up the personality of the man before him. He saw at once Heine's lack of practical sense, his need of money, and all the general and permanent instability of his position. Some time later he profited by one of Heine's acute crises in order to bind him irrevocably by contract to his publishing house. He would pay high prices for a manuscript when the poet had no urgent need to sell, and he would haggle cruelly when he was in crying need. In all the many difficulties which were scattered along Heine's path through life, Julius Campe proved a discreet confidant, ready with his aid—just so long as his own interests were not at stake. The curious friendship survived many quarrels ; it was a marriage of convenience between an author who had all his life to fight against want, and a publisher who made a fortune out of him—but who still imagined himself to be the poet's benefactor.

One day, as Heine lay dying, his brother Max sought to distract his attention from his pain by speaking to him of the literary immortality which awaited him. To eyes which were then almost blind, Max described the monument which his native town of Düsseldorf would erect to him. "I have one already," Heine interrupted with a bitter laugh. "Where do you mean ?" asked his brother. "At Hamburg, dear man. If you turn to the left from the Börsenplatz you will see before you a large house which belongs to Herr Julius Campe, publisher of my

Reisebilder. That house is a magnificent monument in stone erected in grateful memory of the numerous and bulky editions of my *Buch der Lieder*."

Heine's first meeting with Campe took place towards the end of January 1826. In May the first volume of the *Reisebilder* was published by Hoffmann & Campe. It contained the eighty-eight poems of *The Home-coming* and the *Travels in the Harz*, as well as twelve poems from the cycle *The North Sea*. Campe was not mistaken; he had judged better than Heine himself, who had thought that the *Reisebilder* "would certainly not arouse much general interest; it is not a great piece of work, although, taking it as a whole, it cannot be called a bad one."

It was the first time that Heine had submitted a work in prose to the general public. The sensation it caused was as great as that which had followed his first collection of verse. A whole epoch of history was seeking desperately for a means of expression: condemned to inactivity; discontented and swayed by opposing currents; proclaiming its depression and hungry for gaiety; sentimental and ironical by turn; frivolous and yet tormented by a longing to believe—public opinion saw itself reflected in the pages of this book, and acclaimed it as the finest and most faithful of mirrors.

The success of the book amongst intellectuals was equalled by its success as a seller. Berlin found a historical comparison for its author, and was enchanted by it. Heine is the German Voltaire. The doctor in law Heinrich Heine was justified in having refused to become a briefless Hamburg lawyer, even in the eyes of his enemies.

But once more his intimate feelings failed to accord with outer events; not even this success could quench the incurable suspicion which, as Campe said, had something in it of the Italian Middle Ages. One evening, when passing Heine's house, Campe noticed that there was still a light in the poet's window. He called several times, but the only result was that the light was immediately snuffed. Seeing a shop still open which sold spiced cake, and remembering that Heine was particularly fond of it, Campe went in, bought some, and sent it up to Heine with a message: "From Professor Hugo of Göttingen." The next day, when he asked Heine how he had enjoyed the cake, the latter, half laughing and half angry, exclaimed: "So it was from you! Idiot that I am, I thought it was a present from my enemies and threw it into the fire." Campe's laughter did not disconcert him. "I mean it," he said. "I think them quite capable of giving me rat poison."

His fear increased when a Hamburg business man, who thought to recognise himself in a disagreeable character portrayed in *Travels in the Harz*, stopped him in the street, and uttered blood-curdling threats. For months Heine lived in perpetual dread that such scenes might recur. His fevered imagination saw the traps of his enemies everywhere, and he passed sleepless nights in planning how to defeat their manœuvres.

After a summer of repose, spent at Norderney amidst "pretty women, good food, and a divine peace," his old demon of persecution took possession of him again. Again, as always when in trouble, he began to think of living abroad. "I want to leave Germany for ever," he wrote to Immermann. And he confided to Varnhagen, under a vow of secrecy, that he wished "to go to Paris, to use the libraries, see people and the world, and compose notes for a great book which shall be European." Only to Moser did he confess the real reason for his decision: "It is less the desire to go away than the torment of my personal affairs which drives me hence. I have, for example, not rid myself of the Jew in me."

Before leaving he thought he would publish another volume of the *Travel Pictures*. Encouraged by the success of the first, he summoned all his strength to create a really remarkable work.

For the second cycle of the *Nordsee* poems he sought to strike a new note. He also wished to introduce humour for the first time into an autobiographical work. And so the same man who could be thrown into a crisis of insomnia by the words of an angry merchant, prepared to pit his strength against the most formidable forces of Europe—the Catholic Church and autocratic Government, the nobility and its obscurantism, and against the most firmly established literary reputations of his time. He wished his book to include the whole list of his most inveterate enemies, and, as if there were not poisoned arrows enough in his own quiver, he must needs solicit his friends, Varnhagen, Immermann, and others, to lend him the venom of their pens also. Immermann alone acceded to the strange request, and it was his contribution, in the form of some epigrams, which involved Heine in one of the most troublesome quarrels of his life. It was not a question of being blinded by pride in his recent success—his words show that he was all along quite aware of the danger he ran : " My book will cause a great sensation. I have blazed a new trail at the risk of my life."

The book did indeed cause a sensation. It fell like a clap of thunder in the death-like silence which then prevailed in Germany. The papers hardly dared to mention it, but it circulated from hand to hand, arousing everywhere passionate enthusiasm or indignant criticism. The State Governments hastened to ban it—Hanover first of all, on account of the sneers at the local nobility contained in the *Nordsee* poems ; Prussia and Austria followed suit. But, the more it was banned, the better it became known. It was long since the German public had listened to violent attacks upon the " spider's web of Rome," upon class prejudice, the suppression of all opinion and liberty of conscience. The attacks were rendered all the more serious by the glorification of Napoleon which formed the *leit-motif* of *Ideen. Das Buch Le Grand.*

" I can find expression now for everything," said Heine proudly. The book paid scant respect to continuity ; it ranged from stories of his childhood to biting satire on his times, and from the paying off of old scores to the poignant tale of his love for Therese Heine. With this book Heine achieved the mastery of his ironic style ! It is fools who enable me to live, he declared triumphantly ; they it is who supply me with material, and when I see them I laugh at the thought of what they will bring me. Thus that fat Hamburg millionaire will supply me with a night-stool, and that other idiot in Berlin is good for a cask of Rhenish wine. After publication of the first volume, Heine had been acclaimed as Voltaire's successor : in the second he accepted the title. From being a fashionable poet, Heine became at one stroke an important factor in the political life of Germany.

CHAPTER VI

THE COLD WORLD

O, dass ich grosse Lasters säh!
Verbrechen, blutig kolossal.
Nur diese satte Tugend nicht
Und zahlungsfähige Moral.

(*Anno 1829*)

IN THE SAME MONTH in which his book was published—April 1827—Heine embarked for England, the land of liberty as it appeared to the Continental democrats, in the front rank of which he now considered himself to be. It was in his new capacity as a political writer that Heine went to study English ways. He fancied himself playing the part of expert observer of the political and social life of the country he was visiting, and he took his position seriously. All that he managed to see he judged accurately. His *Letters from England*, which were eventually published, contain passages of great discernment. " The Englishman loves liberty as he does his spouse, he possesses it, and if he does not treat it with any great tenderness, he certainly knows how to defend it like a man, when necessary, against any intruder in uniform who tries to push his way into the bed-chamber, whether he professes to come as a lover or as bailiff's man. The Frenchman loves liberty as he does his betrothed. He becomes fired with passion for it, and throws himself on his knees in protestation of his love. He will fight for it at the risk of his life, and for it will be guilty of any foolishness. The German loves liberty as he does his old grandmother."

Heine was stunned by the life of London, the first city to take on the aspect of a modern metropolis. He was astounded and flustered by the traffic, by the crowds of pedestrians dodging amongst the carriages and people on horseback, by the deafening noise of wheels on the cobbles, and by the shouting of the cabmen. He compared this mad haste to the panic on the bridge of Bérésina, where each thought only of saving his own skin and risked trampling on the corpses of others !

He also felt lost in English society life, of which a contemporary traveller said : " There is no country in the world where a stranger may feel himself so completely at home, providing he knows the language, the customs, and the people ; but there is also no country in which he will be so completely alone if he does not know them."

Heine left England with a profound dislike for it. He spoke of it as a country " where machines behave like human beings and human beings like machines." He hated the stifling boredom of " society life " and the chilly indifference and hypocrisy of the English. It is true that towards the end of his life he had the courage to admit that his hatred was chiefly lack of comprehension. " You have never really known us," said an Englishwoman who came to his sick-room—" like a beautiful angel of death," as the poet said. " *C'est vrai, mon Dieu,*" Heine answered, " and I do not know what I have had against the English to cause me to be so harsh with them ; it has been pure spleen on my part ; *au fond* I have never disliked them and I have never known them. I was only once in my life in England, long ago at that, and I knew hardly anybody there. London seemed to me a terribly drab town and the people in the street seemed insufferable."

As an escape from boredom, and to drown a certain humiliation he felt in finding that nobody knew or cared about the successful poet so recently become a hero of liberalism, Heine plunged as usual into amorous adventures. " If I leave England alive, it will not be the fault of the women," he wrote. " I am sunk to the neck in adventures ; by bad luck and stupidity I have lost 300 guineas and count myself fortunate to have escaped so lightly."

Only one of his love episodes in England has left traces in his work, and, by chance, it is one of the rare exceptions in which we know the name and even the address of the charmer. The series of poems known as the " Kitty Cycle " concern a certain Miss Clairmont, of 26 Osnaburgh Street, Regent's Park, as is shown by a letter of Heine's dated Ramsgate, August 19th, 1827.

This letter, however, is a farewell, and sounds the knell of the little adventure in terms which say plainly that Kitty was being jilted by the poet. It is written in French, and in formal terms thanks her for the kindness she had shown him during his short stay. He excuses himself for not having called upon her before leaving London, and winds up with the lame assurance that he " would certainly not return to London without knocking at her door." It seems probable that Heine had left this letter to be posted after his departure from England, and that he had already placed the sea between himself and Kitty Clairmont's kindness before she had a chance to read it.

For a time, however, she was his " lady of the white and slender limbs," the girl with the " doe-like eyes " whose " dark hair hung in curls about her face " ; she whose body was " the fragile shell of a yet more delicate soul." But even here a note of bitterness creeps in :

. . . Du wirst mich reichlich
Beglücken mit Gefühl und Küssen
Und dann verraten wie gebräuchlich.

" You will please me abundantly with emotion and kisses and then betray me as usual."

But in this case at least it was Heine who proved the deceiver. At the time he wrote his lame excuse for not returning to see Kitty in Osnaburgh Street he seems to have been in Ramsgate with another woman, with whom he walked the sands and rhapsodised about the waves lapping the cliffs and the path of the moon across the water " like a silver bridge stretched to the Promised Land."

The letter from Ramsgate does not seem to have proved the end of the episode, however, which may have been deeper than he would have us believe. Some eight years later, when he was assembling the poems of the " Kitty Cycle " for the composer Hiller to set to music, Heine seems to have added to the mystery of this affair by including a verse which obviously was not inspired by Kitty. But from hints elsewhere it would appear that Kitty, whom Heine in a poem had described as weeping bitterly when they parted, and begging to see him again, had in fact gone to see him some years later in Paris. When, at the end of this visit, she announced her intention of returning home, Heine warned her that the separation would be hard :

Doch den Leibern, armen Leibern
Wird die Trennung sehr verderblich,
Haben keine Flügel, haben
Nur zwei Beine und sind sterblich.

Das bedenke, schöne Kitty,
Sei vernünftig, klug und weise ;
Bleib in Frankreich bis zum Frühling,
Bis ich mit nach England reise.

" But for our bodies, our poor bodies, the separation will be very harmful, for they have no wings, but only two legs, and are mortal. Remember this, beautiful Kitty, be sensible, clever, and wise; remain in France until spring, until I can travel to England with you."

But the tone is affected, and smacks of a cynical playing with sentiment. Then suddenly, in this most ordinary of love-affairs, there sounds a note of tragedy. There is only one short poem about it—less a memorial than a somewhat callous record, it would seem.

Kitty stirbt ! und ihre Wangen
Seh ich immer mehr erblassen.

. . . . . .

Kitty stirbt ! und kalt gebettet
Liegt sie bald im Kirchhofsgrunde.
Und sie weiss es ! Doch für andere
Sorgt sie bis zur letzten Stunde.

" Kitty is dying, and I see her cheeks grow paler

and paler. . . . Kitty is dying, and, coldly bedded, she will soon be lying in the churchyard. And she knows it, and yet she cares for others until her last hour ! "

There follows a passage which no man could have imagined in such circumstances without a woman's prompting. Kitty begs that next winter, when she is gone, he will wear the stockings she has knitted for him ! Whatever may have been the truth of this mysterious affair, Heine at least seems not to have been deeply affected by the episode which, begun during an English summer, ended so tragically in the course of a French winter.

After his return, money matters were again the cause of a serious quarrel with his uncle. Before leaving he had asked Salomon Heine for money. " But you have just had some," his uncle replied, having, in a moment of generosity, just made his nephew a handsome present. " I know, but that is for daily expenses," replied Heine. " I ought to have a letter of credit for a fairly large amount if I am to make a good impression on Rothschild. After all, I bear your name." Salomon Heine knew the importance of such things in banking circles, and the argument, in any case, was difficult to resist. He provided his nephew with a letter of credit on Rothschild's bank for four hundred pounds, together with a warmly written introduction to the head of the firm. Salomon stressed the fact that the letter of credit was part of the introduction to Rothschild, and was not to be drawn upon. Heine had received in addition, for his journey, the sum of one hundred louis d'or from his mother. Nevertheless, no sooner had he arrived in London than he cashed the whole of his letter of credit and at the same time asked to see the head of the bank. Baron Rothschild lost no time in inviting such a wealthy young man to his house.

On his return to Hamburg the full force of his uncle's anger fell upon the poet. As a matter of fact, he had not been quite so silly as he pretended ; this was one of the occasions on which he deliberately made himself out to be worse than he was. There is no doubt that he squandered a lot of money during his stay in England, but with the proceeds of the letter of credit he had paid off all the debts he owed to friends, and had had left a sum of eight hundred thalers, which he sent to Varnhagen to keep for him. He could not trust himself: "I spend everything I have on me, and it is safer to have something in reserve," he wrote.

In this sudden fit of prudence there was fear of the morrow; but there was also the determination to change his present life entirely, above all to finish with Hamburg and all that it meant. "I hope to have the strength of mind not to return there," he said in one of his letters from London.

But he did return.

On arriving in Germany, he went to spend a fortnight at Norderney, which his friends considered an act of great courage in view of his attacks on the nobility of Hanover. "If I felt a little anxious before leaving Hamburg, I hope I have now made up for it," he wrote. But, after having given this proof of courage, his apprehension, as he admitted, got the better of him. He left Norderney to go and live amongst the peasants and fisher-folk of the Frisian islands, where he felt alone with the sea.

On his return to Hamburg he met Amalie for the first time after eleven years, and at once all his unhappy past was revived in him. "The world is stupid and tedious and smells of dead violets," he exclaimed. It may have been this encounter which at last broke the spell of his city of misfortune. Or perhaps it was his quarrel with Salomon Heine, whom he afterwards said behaved towards him "like a cad." Or possibly it was his passion for a Hamburg actress which threatened to become too much for him. Or it may have been his love for Therese Heine, which survived all his other infatuations but which now received a death-blow, when he found she was being courted by the jurist Halle, to whom she soon afterwards became engaged. It is not certain what finally decided him to quit Hamburg; the only comment which he himself makes is enigmatic: "Things of surpassing bitterness have happened to me in Hamburg, things which I should have found it impossible to endure had I not been the only person to know about them."

At this turning-point of his life, when the idea of going away had for long been ripening in his mind, chance threw in his path an opportunity to start afresh elsewhere.

Baron Cotta, the wealthy proprietor of the *Augsburger Allgemeine Zeitung*, offered him a post as part editor of the *Political Annals*, which were to be published at Munich, beginning in January 1828. "What a grand idea, to become leader of the liberals in Bavaria," Heine had said in June when Cotta first made his offer. But, he immediately added, "I am ill, ruined, and tied." The mysterious collapse of his Hamburg world had to take place before he could bring himself to accept an offer which presented so many advantages, above all that of the assurance of economic independence.

The poet Heinrich Heine, who travelled slowly across Germany to Munich during that cold, wet November, had by no means the appearance of a man joyously setting forth to take up a good position. Ludwig Emil Grimm's engraving of him at the time—the most popular existing portrait of the poet—shows a romantic-looking young man with a clean profile, a regular and only very slightly Jewish nose, a well-shaped but discontented mouth, and a forceful chin. In the picture he wears a cloak, and his high forehead is crowned with long curls ; there is a general air of haughty melancholy about him, reminiscent of Byron. As if to confirm the artist's reading of him, Heine wrote beneath the portrait :

Verdrossnen Sinn im kalten Herzen legend
Reis ich verdriesslich durch die kalte Welt.

"Harbouring a downcast disposition in a cold heart,
I journey downcast through the cold world."

Munich in 1827 was very busy establishing a new reputation for itself, under the hectic influence of King Louis I. This royal amateur had only one ambition, which was to make Munich the great centre of artistic, literary, and scientific endeavour. King Louis had been born at Strasbourg and brought up in exile amongst French emigrants. A practising Catholic, he had come to hate the French Revolution as the incarnation of all evils. His leaning towards absolutism, which sometimes took the form of a mania for pomp and ceremony, was born when times were bad for kings and when thrones were tottering. His hatred of France as the cradle of revolution was augmented by personal dislike for his brother-in-law, Eugène de Beauharnais. This creature of impatient gestures and an uneasy stare could not forgive the fascinating Frenchman whose charm had so often eclipsed his own. The general trend of the period, his personal antipathies, his sincere and passionate patriotism, and his somewhat boisterous manner, had combined to make Louis I the hope of the young Teuton nationalists, of the clericals, and at the same time of the artists of the Romantic School. This rhapsodist sought to turn Munich into a new Athens and to transform peaceful, phlegmatic Bavarians into enthusiasts for a great artistic renaissance which they were incapable even of understanding. Louis paved the way to this ambition by importing artists, painters, and sculptors. After the manner of Charles V playing with the brush of Titian, he too would mount upon the dais and inspect the work upon the easels. He reduced his military budget and increased his expenditure on public works and on the arts. He was acclaimed the Mæcenas of the age by liberals. Giant schemes and plans which were often absurd took shape in his unstable brain ; he produced verses which violated every known canon of grammar and prosody. They were applauded by his courtiers, but laughed at by all the rest of Germany. Unlike most amateurs of this kind, he had perseverance, and the most ludicrous of his projects became realised in some way or other. In any case, at a time when all the other German States were sunk in the depths of reaction, the reign of this poet-king seemed like a haven of refuge for artistic inspiration, notwithstanding the hold of the clericals and the " Teutomania " of the sovereign himself. Louis chose his Ministers for their poetic ability as much as for other qualities. His Minister of the Interior was a young Rhinelander named Edward von Schenk, a Protestant converted to Catholicism in accordance with the mysticism of the period, who had attracted the King's attention as the author of some romantic dramas.

Heine became acquainted with Schenk through Michael Beer, the brother of Giacomo Meyerbeer, with whom he had had dealings in Berlin. He repaid Beer's introduction by writing an exaggerated eulogy of his drama *Struensee.* Nor did he neglect to burn incense before the Minister himself, calling him " the greatest poet in the world." The meeting with Schenk roused the wildest hopes in Heine. Schenk was a sincere and warm admirer of Heine's poetic genius ; he forgave his political opinions and even excused the absence of any religious feeling in " this lost nightingale." He presented him to the King, and tried to persuade Louis to offer Heine a Chair at Munich University. " You are one of the few who have ever tried to assure my position in the world," Heine wrote to him. " I hope the King of Bavaria will one day also be grateful to you for it."

The rebel of yesterday, the mouthpiece of the common people who felt able to be a leader in the great struggle of his period, seemed to have undergone a rapid change of attitude during the few months of his stay in Munich. With his characteristic facility for adapting himself—adaptations which were always superficial and of short duration—Heine adapted himself to the atmosphere of the Court and of the diplomatic world, with due regard for his possible future professorship and perhaps even the post of laureate. His work as co-editor of the *Political Annals,* in which he collaborated with Dr. Lindner, the author of a plan for the federation of the Southern States of Germany, did not take up much of his time nor call for much labour. From the start Baron Cotta had thought to use him for more important publications, but, despite a tempting offer of 2,000 florins a year, Heine would not bind himself for more than six months at a time, nor accept any responsibility.

This Baron Cotta von Cottendorf was a remarkable

character. Starting life without means, he had studied theology at the university, had become a Deputy for Württemberg, and later, as President of the Chamber, played a considerable part in South German politics. When Heine knew him he was the most powerful newspaper proprietor in Germany, owning, in addition to numerous political and literary periodicals, the *Augsburger Allgemeine Zeitung*, the paper which had the largest circulation in Austria and South Germany. Besides being the publisher of Goethe and Schiller, he was also interested in a number of commercial enterprises. His greatest success had been to persuade Bavaria and Württemberg to join the customs union, which he accomplished in the course of a few conversations, after the diplomats had spent years of work in vain to bring it about. He was a man totally lacking in prejudice, and so indifferent to the tendencies of the period that, as a Deputy, he had several times raised his voice in favour of political and civic equality for the Jews. He was prepared to pay heavily for Heine's services, and pressed him to renew his contract when it expired in June.

But Heine by then had received a formal promise from Schenk, and the decree establishing him in an official position only awaited the King's signature. The son of the small shopkeeper of the Bölkerstrasse was received by Ministers and diplomats ; the King himself showed a kindly interest in him, assuring him that he read the *Political Annals* attentively. " The King is a most amiable man," said Heine. Nor did the fashionable poet lack favour in the eyes of the fair members of the aristocracy. On his arrival in Munich he had written that there was " a fire in his heart " and that his " brain was empty," but a few months later he was boasting of " loving and being loved by the most charming of the aristocrats." The letters, which usually were a stream of lamentations, began of a sudden to thrill joyously. " I find myself here in a calm and most attractive environment. I live like a lord, and the five and a half people here who know how to read hold me in great esteem."

The transformation of the rebellious poet into the docile

future functionary of the Wittelsbachs seemed complete. But it was less so than Heine himself would have cared to believe at a moment when he was seeking to persuade the King that the author of the *Travel Pictures* was more orthodox than his works. The quiet life of Munich would soon have bored him had he not found means to enliven it in accordance with his taste. The counterweight to his sober life in Court circles was a man named Wit von Döring, one of the most curious and suspicious characters which even that era could show.

Ferdinand Johannes de Wit, known simply as Wit von Döring, had been born at Altona when that city was in the possession of the Danes. He was the son of a horse-dealer, descended from the Dutch Marshal Cornelius de Wit. His mother was the daughter of a rich Jewish commercial magnate named Eckstein, whose brother, Baron Ferdinand de Eckstein, was Prefect of Police of Paris and well known there under the nickname "Baron Buddha." Legend and the Prussian police, however, affirmed that Wit von Döring was really the illegitimate son of the future French Minister of Justice, Comte de Serre, who had lived in Hamburg as an emigrant.

In his youth Wit von Döring had been a member of the Union of Irreconcilables, and it was in his rooms that the young radical extremists had planned the assassination of Kotzebue. Von Döring had fled to England, where he got himself acclaimed as a martyr in the cause of liberty. He was still in his teens when he began to lead his double life as revolutionary and traitor. He wrote inflammatory articles under his own name in the *Morning Chronicle*, and at the same time supplied anonymous articles to the official organ which contained revelations concerning his fellow-revolutionaries.

About 1820 he went to Paris, armed with letters of introduction from German radicals, and immediately got into contact with La Fayette, Benjamin Constant, d'Argenson, and others. Finding the French police were on his tracks, he fled to Nice to seek the protection of the Comte de Serre. Whether from paternal duty or merely as a friend of Baron

Eckstein, de Serre called off his police agents and von Döring returned to Paris, to conspire with the members of the Liberal Committee—Rey, d'Argenson, and Victor Cousin—on the one hand, and to betray them in confidential reports to the Comte de Serre on the other. He got into touch with the Italian secret society of Liberals, the Carbonari, and was sent by them to stir up the revolution in Switzerland, staying the while in the castle of the Duchess of Saint-Leu. Again the French police sought him out, and, on his return to Paris, Richelieu, Minister of Louis XVIII, demanded his expulsion. The French spy service gave him a passport and sent him as a secret agent to Piedmont. After being assiduously hunted by Metternich and serving a number of terms in Austrian prisons, he ended his days as a petty official in Vienna.

It seems that it was not the hope of material wealth which induced Wit von Döring to play his despicable rôle in those troubled times. He appears to have indulged in treachery as a fine art and for the sake of excitement. In any case, it brought him far more trouble than money, and his own confession is probably sincere. "I myself never really knew what I wanted," he said. "To-day it was one thing, to-morrow something different—anything so long as it was new and difficult of attainment. I began by using intrigue as a means to an end, but it became for me an end in itself."

He could easily have earned his living as a writer had he not preferred a life of danger. After reading part of his autobiography, Goethe said : "This book attracts and repels at the same time. One cannot remain indifferent to it." And Heine, too, wrote once to Wit von Döring saying : "I will admit that if your pen served a worthier cause we should all agree that you are the best political writer in Germany."

Heine had made von Döring's acquaintance in 1827 at Hamburg. He was a tall young fellow, three years younger than Heine, fair-haired, with quick, piercing eyes hidden behind spectacles, and long, effeminate hands. He talked a great deal, as the police description of him emphasised, and his conversation was often fascinating. "He had such charm," said Heine, "that in talking with him I often forgot his character." The two young men had passed long evenings together at Hamburg, but later, when Campe asked von Döring to deliver a private letter to Heine in Munich, the latter exclaimed: "In God's name, how could you entrust a letter for me to one so irresponsible as Wit?"

Heine's friendship for Wit was inspired by the same psychological cause as that which induced the Grand Duke of Weimar to receive him. Goethe gave the explanation of it: "The Grand Duke is fascinated by the fellow, because he brings with him an atmosphere of danger. Wit is like a domesticated wolf amongst his dogs and sheep. He brings excitement anyhow, and that is the chief thing, whether it be that of love or of hate. In order to fight against depression one must be constantly excited."

When von Döring, during his stay in Weimar in February 1828, begged an audience of Goethe, it was granted immediately. But when, at the end of the conversation, he asked if he might see him again, Goethe replied: "No, sir. This visit is the first and last. You say yourself in your book that you are a dangerous man, and you prove it by your indiscretions. Allow me to refrain from running this risk again and to beg you not to return." "If I was the King," said Goethe to the Chancellor Müller after this interview, "I would have the fellow arrested forthwith, in order to return him to his proper element."

"If I had the power, I would have him hanged," wrote Heine to Varnhagen about the same time. He realised perfectly well that Wit compromised him badly in Munich by declaring that he was his friend. But the risk amused him and the atmosphere of scandal which invariably surrounded Döring "excited him," as Goethe said. He remained true to Wit when the latter was pursued alike by the hatred of the liberals and by the suspicion of official circles. He even promised him his help in the campaign which he waged, with all the bitter malice of his pen, against the King of England and Count Munster in favour of Charles of Brunswick, the notorious "Duke of Diamonds."

In all practical matters Heine was naïve to a degree. He

seemed incapable of realising that his relations with Wit, who was later expelled from Munich, almost nullified the efforts he was making to obtain an official post. Madame Cotta, always jealous of his interests, said later with indignation that von Döring had done Heine enormous harm. Nevertheless, Heine felt sure of his success. Despite Cotta's entreaties, he would not renew his contract with him, and the Baron, provoked by his refusal, terminated the publication of the *Annals*. Heine expected to hear of his appointment within a few weeks, and decided to spend the interim by indulging his craving for travel. He had been thinking for some time of visiting Italy, a project in which he was warmly seconded by Campe, who wrote to Immermann : " I should be most happy to know he was in Italy. With his impressionable mind he would make us see that country with new eyes."

Heine set forth in the month of July, accompanied as far as the Bavarian frontier by his brother, Max, who was finishing his studies in Munich. He was in a state of joyous exaltation. Gone were the cares of the past ; his future was assured ; the present was plagued by no inner conflict or material worry. For once he was able to grasp happiness with both hands. " Those were the best days of my life," he wrote later. " I was intoxicated with the joy of living and the fullness of my own powers. I journeyed through the Alps dreaming dreams of the great deeds I would perform, deeds which should carry my fame to every corner of the earth, even to the furthermost isle, where the fisherman would speak of me around his fireside in the evening."

His route took him through the Tyrol to Trent, thence by Verona, Brescia, Bergamo, and Monza to Milan. From there he visited the battlefields of Marengo, passing on to Genoa and so to Bagni di Lucca, where he spent " the most heavenly time. I bathe and chat with pretty women, I climb the Apennines and commit a thousand follies." In his joy he expanded and became more human, even to the extent of forgetting his old dislikes. From Lucca he wrote the most dignified letter he ever penned to Salomon Heine. At the moment when he felt he would need his help no more, he stretched out a hand in friendship to the benefactor of his early days and his most formidable enemy.

" I wish to forget whatever injuries I might hold against you ; they are perhaps greater than you quite realise. I beg you also, on your side, to forget the causes of complaint you have against me. They all come down to a question of money, and if all was counted to the last centime the total would amount to no greater sum than a millionaire might throw out of the window and forget. But the injuries I hold against you cannot be summed up and totalled, for they lie in the spiritual sphere and have their roots in the bitter hours of my suffering."

It needed only a little happiness to awake in him the generosity which was in his heart, to dispel suspicion and resentment and so to colour his vision that men and things took on a truer, nobler form.

" Ah ! Schenk, my soul is so full, so overflowing, that I cannot do otherwise than write books which will glow with enthusiasm," he wrote from Bagni di Lucca. He was already at work and had a book half finished. It is indeed a work glowing with colour and instinct with life ; the irony in it is light and the characters, too, are drawn from life and no longer seem the creations of a poet's dream. Heine could not draw a character wholly from imagination, but he could reveal to perfection the secrets of the living. The Marquis Gumpelino is the banker Lazarus Gumpel of Hamburg, a rival of his uncle's. Jacinthe Hirsch, the banker's factotum, was, in reality, a broker's messenger with the picturesque name of Isaak Rocamora. Hirsch was a queer mixture of honesty and cunning, wisdom and ignorance, who had stuck in Heine's memory. " My Jacinthe is the only character I ever drew life size and true to life," he said.

It was in this mood that he reached Florence. He did not find there the nomination which Schenk had promised. He began to be uneasy, and waited impatiently for news from Munich. But his high spirits were as yet little damped, and he continued to work at his book. It was in Florence that he heard that Count Platen, stung by the epigrams of Immermann, was preparing to avenge himself by a counter-attack. Heine had no personal quarrel with Platen ; on the contrary, he had once intervened on his behalf with Madame Cotta, when Platen had gone to Schenk and to Baron Cotta for financial help. Heine had heard a rumour of Platen's intentions before leaving Munich, and had spoken of the matter to Baron Cotta, who, in his desire to employ Heine in his publishing house, had asked him to pass judgment on Platen's lampoon before it was accepted for publication. " I had only to say the word and the book would not have appeared," wrote Heine to Immermann. " But I declined the offer, as you can well imagine." The confirmation of the news of Platen's attacks did not at first engage his attention. His new-found store of confidence in human nature was not yet exhausted, and the weeks he spent amidst the beauties of Florence were weeks of happiness.

Suddenly he became possessed by an overpowering desire to see his father. It seemed to him as if he heard through space a desperate cry for help. So imperative did the impulse become that he decided to wait in Florence no longer for the all-important letter, but to return as quickly as possible to Hamburg, where his parents had been since the summer. The agony of apprehension by which he was overcome, and for which there was no apparent cause, even made him rush through Venice without stopping. The historian Ranke, who met him there, describes him as a man in the grip of an irrational anxiety, forsaking the pleasures of Florence without warning in order to chase across Europe for no better reason than a wish to see his relatives.

During the journey Heine received a letter from Max telling him that Samson Heine was seriously ill and promising to send further news to him at Wurzburg. On arriving there he learnt that his father had died.

" I have tried for years to understand this loss, but never have I been able to overcome my grief at it," confessed Heine nearly a quarter of a century later. " It is strange that one can never bring oneself to believe in the death of somebody whom one has not seen die, and that one never really believes that somebody one loves can die. We say to ourselves that it may happen some day, but we do not really believe it, and it is a great pity, for it is the reason why we do not treat those we love as kindly as we should do did we realise fully that we should one day lose them. . . . We are all too often far from being as good to each other as we might be." These words were added after a long interval of silence during which emotion had rendered him incapable of uttering a word.

The sudden death of his father plunged Heine into a bottomless pit of despair. The fall was all the harder to bear because he fell from heights of happiness such as he was only once again to experience in life. It was more than the natural sorrow of a son at the loss of his father. He mourned as though something precious had died in himself also. This feeling of irreparable loss was the more strange since there was no spiritual bond between the humble shopkeeper and the poet of genius, the pathfinder of his time already vowed to fame. But it was on this quiet, good-natured man that Heine, so quickly on the defensive to others, had expended his need to love and have confidence, and all the instinctive tenderness of his nature which he normally repressed so fiercely. The shock of this death brought to the surface the deep resemblance between the two men ; in mourning his father Heine also mourned something in him which he was never to find elsewhere. Rahel, whom he visited in Berlin in February 1829, noted that " Heine is completely overcome by the death of his father ! " She found him physically much changed ; there was a nervous twitching of the corners of his mouth, his complexion was more highly coloured, his fair hair had darkened ; he was more reserved also, and had lost the habit of self-pity.

Added to this sorrow there was his renewed anxiety about the future. He began to understand that his enemies in Munich had conspired to prevent his nomination. He suspected the intrigues of the clericals ; he also suspected the intervention of Platen, who had, in fact, roused his friends against the Jew, Heine. Platen's " revenge," at which he had at first laughed, appeared to him now as a serious matter. Goethe said of Platen that he lacked the inspiration of love ; he was the author of some poetry of a cold and classic style, but he had a morbidly sensitive nature, due, according to Treitschke, to an inner lack of conviction and a realisation that his talent was inferior to his aims. His nervous, effeminate temperament prevented him from realising how exaggerated were his reactions to the pin-pricks felt by his wounded pride.

He knew nothing of the works of either Immermann or Heine except for a few poems. By the time he read the *Travel Pictures* he had already sent off his manuscript of *The Romantic Œdipus*. He knew, however, that Heine was a Jew, and that was enough for him. The man he attacked was unknown to him by his works, and had done nothing more than insert a few of a friend's epigrams in his own book. But he was a Jew, and that sufficed to enable Platen to write of " the Pindar of the Tribe of Benjamin, the pride of the synagogue, whose kisses smell of garlic." His malicious thrusts quickly went the round of Heine's literary enemies, and even of his friends. Campe showed himself eager to encourage a great literary scandal, and to this end brought Heine a copy of *The Romantic Œdipus* when he visited him in Potsdam in June 1829. Heine at first scarcely glanced at it, and mastered his annoyance in front of the jubilant Campe. Salomon Heine was worse. " Harry, without wishing to flatter you, Platen has drawn a pretty fair portrait of you," he said, when his nephew reached Hamburg in August.

When at last Heine began again to work, after ten months of idleness due to grief, the first part of his Italian journey had already begun to appear in the *Morgenblatt*, under the title : " A Journey from Munich to Genoa." He made up his mind to reply to the meanness of Platen with a vigorous attack. " I am starting work again on my Italian journey, in which I intend to have a wholesale reckoning with my enemies. I have already made a list of those who have tried to do me harm, in order to be sure that, in my present sentimental state of mind, I shall omit nobody." But as the work proceeded this settlement of accounts resolved itself more and more into an attack on Count Platen. The affair had become for him greater than a mere literary battle or the satisfaction of a personal grudge. Platen had touched him on what was always his most sensitive spot—his racial origin. " When the priests of Munich first attacked me as a Jew, I laughed," he explained later. " I thought then that it was just a piece of stupidity. But when I discovered that it was a plot, when the absurd nightmare became a vampire and when I discovered the real intentions of Platen's satire, then I took up my weapons and struck as hard and as quickly as possible."

Platen had been the first to base his attack on personal grounds : Heine replied by using the same method. And in his turn he sought Platen's most vulnerable spot—his homosexual habits. It was not only Platen at whom he wished to strike, but at the whole crowd " of shavelings, barons, and homosexuals who are far more widely spread and more powerful than is generally believed." " Do not laugh," he wrote to Immermann ; " I am serious ; the homosexuals are the Servite Brethren, the liaison officers in this great union of Papists and aristocrats."

The summer of 1829, during which his book *The Baths of Lucca* was brought to completion, was passed in a state of sadness and nervous weakness which he found it impossible to master. To this was added physical illness and worry about money. His nerves were so on edge that the atmosphere of Berlin became unendurable, though he had gone there in the hope that the change would allay the depression caused by his father's death. But he found the vapid conversation and pretentious tone of the *salons* exasperating ; he quarrelled even with Rahel. He left Berlin to go and live in Potsdam " like Robinson on his desert island." His financial situation was so desperate that once he wrote to Moser, " Unless you send me forty thalers immediately I shall starve to death at your expense." A little later he had resort to his infallible cure, sea-bathing, and in Heligoland body and soul were again restored to health, and *The Baths of Lucca*, which ended with the " execution " of Platen, was completed.

The book appeared in December 1829 and roused a tempest of indignation throughout Germany. Never had a polemic been carried to such lengths ; never had a man's private life been so cruelly flayed in public.

Heine's first reaction to the general indignation was wholly characteristic both of his personal pride and of that of a member of a persecuted race. " God be praised ! Nobody any longer talks about that poor Heine, or poor Immermann. That pity was intolerable." But he soon had cause to realise the full extent of what he had done. " Nobody knows better than I that I have done myself enormous harm by the chapter on Platen." Michael Beer told Heine that he had put on his gloves to read the book. Immermann, who had also replied in a pamphlet to Platen, declared that " Heine's attack is indefensible," though he added that it must not be forgotten that Platen himself had first indulged in personalities to a revolting degree. Heine even fell out with Moser as a result of some harsh comments he made. Only one of his friends took up the cudgels on his behalf in the storm he had roused against himself. The eternally censorious Varnhagen published an article in the *Gesellschafter* in which he sought to justify his friend. " We do not wish to expatiate on the guilt or innocence of the accused ; let us simply note the fact that an execution has taken place, the executioner has shown himself to be an expert, a head has fallen. . . ." He added that if Platen had tried to copy Aristophanes in his stilted, empty verses, Heine had beaten him even at that. Heine had annihilated his enemy precisely because he had " exposed his incompetence in the sphere of which he was most proud ; had far outshone him, not only in the fury of his satire but in artistry of expression, in the art of Aristophanes himself." It was Varnhagen, too, who drew the attention of the public to the fact that the third volume contained much else, and much of higher value than the polemic with Platen. But those qualities remained unnoticed ; the literary world concentrated all its attention upon the quarrel between the two poets. Platen's first impulse was to take the matter to the courts, and his friend, Count Fugger, instituted proceedings for slander. But Heine was prepared to prove his statements, and Platen, better advised than was Oscar Wilde in later years, preferred to drop the case.

The universal reprobation roused by his book naturally served to accentuate Heine's isolation in Hamburg. " Everybody here is against him," wrote Varnhagen's sister, who lived there. Heine was living at that time with his mother, who had been left alone when the two younger boys had gone out into the world. Gustav the adventurous had hitherto made a failure of everything, and, after the collapse of his last commercial venture, had enlisted in the Austrian army. He had adopted his mother's maiden name, which sounded better than Heine, especially when the " van " was changed to the more aristocratic " von " Geldern. Gustav rapidly climbed the ladder of military promotion and was soon an officer of dragoons. This brother of the arch-enemy of Austrian absolutism eventually became editor-in-chief of the official paper, and was rewarded for his services to the reactionaries by being given a title, thus justifying the one which he had earlier stolen. The younger brother, Max, had gone to Russia, where he became a military doctor and took part in the war against Turkey. Two years later, at the very moment when Heinrich Heine, in company with all German liberals, was expressing his enthusiasm for the Polish insurrectionaries, Max was accompanying the Russian punitive expedition against Poland. He later settled in St. Petersburg, where he married the widow of the private physician to Tsar Nicolas I, Henriette von Arendt. Thus were the young German Jews obliged to leave the country of their birth in order to attain success, and, like Gustav and Max Heine, they often acquired it by becoming the defenders of reaction and of the established order of society. . . .

The idea of leaving Germany again revived in Heinrich Heine, but he was perplexed by the problem of finding a country of adoption. At first he thought of Italy, but reflected that an Austrian sentry-box stood in front of every lemon-tree. England? "They ought to pay people to live there, but the cost of living is twice as high as elsewhere." In America? "Liberty's great prison, where profit is the only religion and money the only omnipotent god." France then, perhaps? But there reigned those "whose heads were cut off fifty years ago." . . . And in his distress he cried: "Liberty, Liberty, thou art but a restless dream!"

For distraction he turned, as usual, to the company of those eccentric characters who always appealed to him. One was the deaf painter, Johann Peter Lyser, whose wild humour amused him. The painter lived in one wretched room overlooking the canal, where, from time to time, Heine would seek refuge from his own more noisy quarters. Often he would spend the whole day there, reading or writing, whilst Lyser sketched away in his corner trying to make as little noise as possible. In the evening they would eat together, Heine going out to buy a herring and Lyser boiling a few potatoes and making the tea. After this frugal repast Heine would seek relief from the day's silence by going to some popular dancing-place.

Another of his encounters of this period was with the more picturesque Paganini. The violinist always wore a long grey redingote, which flapped about his thin legs as he walked and made him seem immeasurably tall; his long black hair fell in uncombed profusion on his shoulders, in striking contrast with the deadly pallor of his face. His movements were stiff and jerky, giving the appearance of invincible shyness. In the raw light of day this strange figure appeared to Heine like a ghost. "They say that Paganini has sold his soul to the devil," Lyser would whisper in Heine's ear; "they say he sold it in order to escape from the galleys in which he was serving sentence for the murder of a faithless mistress, and also in order to become the greatest violinist in the world and amass millions thereby. . . ."

Heine spent a number of evenings in the company of Paganini; a friend who was there relates how he watched the great virtuoso's every movement, as if to fix his image in his mind for ever. He intended to write a monograph on Paganini, but gave the subject to August Lewald at his entreaty, and abused him roundly later for not having used it. He himself has given a magnificent description of a concert by the great artist in his *Florentine Nights*.

In the course of the first half of the year 1830 Heine became possessed of a curious disquietude. "Just as there are birds which sense the coming of nature's revolutions, such as storm or floods, so there are men who feel in advance the coming of social revolutions. Such creatures at such times are paralysed and distraught to the very depths of their being," he wrote later in describing his earlier state of mind.

In the *Journey from Munich to Genoa* Heine had already outlined his anticipation of the great movement which he thought would captivate humanity, leading it by more or less violent stages, with halts, hesitations, and retreats, yet surely and inevitably, towards the transference of the political axis from the national to the social sphere. " Europe is no longer composed of nations, but of parties," he wrote. And again, in another passage, he asked, " What is the great task of our era ? It is the emancipation of the entire world, but above all of Europe, which has become the chief continent, from the thraldom of the privileged aristocracy."

This task appeared to him of such overwhelming importance that he came to dedicate more time to it than to his mission as a poet. As he once said : " I do not know that I deserve a crown of laurels on my grave. Much as I have loved poetry, it has never been more to me than a sacred toy, a blessed means to divine ends. I have never attached much value to my fame as a poet, and I care little if my poems are praised or condemned. But lay a sword upon my coffin, for I have been a worthy soldier in the struggle for the liberation of mankind."

This idea of his part as emancipator was no doubt made possible by his imperfect comprehension of his own character, combined with unusual sensibility to the deeper tendencies of his times and a curious facility for being carried away by his own vision of the future. One of his friends of this period, Ludolf Wienbarg, philosopher and man of letters, and later one of the leaders of the literary school of young Germany, saw more clearly than Heine himself: "If it had depended upon Heine to destroy the established order of society, to change the face of the world and, with one stroke of the pen, establish a regime to all appearances perfect, he would certainly have hesitated. Life and the world gave him material for his satire, for his vivid descriptive writing and his poetical outpourings; he had strongly pronounced sympathies and antipathies; he was capable of great enthusiasm for great characters and for great historic forces; but an abyss separated him from the struggling masses and from their leaders in action."

Wienbarg listened with a little smile when Heine told him of the nightmares from which he suffered after reading the accounts of Thiers and Mignet of the French Revolution. The decapitated heads of the victims of the Terror had danced a saturnalia round his bed; in his dreams he heard the bloodthirsty howling of the mob and the dry click of the blade of the guillotine. These histories whose reading so disturbed his sleep were his chief occupation during the spring and early summer which he spent in Heligoland.

When he heard the news of the July Revolution he was struck by the coincidence of events with his own reading. "It seemed to me the most natural thing in the world, like a continuation of my studies." He became at once intoxicated with enthusiasm for the cause of the revolutionaries. The bundles of newspapers which came for him he described as "rays of sunshine wrapped in printed paper; they light the wildest fire in my breast." His first impulse was to rush to Paris in order to watch the great events at close quarters. "I know what I want and what I ought to do at this moment. . . . I am all joy and song, all weapon and all flame." But the inertia which overcame him at the thought of taking decisions led him back to Hamburg first.

Pogroms broke out there during that month of September. At nine o'clock—the day's work being over, as Heine remarked ironically—the crowd gathered in the streets, pressing into taverns and all public places and bullying anyone who looked like a Jew. Stones were thrown through the windows of Jewish houses, including Salomon Heine's. For two days any Jew who was unable to produce his certificate of baptism was attacked as soon as he appeared on the street ; many houses were broken into and pillaged ; glass littered the pavements, and the Jewish quarter looked like a battlefield, until, in the end, the Government decided to intervene. Guards quickly cleared the streets ; they had only to show themselves for order to be re-established without trouble or bloodshed.

These events impressed Heine all the more deeply because after the July Revolution in France, a wave of liberalism had swept across Germany which promised to banish the old prejudices. Nevertheless, he made a desperate effort to find a post in Hamburg, for he was in great financial difficulties, having broken with his uncle and having quarrelled with Campe. On one occasion he was so lacking in funds that he wrote a begging letter to a man whom he hardly knew : " Send me any sum you can spare, however small ; fix the amount yourself." He justified his importunity by quoting from the doctrine of the followers of Saint Simon : " The courage to go begging is the highest state of their sublime devotion."

He realised acutely, however, that his plight was his own fault : " Rage at my own incapacity, at my mistakes and my stupidity, torments me more, even, than destitution itself."

But he also realised that there was no longer room for him in Germany. " I believe there will be another wave of reaction and am filled with evil forebodings ; I dream each night that my trunks are packed and that I am leaving for Paris, to breathe fresh air and consecrate myself entirely to my new religion, perhaps even to become ordained its priest." This was written in April 1831.

This time the decision was finally made and realised. In May he left Hamburg and, after only a short stay in Frankfurt, crossed the French frontier. The state of mind in which

Heinrich Heine crossed the Rhine may be seen in the concluding words added to his *Letters from England* immediately before publication: "Liberty is the new religion, the religion of our day. . . . The French are the chosen people of that religion, for in their tongue are written its first gospels and its first dogma: Paris is the new Jerusalem, and the Rhine is the Jordan which separates the holy land of liberty from the country of the Philistines."

CHAPTER VII

VIVE LA FRANCE, QUAND-MÊME

"He who knows the watchword of the future has little to fear from the thieves of the day."

(Letter to Laube, *November 28th, 1833*)

DAY IN DAY OUT Heine could be seen strolling along the streets of Paris, clad in the latest fashion, a blue jacket and a coloured waistcoat, absorbed by new sights and sounds. The French writer Philarète Chasles first met him on one of these excursions. He seems to have been struck by Heine's queer, dragging walk, and the curious smile which played about his lips. A sharp shower drove them to seek shelter under a wall: "As soon as the sun had come out again the individual who had attracted my attention hunched his shoulders, stuck his hands deep into his pockets, and set off again about his business. This business appeared to consist in staring at the things about him. I in my turn stared at him. I walked slowly a few paces ahead of him, turned about, and even walked round the observer, whom I was observing. I was struck by his unusual appearance, and wished to find out more about this enigmatic person."

Heinrich Heine, whose "business it was to stare about him," was enchanted by the seductive city. He liked its unforced, impersonal gaiety, like the smile of an unknown woman. "Here you can live without being happy," he said, quoting Madame de Staël, and he welcomed each new impression with that eagerness common to most foreigners who visit Paris for the first time. "If anyone asks you how I feel here," he wrote to a friend, "say that I am like a fish in water; or rather, say that if a fish in the sea were asked how it felt, it would answer: 'Like Heine in Paris.'"

As an exile, even though a voluntary exile, he found all

doors open to him during the restless period that followed the July Revolution. Like others who disagreed with their own reactionary Government, he was introduced to that caravanserai of revolutionary Europe, the house of La Fayette, who was the hero of the Old World and the New. Each Tuesday evening, from eight o'clock onwards, the reception-rooms of his house in the Rue d'Anjou-Saint-Honoré were packed with an international crowd of visitors. Like his friend Washington, La Fayette lived up to the first canon of democracy, which is to be accessible. He was encouraged to do so, no doubt, by his strong liking for personal popularity. In his puritan bourgeois *salons* were herded together the outstanding figures of the day, and of yesterday ; those of the class from which La Fayette himself came found themselves cheek by jowl with those who acclaimed him as the prophet of a new religion. The faithful rubbed shoulders with the merely curious, enthusiasts with climbers. " I have, in one of these *salons*," said Heine, " seen old musketeers who, in their time, had danced with Marie-Antoinette ; moderately orthodox Republicans who had been the idols of the National Assembly of Montagnards, ' without pity and without reproach ' ; ex-members of the Directoire who had sat in judgment in the Luxembourg ; high dignitaries of the Empire before whom all Europe had trembled ; Jesuits, all-powerful under the Restoration ; in fact, every kind of idol, mutilated, discoloured, of every age, in which no one believes any longer. Their names cry out when they approach one another, but the owners of these names associate peacefully and amiably, like the antiques in the shop-windows of the Quai Voltaire."

The advance-guard of Fame could be seen in La Fayette's dining-room—middle-class Generals like Lamarque and Dumas, old Dupont de l'Eure, Victor de Tracy, and Cavaignac. Side by side with them were foreign revolutionaries, whose style of hair-dressing, " à la malcontent," proclaimed their convictions. The champion of liberty himself, the white-haired La Fayette, an old man of big stature, his face square and pale, the top of his head too narrow and scantily covered with a brown wig, stood in the middle of the room attended by a crowd of pretty nieces, and surrounded by a triple row of his admirers.

The strangest figure of this mixed company was a woman —the revolutionary aristocrat, Cristina Belgiojoso. "In appearance she seemed to belong rather to the realm of poetry or of dreams than to everyday life," wrote Heine. "Her face recalled Leonardo da Vinci ; a noble oval face with pretty dimples, and the little, pointed, sentimental chin of the Lombard school." But the crown of her head was like a dome that surmounted a high, arched forehead, framed in black ribbons. Her dark, straight eyelashes gave her enormous eyes an energetic appearance. Their fire seemed to devour the pale face. Under artificial light her pale complexion assumed an almost greenish hue, in strange and striking contrast to her dark eyes and jet-black hair. It was whispered that her curious colour and the brilliance of her eyes were due to a drug to which she was addicted, called datura stramonium.

Princess Belgiojoso was descended from the proud House of Trivulzi. She had been brought up by her stepfather, the revolutionary idealist, Visconti d'Aragona, and given a modern education in accordance with the liberal ideas of the period. At thirteen she had studied Latin and numismatics, later medicine and philosophy, and, at an early age, this girl with the figure of a boy and the brain of a man had followed her stepfather's example and plunged into political life and the struggle for Italian liberty. Scion of one of the great families of her country, and heir to a vast fortune, she became a member of the secret societies, and placed all her innate daring at the service of the dangerous and clandestine operations of the *carbonari*. She had married a young waster of the aristocracy, Prince Emile Belgiojoso, who divided his time between amorous adventures, dabbling in art, and the exercise of vague political ambitions. The girl was fully conscious of her intellectual superiority, and believed that she had sufficient influence over the young man to induce him to mend his ways, join her in her conspiracies, and perhaps become a hero or martyr in the cause. But she had been quickly disillusioned, for the handsome young princeling soon relapsed into his old habits. Cristina Belgiojoso had been mortally wounded alike in her pride as a woman and in her hopes as an idealist. When, many years later, she became a novelist, she described the heroine of her story, in a letter to Heine, as a woman " who was convinced that she was the most faithful in the world and could only love once, and for this very reason accepted one lover after another."

After the bitter disappointment of her marriage, with its subsequent break and superficial reconciliation with her husband, Cristina had launched more desperately than ever into political adventures, and showed a preference for the most dangerous missions. It was solely because of the charm she always exercised, even upon her adversaries, that she escaped imprisonment, or even death, and that she was, in the end, able to leave Italy.

She reached Paris in bad health, and without any money whatever. But she was in Paris, of which she said that it " served as hospital for the political wounded of all Europe." She lived at first in a wretched garret in an outlying quarter, and the card pinned on the door bore the inscription " La Princesse Malheureuse." She earned a living by painting fans, and, whilst her thin, artistic fingers laboured at this work, her friend Thiers would be cooking the eggs for supper in her tiny kitchen. She obstinately refused the pecuniary aid pressed upon her by La Fayette and other friends. In the end, she succeeded, through social influence, in re-obtaining possession of a part of her lost fortune. At once, and as easily as she had accepted poverty, she took up again her luxurious style of living. Her mansion, situated near that of La Fayette, soon became a centre of political and intellectual life. A legend grew up about her, composed as much of envy as of admiration, but she herself encouraged the legend, for she was ever ready to meet a new sensation half way.

Her *salon* is described by contemporaries with agreeable thrills of disapproval. It resembled a romantically decorated mortuary rather than the drawing-room of a woman of the world. The walls were hung with black velvet, picked out with stars of unburnished silver. The dark wood furniture, draped also in velvet, was scarcely discernible in the gloomy light. Cristina appeared in these weird surroundings like the priestess of some unknown divinity, clad in a robe of black velvet, which hung in folds from her slender shoulders, and with a filigree of golden flowers around the black coils of her hair. " How beautiful must this woman have been when she was alive," said Ancelot wickedly. Her more intimate friends were received in a bedroom hung with white satin, filled with silvered reflections from the white silk of the great bed, on which Cristina lay, clothed in a long white robe, as though in a bowl made of mother of pearl.

Amongst these more intimate friends was Heinrich Heine. The woman appeared to him as the revelation of a world which had existed only in his dreams. All the qualities which most struck his imagination seemed to be united in her—a masculine mind ; a knowledge so wide that it recalled the culture of Italian princesses of the Renaissance ; a passionate interest in the problems of the hour ; and a sensibility so abnormal that he felt that with her he scarce needed to clothe his thoughts in words. This instinctive mutual sympathy began as a passion but developed into a friendship which lasted until his death. It was perhaps because Cristina Belgiojoso too closely resembled the ideal woman of his poetic imagination that Heine's relations with her remained above the plane of sensuality and crystallised into enduring friendship. " She is the most beautiful, the noblest, and the most intelligent of women, but I am not in love with her," he confessed to Laube. His robust desires were not of a kind for which her morbid charms would hold appeal. Perhaps Cristina Belgiojoso also sought security in love rather than emotion.

Another intimate friend was Alfred de Musset—" the young man with a brilliant past," as Heine called him maliciously, not without a touch of jealousy. Musset described the Princess as having the terrible eyes of the sphinx—

"so deep, so large, that I have lost myself in them and can find my way no more."

But there was one more favoured than either of the two poets—the historian Mignet. This tall and handsome permanent secretary of the French Academy, with his carefully trimmed beard, his polite smile, and the delicate hands which seemed to deny his humble origin, contrasted with most of those who frequented a society to which the tongue of scandal attributed all the vices. Mignet, with his unvarying correctitude and coldly distant kindliness, also contrasted strangely with the capricious woman who was subject to fits of epilepsy. Probably it was this even constancy which won for him Cristina's troubled heart, a favouritism which Alfred de Musset accepted with far less good grace than Heine. With the perversity of a disappointed lover, Musset attached himself to her husband, Prince Belgiojoso, who lived on sufferance in his own house, and consoled himself for his broken marriage by indulging in a life of pleasure. His own health, however, was made to stand the round of nightly orgies better than Musset's frail constitution, which gradually went to pieces under the life of debauch. Musset avenged himself for the bitter resentment he felt against Cristina in his poem dedicated to "a dead woman."

> "She would have loved had not her pride, like a useless lamp lit by the side of a coffin, watched over her sterile heart. She is dead who never lived, who only made pretence of living. From her hands has slipped the book in which she never read."

The woman whom Musset accused of being inhuman was in reality the best of friends, one whose advice was always sound, and whose help in time of trouble was never asked in vain. Augustin Thierry, the historian, would have died destitute and alone but for her friendship. When he was blind and helpless, Cristina installed him in a little house adjoining the one she herself occupied in the Rue de Montparnasse, after she had left her mansion in the Rue d'Anjou.

Throughout the whole of his life Heinrich Heine also had cause to be grateful to Cristina. He appealed constantly for her help, whatever the material or moral difficulties which beset him. Always she found a way out, using her friends and her connections on his behalf, and consoling him at every turn in his most intimate worries. The friendship between them remained unchanged despite the vicissitudes of their lives, despite separation and every shock of the troublous times in which they lived. When Heine lay dying, racked with pain and clinging with all the strength of despair to the idea of survival after death, it was to Cristina that his thoughts turned. " I have lately promised a certain woman that I shall come back, if perchance our atoms can materialise again after death : and this woman has all the necessary courage, it is the Princess Belgiojoso."

It was in Cristina's house that Heine made the acquaintance of Thiers, whose talent as a historian he had long admired. He called him the most hardened of sceptics, a political Goethe. Thiers enjoyed Heine's brilliant wit, and spent hours in conversation with him. He received him at his house, and supported every step Heine undertook on behalf of the German *émigrés*. One of the spies whom Metternich had set to dog the heels of the German exiles, reported to his master : " The worse of it all is that Heine is on such intimate terms with Thiers."

It was not only as a German liberal *émigré* that Heine was sought after by the eminent Frenchmen of the day. He was, above all, the poet of romanticism whom the new movement, flushed with its first victories, eagerly acclaimed as one of its own. He came from a country which had been discovered by Madame de Staël, and which was, for a time, the Holy Land of the new literary religion. None of the great writers of the Romantic School understood German, not even Sainte-Beuve, and very few of them had even read the translations of the great German poets. But all knew that the kingdoms of the heart and of the imagination lay beyond the frontiers of the kingdom of rationalism.

Heine's personal qualities greatly helped him to benefit

by the wave of enthusiasm which rose to meet him. " He was a handsome man, with all the appearances of robust health," said Théophile Gautier of him. " He seemed like a German Apollo with his high forehead, clear as a piece of marble, and shaded by a mass of fair hair. His blue eyes sparkled with inspiration, and his round and fresh-coloured cheeks had nothing of the romantic leaden hue that was then so fashionable. A very slight Hebraic curve changed without affecting the purity of his almost Grecian nose. His shapely lips —' as well-matched as two good rhymes,' to use one of his own phrases—had in repose a pleasant expression, but when he spoke the barbed and pointed arrows whistled forth from their red bow ; winged darts of sarcasm which never failed to reach their target, for never was anyone so cruel to the stupid ; to the divine smile of the leader of the Muses succeeded the mocking laughter of the satyr."

Théophile Gautier was one of the first friends Heine made in Paris, and remained one of the most staunch. Heine had a particular attraction for the young painter who was about to turn to literature. Gautier himself possessed few ideas and less imagination ; his gifts consisted solely in his eye for form and colour ; he found in Heine the qualities which he himself lacked, and was fascinated by his brilliant wit and constant flow of ideas and impressions. Moreover, he had the attraction of one who comes from afar—a little of that exotic quality which Gautier appreciated above everything. " Le bon Théo " was one of the first to blazon abroad the glory of Heine in France, at a time when all that was yet known of him was an abbreviated translation of the *Travels in the Harz*, which had appeared in the form of articles in the *Revue des Deux Mondes* and *L'Europe Littéraire*. Théophile Gautier showed an unswerving affection for Heine throughout his life. Long after the death of the German poet he spoke of him with emotion, and when the war of 1870 broke out he declared that he could not find it in him to denounce a country which had produced a Heine.

Shortly after his arrival in Paris, Heine became acquainted

with the most eminent of all the French romanticists, Victor Hugo. He joined the illustrious group which gathered regularly in his *salons*, and, during these first years, the most friendly relations existed between the two poets. But by degrees they drifted apart, and Heine's attitude towards Hugo became increasingly critical. In an article which he wrote in 1837, Heine called Hugo the greatest of French poets, " and he should be numbered also amongst the first poets in Germany, which is saying a great deal. He has imagination and feeling, and also the tactlessness which is common to us Germans, but which is never found amongst the French." Although Heine declared that Victor Hugo was not appreciated at his full value in France, on account of the political animosity which he had aroused, he recognised (and said so too) that it was through his own fault that his best friends had deserted him. They had been offended by his egoism, " which can be very useful in creating a masterpiece, but is very harmful in personal relations." Later Heine published a diatribe against Hugo : " He is cold, cold as ice even in his most passionate effusions. His enthusiasm is a phantasmagoria, coldly calculated and without fire."

Another literary figure whom Heine cultivated was Alfred de Vigny. Sandeau said maliciously in his speech before the Académie Française, addressed to Vigny's successor, that " M. de Vigny was intimate with nobody, not even with himself." The gatherings at his house were famous for the formality and reserve with which they were conducted. The host himself rarely took part in the conversation, but Heine for some reason was always exceptionally animated there. A contemporary who met him at Vigny's has put it on record that "nowhere, not even in the company of his ' little friend ' Thiers, was Heine enabled to be so witty, nor to discourse at such length in his German way, hands deep in his pockets, expounding his views on Spinoza."

The most fruitful, however, of all the friendships he formed in Paris was probably that which he made with Balzac. Heine was amongst the first to acclaim the great novelist at his true value. It mattered little to him that Balzac's political opinions were the exact opposite of his own, nor that he detested most of his best friends, especially Thiers. As for Balzac himself, the terms in which he related one of his first meetings with Heine say everything : " Ah ! the other day Henri Heine, the famous Heine, Heine the powerful, came to see me. He came unannounced, and although, as you know, I am myself not a nobody, still, when I heard who it was, he took possession of my entire day." They often went out together to saunter on the Boulevards, an ill-assorted couple in appearance. Heine elegant and still slim, strolling beside the tun-bellied silhouette which was Balzac ; the " German Apollo " accompanied by the man with the domed brow crowned with a tangle of black hair, the huge square head poised upon a bull-neck, " smooth and white as a pillar," as Gautier said. But the two figures walked in step, both burning with the same intense curiosity for all that they observed in the streets of Paris. Balzac gesticulated incessantly, his fat little hands, on which rings disputed pride of place with ink-stains, helped out the rapid flow of words with which he explained to Heine the actors and walkers-on in the human comedy around them.

Balzac's book, *Un Prince de Bohème*, bears the following dedication : " My dear Heine, this study is for you, for you who represent in Paris the spirit and poetry of Germany, as in Germany you represent the sharp and witty critical faculty of France. I dedicate it to you, who know better than anyone what there is in it of criticism, of jesting, of love and of truth."

The only writer of the new France whom Heine believed comparable with Balzac was George Sand (Aurore Dudevant) : " That terribly lonely genius." " Her appearance is like the genius shown in her works, it is beautiful rather than interesting," he wrote in *Lutèce*. " The interesting is always a graceful or witty deviation from beauty, and the features of George Sand are cast in the mould of Grecian regularity. But their outline is not hard, and is attenuated by the sentimentality which covers them like a veil of suffering. Her forehead is not high, and her exquisite chestnut hair is parted in the centre and falls in ringlets to her shoulders. Her eyes lack lustre, their fire perhaps has been quenched by tears or has passed into her works. . . . The author of *Lelia* has soft, ineloquent eyes which speak neither of Sodom nor of Gomorrha."

George Sand often received Heine at her home. He would enter her small apartment unannounced, and find her sitting in an alcove in her *salon*, dressed as a monk or in man's clothing, her slender fingers busy rolling endless cigarettes. She always welcomed him with the same happy smile—he was her "dear cousin," her hand would pass tenderly over his hair. Her tenderness had indeed something animal about it, but something maternal too, which the gesture and the smile expressed. She spoke little—"from avarice," as Musset said spitefully to Heine, adding : "She has the great advantage over all of us that she gives nothing in conversation, but always takes something."

For some time Heine was her special favourite. He enjoyed the privilege of the imaginary relationship conferred on him, he played with and spoilt her pretty children, who welcomed with shouts of joy the visits of this jolly uncle who was always so full of exciting stories.

"We have been, and we still are, very fond of one another," said Heine later on. But, if Cristina Belgiojoso seemed too much his ideal woman, Aurore Dudevant perhaps reminded him too forcibly of his own life of adventure in search of love. "Heine seeks love in order to escape from his internal conflict ; it is his means of getting away from himself, of surmounting that dualism of his nature which creates in him a ceaseless violent struggle," said Alfred Meissner, one of those who best understood the poet's complex temperament. George Sand had likewise an internal struggle to appease—the struggle between her creative power, which tended to satisfy her, and her woman's nature which summoned her to give herself, to pour out her passion in the form of tyrannical domination. Heinrich Heine and George Sand sought the same objective—somebody whom they could possess entirely. They could not, therefore, give themselves to each other. But, if their passion was abortive, it was replaced by a deep and understanding affection for each other. Heine stood faithfully by her in all the vicissitudes of her amorous life, quick to defend her against calumny, to attack her enemies with all the gall of which his pen was capable, and ready always to sing her praises in the papers to which he contributed. Only from time to time did a tinge of jealousy seem to colour his remarks, as if in regret for a lost opportunity.

Heine's friends in Paris were not confined to politicians and writers, he was also seen in the world of music. " Has music ever really interested you ? " a composer once asked him. " Only through its exponents," was the reply. One who interested him most was Hector Berlioz, whom he knew when he still wore " that enormous bristling mop of hair which rose from his forehead like a forest from the edge of a steep cliff." When Berlioz married Harriet Smithson, this outward form of turbulence became subdued. The marriage took place in the autumn of 1833, with Heine as witness. Berlioz had first fallen in love with the English girl six years earlier, when she had taken Paris by storm in the rôle of Ophelia.

Another close acquaintance of Heine's was Giacomo Meyerbeer, from whom he later accepted, and even asked, financial help. The *maestro* gave it to him, partly from admiration of his genius and partly from fear of his pen. The acquaintance lasted many years, though the two men had little in common. It was finally broken by Heine quarrelling violently over two badly situated theatre seats for which Meyerbeer had sent him tickets—two miserable seats which earned the musician several fiercely satirical poems !

A somewhat mischievous quality which rumour began to attribute to Heine was by no means displeasing to the Parisian circles in which he moved. Flattered in the *salons*, admired by his literary colleagues, he was at this time truly the great, the powerful, Heine of whom Balzac had spoken. " You have no idea what an enormous reputation I have here," he wrote, without boasting, to his brother Max. "I am almost overwhelmed by the expressions of esteem which are showered upon me."

It was curious that in Germany, where the public devoured all he wrote, the admiration shown for the poet was not translated into personal success for the man. After his return from Italy, the *salons* of Berlin, which had received his first efforts so rapturously, had proffered him little more than jealousy and disparagement. His personal success at Munich had barely lasted the short time it took him to deny his own personality. At Hamburg he had lived merely on the fringe of society. But in France, where nothing was known of his work and where he lived solely on the reputation he had acquired in Germany, he at once found all the sympathy for which he had hitherto searched in vain.

His first literary work in France, designed for French readers, was a series of articles entitled " De l'Allemagne," which began to appear in *L'Europe Littéraire* in March 1833. They were written in German, and appeared later in that country under the title *The Romantic School.* At the same time the *Travels in the Harz* was being translated by Baron de Loeve-Weimars for publication in the *Revue des Deux Mondes.* But Heine's prose remained almost as impossible to translate as his poems ; until the end of his days he lamented that he was "the German nightingale obliged to nest in M. de Voltaire's wig."

Heine accepted the adulation with which he was surrounded with an assurance which betrayed no memory of the painful rebuffs of the past. Gone are the sudden transitions from timidity to pride, and the moods which used to plunge him from gaiety into the pit of despair. He had never been so much at ease in life or so fully in accord with his environment. True that at the very beginning of his stay in Paris he had had a warning of the terrible fate which awaited him. For a time he had suffered partial paralysis of two fingers of his left hand, but the symptoms had quickly disappeared, and his headaches with them. He felt better in health than he had felt since the days of his youth. It was the most varied and colourful time of his life : " I live where time itself does not take time to rush past."

His old habits of changing his quarters had at first possessed him, and he had wandered from hotel to hotel, from one set of furnished rooms to another, first on the left bank of the river, then on the right. Finally he settled on the right bank, taking rooms let by an old woman in the Rue de l'Echiquier, situated on an inner courtyard sown with grass and far enough from the centre to make him inaccessible to unwelcome visitors. In this apartment, waited upon by a hideously ugly negro, he found at last the peace and quiet for which he had long searched. " La Vie de Paris " was there too for his pleasure, a life of easy indulgence in the kind of love which cast no shadows. Albeit, Heine was not immediately captivated by the charms of French women. " When one has been accustomed to long German legs, this place takes some getting used to," he said to a friend, with a wave of the hand towards the caryatids of the Palais Royal, which reminded him of his last adventures in Hamburg. However he soon forgot his earlier tastes and became adapted.

The customary discretion with which he concealed his love-affairs makes it impossible to discover anything about the originals of the little poems whose titles read like a daintily chosen list of feminine names : " Angélique," " Hortense," " Yolanthe," and " Maria." They all, however, are written in the same tone of amorous *badinage* which borders upon libertinism ; they all have the same note of pleasure combined with satiety, like a fire which bursts quickly into flame and as quickly dies down. Their sensuality seems pierced by the agony of unassuaged desire, and by disgust. He had already written, in *Ideen. Das Buch Le Grand* : " Madame, if you wish to be loved by me, you must treat me *en canaille*." But the poems which Heine wrote during his first years in Paris were few in number. He says himself, in " Angélique I," that on the day on which the God of love grants him everything he is dumb, whereas when love was refused to him he had sung his despair aloud and unceasingly.

Generally speaking he had little success at this time with works of pure imagination. " I have had little luck these days with pure fiction," he confessed. " The whirlpool in which I swim is too strong to permit of free poetic work." He failed also to write a novel of which he had formed the plot, and for this he consoled himself by saying : " I am here in Paris in the centre of great events ; I watch world history unfold itself before my eyes ; I am on terms of friendship with the world's most illustrious heroes, and, if I live, I shall one day be a great historian."

It was precisely in the field of world politics, however, that Heine experienced his only disillusionment in Paris, where, in every other respect, he satisfied all his ambitions, both as a man and as a poet. The " son of the Revolution," who had crossed the Rhine in a transport of enthusiasm in search of the promised land of liberty, was quickly brought to earth. " From the first day of my arrival in the capital of revolution, I perceived that matters bore a very different aspect from that which they had presented from afar in the light of my enthusiasm." He noted that the current of the great week of July had turned aside from its expected course, and that Louis Philippe was endeavouring to come to terms with absolute dynasties abroad, in order to secure the outward semblance of legitimacy. Heine was the regular correspondent in Paris of the *Augsburger Allgemeine Zeitung*, and in his first article for it, dated December 28th, 1831, he had written : " Louis Philippe, who owes his crown to the people and to the barricades of July, is an ungrateful creature whose desertion becomes more hard to bear the more it is realised how grossly the people have been deceived." *Le Temps* became indignant at this sharp criticism : " The *Augsburger Allgemeine Zeitung* has begun to print letters from Paris which are very hostile to the Royal Family," it wrote. " It appears that the censor, who allows no word to be printed which is unfavourable to the Emperors of Russia or Austria or to the King of Prussia, does not think it worth while to defend the interests of a citizen King." In his second article, Heine replied to the attack in *Le Temps*. " It is certain," he wrote, " that Louis Philippe is honourable as an individual, and that he merits esteem as a family man and a worthy husband, but it is regrettable that he allows all the trees of liberty to be cut down and robbed of their foliage to make props for the tottering House of Orleans."

It was not only the defenders of the middle path who attacked Heine. The republican paper *La Tribune* also entered the lists against him. It reproduced his articles in a deliberately falsified translation, adding that their author was under the " direct influence of the Austrian Government." " This manœuvre has been undertaken by agreement with the German Jacobins," Heine wrote to Baron Cotta. " They know I am the author of the articles, and are trying to compromise me in such a way that I shall be obliged to pronounce myself for or against them. I am not the sort of man to allow my hand to be forced, and they will attain only one result—that, out of disgust for Jacobin dishonesty, I shall become more moderate than I really am." But, whilst he parted company with the republican movement, Heine realised that a new and decisive factor had entered political life, and that the power of money was corrupting it more even than the personal interests of autocratic sovereigns. " Never has France sunk so low in the eyes of the world. We see now that there is something worse than the rule of mistresses. There is more honour to be found in the boudoir of a woman of easy virtue than in the counting-house of a banker." He began his article on the death of Casimir Périer with the words : " Casimir Périer lowered France in order to raise share prices on the Bourse. He tried to sell the liberty of Europe for the price of a brief and shameful peace for France."

This article, dated May 27th, 1832, was the eighth which he sent to the *Augsburger Allgemeine Zeitung*, and was the last one to be published. Gentz had in the meantime written an indignant letter to Baron Cotta, which the latter interpreted as a direct warning from Metternich : " Now the cup is full. It passes my understanding how your paper, hitherto inaccessible to such insolent vulgarities, can print the scandalous articles which Heine throws off like firebrands, and, above all, that you yourself, my noble friend, should tolerate such venomous stuff, assuredly against your own inclination ! I will not ask, for it would be too easy to guess, what a common adventurer like Heine desires and is trying to do by dragging the French Government through the mud. . . . For a long time now the cry has been, 'Away with the clergy and the nobility, they have had their day, *requiescant in pace.*' But where it is sought to rouse hatred against such men as Périer and his supporters, that is to say, against employees, bankers, landed proprietors, and shopkeepers, more even than against the previous regime of princes and barons, one may well ask, Who, then, is to be allowed to govern the nations ? "

About the same time judicial proceedings were begun in Paris against the *Tribune* for having reproduced Heine's articles. Almost at the same moment in which Gentz intervened with Cotta against " the common adventurer Heine," the *Tribune's* counsel pleaded on behalf of his clients that the author of the article in question was an enemy of France, a Prussian-Russian-Austrian agent ; and the jury rallied to the same view and acquitted the *Tribune.*

The *Augsburger Allgemeine Zeitung*, which knew the whole truth better even than the chief interested party, contented itself with commenting on the case : " The *Tribune*, the jury, the court, the Press, and the public have all been misled in this matter."

Once more Heine became the victim of the position he had adopted between two opposing camps. On the one hand he had been deprived by Gentz of his post with the Augsburg paper, and on the other he was accused of being an Austrian agent. He was, in addition, being shadowed by an Austrian Government spy, whose activities he did not succeed in unmasking until twelve years later.

" Royalist by inclination, I have become royalist in France by conviction," he wrote, in one of his first articles. " But, doubtful though I am of the prosperity of a republic in France, one cannot deny that everything here tends towards republicanism. The respect for law, which is a republican sentiment, has in the best circles replaced the purely royalist cult of persons." Later he explained his view of the difference between royalism and republicanism in the following terms: "The royalism of a people consists in the fact that they respect authority and believe in the persons who represent it, and that, imbued with this confidence, they become attached to the persons themselves. The republicanism of a people consists in the fact that republicans believe in no authority, and have respect only for laws, that they constantly demand that their representatives shall justify their actions, that they watch over them with suspicion even as they control them, that they are no respecters of persons, and that, the more their representatives are above the common average of the people, the more they seek to bring them down, to mistrust and gainsay them, turn them to ridicule, and even persecute them."

It was precisely during this period that a republican movement began to take shape in Germany. Heine rubbed his eyes, and asked if he was dreaming. In the Palatinate the movement spread rapidly under the joint leadership of Dr. Wirth, a jurist and editor of the *Deutsche Tribune*, and Dr. Siebenpfeiffer. In February 1832, Dr. Wirth wrote to Heine and Ludwig Börne, the two most eminent German *émigrés*, asking them to come to live in the Rhineland "in order to take an active part in the liberation of the Fatherland." "It is the decisive moment," wrote Wirth, "and Germany has need of all her strength, especially of men of great talent on whom all eyes are fixed and whose example would double our power."

As a means of propagating the movement still more widely, Wirth and Siebenpfeiffer decided in 1832 to organise a great public demonstration in the castle of Hambach, in which Heine and Börne were asked to participate. Börne alone attended this great manifestation of republican sentiment, the first to take place in Germany, and for long the only one of its kind. Twenty-five thousand people gathered in the pretty little town, coming from every direction; bells rang and cannon thundered, and at night there was singing, and bonfires were lit upon the surrounding hills. Wirth harangued the enthusiastic crowd in a speech which culminated in a vision of the union of the free German States and a European republican federation.

About this time Heine wrote : " I do not believe in a coming German revolution, and still less in a German republic ; the latter especially I feel sure I shall never see in my time. I am convinced that long after we have all rotted in our graves they will still be fighting for the republic in Germany—fighting both with weapons and with words, for the republic is an idea, and the Germans have never abandoned an idea without having fought for it to the bitter end. . . . But what is half a century, or even a whole century ? The peoples have time enough in front of them, they are eternal ; only kings are mortal." Heine knew that, for the moment at least, the German people were not ripe for revolution ; " The Germans still believe in individuals, in authority, in the police, and, above all, in parchment titles." He believed that a blind faith and respect for authority was ineradicable in the Germans and that it would crop up even if revolution did one day break out in Germany. In a satirical poem, written later, which he called " 1649—1793—? ? ? " Heine drew a comparison between the revolutions in other countries and the vision of a future German revolution.

Franzosen und Briten sind von Natur
Ganz ohne Gemüt ; Gemüt hat nur
Der Deutsche, er wird gemütlich bleiben
Sogar im terroristischen Treiben.
Der Deutsche wird die Majestät
Behandeln stets mit Pietät.
In einer sechsspännigen Hofkarosse,
Schwarz panachiert und beflort die Rosse,
Hoch auf dem Bock mit der Trauerpeitsche
Der weinende Kutscher—so wird der deutsche
Monarch einst nach dem Richtplatz kutschiert
Und untertänigst guillotiniert.

"Frenchman and Briton are, by nature, quite without feeling. The German alone is a man of feeling and will remain so even amid the Terror. The German will always treat Majesty with respect. In a coach and six, the horses black-plumed and decked with crape, the coachman will sit high up on the box, weeping, a piece of crape tied to his whip. Thus will the German monarch be driven to the scaffold some day and be obsequiously guillotined."

It was this instinctive knowledge of the German character, and his pointed manner of summing up the potentialities of his nation, which distinguished Heine from the other German *émigrés* in Paris. These others had the usual naïveté of refugees, always ready to make their wishes father to their thoughts. When Ludwig Börne left Germany, in May 1831, he declared that "things here have taken such a turn that I expect the revolution to break out any day, any hour even. It cannot go on more than four weeks longer, the smoke of indignation will burst into flame behind my coach." This capacity for self-deception and eternal confidence in illusions were just what made the strength of a man like Ludwig Börne. They enabled him to throw himself unreservedly into action and to establish contact with the masses, whereas Heine remained aloof, separated from these "wandering knights of liberty." He knew too well how to measure the distance which separated the present from the future. "In politics, as in life," he said, "one should desire only that which is attainable."

Nevertheless he at first gave way to the importunities of German refugees who desired to gain at least his name in support of their cause. He became a member of the Press Union, which fought for liberty of the Press in Germany. Gutzkow relates that : "Of a sudden a fever for banding together in associations took possession of the Germans living in Paris, the numerous artisans, clerks, and savants who had taken refuge there undertook to sustain the cause of liberalism beyond the Rhine by issuing a flood of petitions and manifestos ; those who would not subscribe to them quickly became the prey of the suspicion with which that over-excited atmosphere was charged. Heine was much embarrassed by the countless requests which were made to him as the poet of liberty. His experience of the business world had made him extremely cautious about putting his name to any documents. But now never a day passed without an attempt to dethrone some prince by means of a manifesto, or in which some new subscription list was not opened. At every other moment he found himself called upon to take his pen and sign his name, and it exasperated him."

Finally, he lost patience. He was seated one day at the same table as Börne, in a restaurant much frequented by German exiles. Between the courses the inevitable daily manifesto was circulated for signature—this time it was a protest against the political attitude of the Pope. " In the name of wonder, what has the Pope to do with you ? " cried Heine. He refused to give his signature, and after that would sign no more proclamations. At the same time he was pursued by a crowd of people asking for money, or begging him to intervene with the French authorities, or with his influential French colleagues, on behalf of this or that. He did, in fact, use his influence freely in regard to the withdrawal of orders of expulsion issued against his exiled fellow-countrymen. An example was his request to Thiers in favour of Venedey—the same Venedey who later fiercely attacked him. He also gave his money, as long as he had any himself. He gave it " like an old woman," as he said, to the worthy and the unworthy alike, and with the same embarrassed haste he always showed when he helped the needy. He could not bear the sight of misery in others. But at the same time he dissociated himself more and more from the atmosphere of estrangement from the world around them in which the majority of his compatriots lived. This was partly because he himself was more assimilated to French life than any of them, and partly because of the increasingly strained relations which grew up between himself and the spiritual leader of the German exiles, Ludwig Börne.

Börne, under his real name Löw Baruch, had been a police

official in Frankfurt during the period of French domination. After the wars of liberation he had been deprived of his post, and brutally reduced to the usual status of a Jew. He had turned then to liberal journalism, had become converted, and changed his name, in order that it should not be said that his attacks on the reactionaries were inspired by resentment (like Heine, he declared that he regretted the money his baptism had cost him).

His ability as a writer, the vehemence of his criticism, his profound erudition, and the integrity of his character combined to draw upon him the attention of the Austrian Government, which tried to buy him, as they had bought so many independent spirits of the day, with the offer of title and rank of Imperial Counsellor. But Börne refused, saying, "In whom could the people ever have confidence again, if I betrayed the good cause?"

After the July Revolution he went into voluntary exile in France. The political *salons* of Paris opened their doors to him as they did to Heine. But Börne always felt out of place and a stranger in that world, and his increasing deafness tended to isolate him still more. After years of residence in Paris one of his intimate friends could write that "Börne remains as much apart from Paris society as on the day he arrived in the capital." He had few French friends, save Raspail and David d'Angers, and he attached exaggerated importance to everything which happened within the narrow circle of the German exiles. Heine he observed with particular attention—an attention which soon grew into suspicion, and the suspicion into an obsession. "I note with care all that others tell me about Heine, and all that I can observe for myself," he wrote to his intimate friend Frau Strauss-Wohl in Frankfurt. He himself felt that this form of espionage would seem repulsive to others, and he excused himself by adding: "Do not think that I take pleasure in speaking evil of him, that is not the case. But he interests me as a writer, and, therefore, also as a man. He is like Robert le Diable—he has no soul." Before long he formulated the great accusation, albeit in admitting regretfully that he had no proof that Heine had sold his pen. Nevertheless four days later he wrote, in a letter to his friend, " I am sure that he has received money."

Börne had no proof, but Heine himself hastened to reinforce his suspicions, "Poor Heine is constantly subjected by me to chemical analysis, and he has not the remotest idea that I am carrying out endless secret experiments upon him," wrote Börne. But Heine's usual intuition did not fail him ; he was so well aware of the fact that he was being watched that he adopted his customary tactics when confronted with suspicion—he did his best to justify them. He assured Börne incessantly that he was always ready to sell himself, until his invigilator cried : " If Heine is only half the wretch he confesses to being, he deserves five gibbets and ten decorations." He seems to have felt some doubt himself as to the value of such confessions, for he added, possibly by way of convincing himself that his suspicions were justified : " The fact that he speaks openly, and of his own accord, about his baseness is no proof against the gravity of the avowal."

Yet, at the same time as Heine boasted of his venality to Börne, August Lewald, who had known him in Hamburg, and who spent whole days with him in Paris, could write : " Heine avoided all contact with corruption . . . I have myself seen him refuse the proposals of publishers which did not seem to him quite above suspicion."

The hatred of Börne for the poet increased daily. In the isolation in which he lived, the slightest event was magnified and echoed back again ; each day he sought and found some new fuel for the fire within him. He was ill and coughed incessantly, red fever spots shone in his sunken cheeks, but, with shoulders hunched and his piercing eyes fixed upon the speaker's lips, he sought out all who would talk to him of Heine. He also sought his company himself, hoping at each meeting to discover some fresh confirmation of his *idée fixe*. Gutzkow relates that Heine tried to avoid Börne, and was greatly embarrassed by the other's pursuit of him. " Börne would inform himself of all his haunts. He insisted on eating where Heine ate ; at length his intimates tried hard to restrain him from the veritable hunt he carried on after Heine."

In all the fuming hatred and suspicion that Börne felt, there was more than a little of the jealousy felt by a man who was deprived of the good things of life, for one who could possess and enjoy them.

In later years Heine interpreted his struggle with Börne as a manifestation of the eternal conflict between two types of humanity—the Nazarenes and the Hellenes, as he called them—that is to say, " those of an ascetic, iconoclastic, spiritual tendency opposed to those who are greedy for life, sane and realist."

Heine had no doubt at all as to the superiority of his Hellenistic temperament over such sour natures as that of Börne, but at the same time he envied Börne's power of action, and, above all, the influence he was able to exercise upon the masses. One day he heard him address a meeting of German workers in the Passage Saumon in Montmartre. In spite of himself he came away much moved by the speech, which he called " bald and artless, in the tone of the Sermon on the Mount." Börne cared nothing for individuals ; he once wrote that " the difference between men of the same kind is so infinitesimal that to study their shades of difference tires me, like reading print which is too small," but he could read the mass mind like a book. When he spoke he appealed to the simplest emotions, stirring his audience to enthusiasm or to indignation in turn, awakening hope or arousing the spirit of sacrifice. On such occasions his power over his audience was absolute, and in that respect Heine recognised that he was a master. He confessed that immediate and direct success such as Börne enjoyed tempted him more than the laurels of a poet, and that his secret ambition had always been to speak to the masses—" to have the great word at my call which arouses passions or allays them, but which in any case produces immediate effect."

Born artist though he was, he longed, throughout his life, to be a man of action ; an individualist to the bone, he yet felt a constant need to identify himself with the masses, though actual contact with them repelled him. But, regret as he might the quality he so much admired in Börne, it was his lack of it which freed him from the pressing pre-occupations of the moment, and enabled him to see more clearly into the future.

The views of Börne had their roots in the eighteenth century ; his opinions were founded on *Le Contrat Social*, and his demands did not go beyond the postulates of the French Revolution. His fervent admirer, Gutzkow, said of him that " his feeling did not allow him to define the new State in any other form than that based on the Rights of Man." In this he was again at variance with Heine, who bluntly wrote : " We are not fighting to give the rights of man to the peoples, but to give divine rights to man." Heine had been profoundly disappointed by the middle course of the new regime in France, and the conflicting vague ideas of those, on the one side, whom he called " the plagiarists of the past," and, on the other, the republicans who expected that a mere change of regime would of itself bring the millennium. Only amongst the followers of Saint-Simon did he find realisation that the fundamental flaw in human society was the injustice between the classes. " What does it matter if the flag be white or tricoloured, if it is not the symbol of a new order ? " Heine read in the *Globe*, a paper edited by his great friend Michel Chevalier, " one of the noblest men of my acquaintance." " The Saint-Simonists are on quite a different plane to those who understand only the externals of the revolution, and not its deeper problems," he wrote to a friend. " Those problems concern neither the form of government nor the personalities of rulers ; it is not a question of the setting up of a republic or the limitation of the monarchy, the real problem is simply a question of the well-being of the people as a whole. Religion has hitherto served a useful purpose, for the majority of mankind were forced to live in misery, and needed the consolation of the idea of a God who would make amends. But now that the development of industry and economics makes it possible for the material burden to be lifted from man's shoulders, and opens the possibility of happiness for all in this world, now that—— But you know what I mean. The people will understand us if we tell them that they can eat beef instead of potatoes, that they can work less and dance more. Believe me, men are not asses."

Heine attended the meetings of the Saint-Simonists in the Salle Taitbout ; he was present when the authorities cleared the hall, in January 1832, and dissolved the new group. He wrote to Varnhagen on that occasion : " The fact that the Saint-Simonists have given way can only be good for the doctrine itself ; it will now come into the hands of more intelligent people, especially the political part of the doctrine. The question of property can now be worked out better."

Rahel von Varnhagen replied enthusiastically, in a letter which shows the appeal which the tenets of Saint-Simon had at that period : " It is the new instrument, the great discovery which at last touches the old, enormous plague-spot covering all the history of man on earth. This instrument is working, and sows its seed ; it has brought to light indisputable truths, and relegated to their rightful place whole categories of questions. . . . All winter these writings, the *Globe* especially, have been my nourishment, my distraction, and my occupation, impatiently I have awaited their arrival. To beautify the earth, that is my old subject. Freedom for the development of human talent."

It was this energy, latent in the new religion, which Heine opposed to the old liberal doctrine to which Börne remained attached. " We do not want to be sansculottes, or grim citizens, or cheap presidents. We are organising a democracy of gods, all equally holy, equally magnificent, and equally happy."

The conflict between Heine and Börne broke into open quarrel in 1833, after Börne had publicly attacked the book *Französische Zustände*, in which Heine had re-published his articles from the *Augsburger Allgemeine Zeitung*, preceding them with the motto, " Vive la France, quand-même ! " Börne called Heine the Jesuit of liberalism. " To us ordinary mortals, nature has fortunately given but one back," he wrote, " and that is the reason why we need only fear the blows of fate from one side. But poor Heine has two backs, and he must fear the blows both from aristocrats and democrats. To avoid them he must try to go forwards and backwards at the same time."

At the very moment in which this diatribe was directed against him by Börne, Heine was engaged in formulating his political views in a manner which could leave no room for doubt as to where he stood. The letter in which Börne attacks Heine is to be found in the sixth volume of his collected *Letters from Paris*, and is dated February 25th, 1833. But as early as October 18th, 1832, Heine had written a preface to his book, *Französische Zustände*, in which he plunged into the fray.

There was no longer any point in the moderation and discretion which the articles showed, for Metternich had already succeeded in destroying all liberty. The resolutions of the Bundestag of June 18th, 1832, constituted the annihition of the moderate forms of liberalism. Using the demonstration at Hambach as a pretext for his action, Metternich had forced the decision that all power should be concentrated in the hands of the sovereign alone ; that the Bund should be authorised to annul the laws of the various State members of the Bund ; that the Bundestag alone should be enabled to interpret the laws of the Bund ; and that the committees set up by the Bund would have the right to supervise the State parliaments. Another decree, dated July 5th, tightened up still more the already stiff censorship of the Press. Treitschke wrote of it that it was " the most ignoble Constitution which has ever been imposed on a great and cultivated people by its own rulers."

Heine was revolted by this drastic destruction of such poor remnants of liberty as had still remained in Germany. He therefore hastened to add a preface to his book which was an impassioned denunciation of the reigning German sovereigns. It was written in a style which none of his contemporaries could hope to rival—with a dialectic skill and a mastery of technique which he reached only in his most inspired moments.

" In accordance with my duty as a citizen, I protest against all the interpretations which the Bund, by its decisions of June 28th, puts upon this document. In my capacity as a writer and a mouthpiece of public opinion, I accuse the authors of this document. I accuse them of having abused the majesty of the people ; I accuse them of high treason against the German nation ; I accuse them ! " He evoked before the eyes of the German princes the nightmare of mass-vengeance. In words which quiver like red flags in a riot, he drew a picture of a German populace which would be no more a fool in multi-coloured coat, but a mighty avenging force which had thrown off its servile trust and its trusting servility. " Have you no fear that the simpleton will tire of his burdens, will scatter your soldiers and seize your persons, and amuse himself by cracking in your skulls with his little finger till your brains splash up to the stars ? "

" With this preface I intended to make it clear that I am no mean hireling," Heine wrote to Immermann. But when, at the end of December, the printed volume reached him, he saw to his horror that his words had been distorted so as to give the impression that he was actually flattering the King of Prussia. In furious indignation, Heine wrote to Campe : " It is just because the cause of liberalism is at its lowest ebb to-day that *everything should be done*, now, at this moment. I know that I shall never be able to return to Germany if this preface appears, but appear it must in its entirety, and with a preface to the preface. I cannot sleep with an easy conscience so long as this preface is not published."

That was his first reaction ; soon after, prudence returned, and the courageous course appeared almost too dangerous. He was seriously afraid of being arrested by order of the Prussian Government, and he knew himself to be surrounded by Metternich's spies. Hurriedly he wrote to Campe, asking him to destroy all the copies of the preface. But this fit of anxiety passed, too, in its turn, and in July the book appeared in French, with the preface complete. At the same time a publishing house in Paris, which was a secret branch of Campe's firm, issued the original German text as a separate booklet.

In the preface itself, Heine attacked German reaction; in the preface to the preface, he turned on the Germans who called him "the head of the French party in Germany." Accused by the *Tribune* of being an enemy of France, he was accused by the German nationalists of being an advocate of that country. "You are playing upon the worst qualities in the German people," he replied to his slanderers; "upon nationalist hatred, upon religious and political superstition, and upon stupidity in general."

About the time his collected articles on France were published, he undertook the writing of a monograph on Germany, which appeared as a sequel to his articles in *L'Europe Littéraire*. "I have worked for long on my attempts to make France understood in Germany, and to destroy the barriers of nationalism which despots know so well how to exploit for their own ends. Now I am undertaking a similar and no less difficult task in attempting to explain Germany to the French." The quotation is taken from the preface to the French edition, dedicated to Prosper Enfantin. He added: "Until recently the most profound ignorance of intellectual Germany prevailed in France, an ignorance which has been disastrous in time of war. To-day there is growing up a kind of half-knowledge in the form of erroneous interpretations of the German mind, and a confusion over Teutonic doctrines which is just as dangerous in time of peace." The first part of the book was devoted to German art, especially to romanticism; the second part dealt with the history of religion and philosophy in Germany.

Heine was neither an historian, nor a philosopher. It is the more surprising, therefore, that he was able to perceive so acutely the menace which lay in the dynamic qualities of the German nation, then still latent in German thought. The place ascribed to Luther in the national development is curiously accurate. "He was," says Heine, "not only the greatest man, but the most German man in our history," in whose character were combined " all the virtues and all the vices of the Germans to a magnificent degree. . . . Since Luther, Germany has produced no greater nor better man than Gotthold Ephraim Lessing." Heine describes the revolution in the world of thought created by Kant, and explains the consequences of Hegelian philosophy, as well as the predominant place still held by pan-Germanism and paganism in the German mind. " It is the greatest merit of Christianity," he writes, at the end of the book, " to have assuaged the joy of the German in brutal bellicosity, but it has not been able to eradicate that joy completely, and when, one day, the Cross of Christ is broken, the savagery of the old warriors, the wild Berserker wrath, will break forth anew in all the barbaric fury of which our Nordic poets tell in song and saga. Even to-day the talisman of Christianity has begun to rot, and the day will come when its power will piteously collapse. Then will the old stone gods arise from under the accumulated rubbish of the past, and rub the dust of ages from their eyes. Thor will leap forth, brandishing his mighty hammer, to break the Gothic cathedrals. Neighbours! When that day comes, and when you hear the hurly-burly and the rattle of arms, take good care, Frenchmen, and do not interfere with those affairs which we are settling amongst ourselves. If you interfere, you will have cause for repentance. Take care neither to fan the fire nor to quench it : you may easily burn your fingers in the flames. Do not laugh at my advice—the advice of a dreamer who warns you against the disciples of Kant and Fichte, and the pantheist philosophers. Do not sneer at one who foretells the same revolution in the world of action which has been accomplished in the world of thought. Thought precedes action as surely as lightning precedes thunder. German thunder is admittedly German : it is not very agile, and it rumbles a bit slowly : but it will come one day, and, when you hear an explosion such as has never yet occurred in the history of the world, then you will know that it is German thunder. . . .

" The hour will come, and like spectators in an amphitheatre, the nations will crowd round Germany to watch the great tourney. I warn you, Frenchmen, keep quiet, and, above all, do not applaud. We might easily forget ourselves and put you roughly in your place, rudely, according to our custom, for in other times, when we still lived in sullen servility, we were able to get the better of you. We shall be able to get the better of you all the more when we are intoxicated by our new-found liberty. You yourselves know well what can be done in such a state of mind, but you yourselves are no longer in that state. Take care ! I wish you well, and for that reason I tell you bitter truths. You have more to fear from a liberated Germany than from the entire Holy Alliance with all its Croats and Cossacks. For, to begin with, you are not liked in Germany ; though its seems hard to believe this, in view of your charm and the trouble you took, while you were in Germany, to please at least the better and more admirable section of the German people. But, even if that section does like you, it is one which does not bear arms, and one whose friendship could be of little use to you. I have never myself understood exactly what it is we have against you. One evening, in a cellar tavern in Göttingen, a young 'old German' said to me that we must avenge Conradin von Stauffen, whom the French beheaded in Naples. You have doubtless long forgotten the incident. But we, we forget nothing. Thus, you see, if at some time we take it into our hands to quarrel with you, we shall not lack reasons. In any case I advise you to be upon your guard. Anything may happen in Germany—the Prince of Prussia may come to power, or it may be Dr. Wirth : but you, keep your arms, stand quietly at your post with your musket on your shoulder. I wish you well. And I was terrified the other day when I heard that your Ministers were intending to disarm France. . . ."

CHAPTER VIII

IN THE VENUSBERG

Sie lacht so gesund, so glücklich, so toll
Und mit so weissen Zähnen.
(" Der Tannhäuser ")

SHE HAD THE BUILD of a country girl, well proportioned; a skin like satin, transparent and pulsating with health ; a small head covered with brown hair, with the locks falling about her neck ; straight eyebrows above large, wide-open eyes, brown like her hair : such was Crescence Eugénie Mirat, when Heine first met her. But it was her smile that drew customers to the little glove-shop in the Passage Choiseul, though her looks and her smile could scarce be separated. It danced in her large soft eyes and was rarely absent from them, but its real playground was around her mouth, as the red lips parted to disclose the whitest ivory of her teeth, and the dimples trapped it in their shadows. It was an effervescent smile with no depth in it, made up of animal high spirits, like the gambols of a kitten. Yet it served, somehow, to give its owner the charm of mystery. It was not a well-guarded smile, kept for special occasions or persons ; it was spent prodigally on all and sundry—on passers-by and upon customers, on the cat sleeping in the spot of sunlight, on things even. She was nineteen years old, and had only recently come to Paris from her native village of Vinot, in the Department of Seine-et-Marne ; her aunt had brought her to serve as assistant in her shop, also hoping that her youth would help to draw custom.

It was in the autumn of 1834 that Heine met her during one of his customary wanderings on the boulevards. At first it was no more to him than similar encounters, the charm of which lay solely in their sudden beginning and undelayed conclusion. This time, however, his self-love was roused by the resistance which the young girl showed. Mathilde, as he came to call her—for her rather uncouth name stuck in his throat—condescended to let this polished foreigner pay court to her ; she rewarded and overwhelmed him also by melting glances and generously proffered smile. She listened only half understanding to his ardent words, and, no doubt, in listening she dreamed dreams of the world of wealth and leisure from which he seemed to come. But her smile, which gave consent, remained deceptive. Despite the trouble of her wakening senses, Crescence Eugénie Mirat set a price upon her virtue, and the price was marriage, or at least a lasting union. She came of hard-working, thrifty peasant folk, and knew from experience how bitter the struggle for existence could be.

Nor was it the resistance of the little shop assistant alone which changed Heine's whim into passionate desire. He felt in her a raw vigour of sensuality such as he had found in no other woman. Fierce emotions dwelt in this body like wild beasts in a cage ; they possessed her without warning and she expressed them without reserve. She was a child of nature, magnificently savage ; she could neither read nor write, she could hardly think, but the untapped reservoir of her passion swept like a tempest through the poet and overwhelmed him. Reason and will were lost, and destiny took charge.

Heinrich Heine knew from long experience that in such an environment money can open all doors. In the little room behind the shop he bought the aunt's complaisance for a considerable sum, thinking, perhaps, that by this deal he also bought security against any further surprise. But he reckoned without Mathilde.

She did not seem to have noticed the little conspiracy which had gone on behind her back. It seemed that she only surrendered to the good advice and understanding winks with which her aunt encouraged her. But on her first night of love, as Heine lay spent beside her, he saw Mathilde sit up suddenly in bed, round-eyed and puzzling to express herself. " Don't think that I don't know you bought me from my aunt ; I'm not as stupid as that," she said, between laughter and tears. " But, whether you paid for me or not, *I* have not been bought. You alone have pleased me of all the men I have met. They tell me, too, that Germans are more faithful to their wives than Frenchmen. I have now given you all a girl has to give a man. And I will never leave you. Whether you love me or not, whether you are good to me or not, whether you marry me or not, you hear me, Henri ? " The little, empty face had taken on a look of tragedy. " I'll never leave you, never, never." The words rang through the silent room like a vow and struck his drowsy mind as though through a fog. He laughed, but the laugh sounded lifeless. " But I love you. I don't want you to leave me." " And if I didn't love you, should I have done what I have ? But you understand, it's for always, even if you don't love me any more. I'm your wife, and your wife will follow you everywhere. Do you hear me ? " She was staring close into his face, shaking him by the shoulders. " And what would you do if I left you ? " he asked. " I should kill myself." The words came hoarsely, and her fingers gripped tight, as though it was not she alone who was threatened with death. " I believe you're making a scene already ! " Heine tried to joke. But Mathilde was crying ; big tears of self-pity filled her eyes and rolled down her cheeks on the pillow.

Alexandre Weill claims that this scene was told him by Mathilde herself. A brain as sophisticated as his could hardly have invented such primitive expressions. Destiny came to Heine on that night, and his conscious life was wholly submerged in his passion. The world fell away. His friends were forgotten. The strong round arms of Mathilde formed his only horizon. His enchantment was so complete that even when he woke up after the voluptuous exhaustion of the night he could think and talk of nothing else. " Since October nothing has mattered which was not directly connected with my passion. Since then I have neglected everything and I see nobody ; only from time to time I sigh a little at the thought of my friends. And that is all I have to tell you at present " (letter to Lewald).

Mathilde's hunger for life had been much sharpened since her change from countryside to town, and showed itself in her demands. Not only in her love was she exacting, but in her claims for all the pretty things which she had never been able to afford. Her tastes, too, developed rapidly. She came to enjoy good cooking, and her peasant's appetite was not quickly sated : she could eat two large beefsteaks for her lunch on any day. Wine, too, she enjoyed, both the soft taste of Sauterne running like fire through her veins, and the gaiety of champagne, which she could drink like water. The theatre enchanted her, especially the vaudeville shows, with plenty of light music and songs. She liked to stroll on the boulevards upon her Henri's arm, to be stared at by the men and envied by smart women ; she liked fine dresses and new hats and silken stuffs which clung to the contours of the body of which she was so conscious. But most of all she loved to dance and abandon herself to the sense of rhythm and movement, and the slightest contact with another set her veins tingling.

It was this diffusion of sensuality throughout her being that Heinrich Heine did not at first understand. His desperate passion was shot through with jealousy and jealous fear. He watched on tenterhooks the girl who seemed to surrender herself with every look, in every strangled laugh, the very tone of whose voice was a caress exciting desire. He knew that his child-wife had no awareness of right or wrong ; he knew there was no scruple nor power of resistance in her which could oppose the fire of her animal passions. And therefore he, the cynic and atheist, took good care to keep from shaking the slender moral sense which was given her by her simple faith in God, a good God who was as strict as a country schoolmaster, and especially exacting as regards the forms of His worship.

It was, above all, the fear of leaving her alone, the thought of what she would be doing if he was not there, which caused him to break entirely with his friends and past life. For months he never let her out of his sight, going wherever the madcap girl had a mind to go. Dimly he felt that the violence of her passion was centred upon himself only so long as he was there, that her wild spirits would automatically spend themselves on all around her. But he did not yet understand that in the narrow circle of her conscious life nothing was permanent, that nothing even fixed itself in her memory. He did not yet know—perhaps, indeed, he never fully realised—that Mathilde's sensuality could draw voluptuous satisfaction from the air around her and from every simple pleasure of her daily life, and that she therefore did not need to deceive him.

Despite his jealousy, her reckless carelessness enchanted him. But while it spoke to him of a femininity very close to nature, it imposed upon him worries of another kind. If her heedless manner was a part of her, so was her selfishness. She was incapable of making the least sacrifice for anyone, or even of conceiving of anything outside the narrow scope of her own existence. Only much later did Heine become resigned to Mathilde's complete egoism ; at this time it caused their first quarrel, but until the very end the most insignificant whim of her own took precedence over her sincere affection for her lover.

The exact cause of this first quarrel is uncertain ; it had consequences, however, and it seems to have been due either to some caprice of Mathilde's or to suspicion of her infidelity on the part of Heine. There is a passage in his book *Die Romantische Schule* which is so obviously an inappropriate insertion that it can only be considered as the echo of a personal experience. " More painful even than loss caused by death, is loss caused by life," he wrote. " For example, if the woman you love leaves you with wild heedlessness, if she turns another way, if she persists in going to a dance to which no respectable man could go with her ; and if, extravagantly dressed up and her hair provocatively curled, she goes with the first rascal who comes her way, and turns her back on you . . . ! "

Whatever may have been the reason, Heine left Mathilde, sobered for a moment, ashamed, humiliated, and profoundly hurt. It was a painful awakening after so many months spent in mad passion. Suddenly he saw his adventure from outside ; saw Mathilde, too, as others saw her, and felt he had escaped from a catastrophe.

It was in April that he came to his senses, like Tannhäuser escaped from the Venusberg. He had neglected his friends so long that he no longer dared to face their quizzical glances. Least of all did he dare to present himself before the mocking eyes of the Princess Belgiojoso, so pitiless towards all exhibitions of weakness. He found it easier to confess himself first to a man, and went off at once to relate his humiliating story to Mignet. Mignet told the Princess, who then showed an understanding of which Heine had not thought her capable. It is possible that she too had experienced the desire for a purely animal passion, she from whom the unshakable correctitude of Mignet had once drawn the cry, " Give me a stonemason or someone who doesn't think." Perhaps she was also more fond of Heine than he knew ; there is clear evidence of great affection in the letter she wrote him : " Dear friend, M. Mignet has told me of your misadventure and I pity you with all my heart. I am not laughing at you, and I beg you not to take the matter too seriously or too hardly. Would not a breath of country air do you good, to stretch yourself at length in the grass, with trees rustling overhead ? Come to lunch in any case on Monday at La Jonchère. Leave all your cares behind you in the city and be sure I shall not mock you."

Heine accepted the invitation gratefully, and spent many weeks at La Jonchère with the Princess. In her company, watching her impenetrable smile and listening to her conversation, Mathilde and her childish tantrums seemed very far away. Soon he was writing : " My peace of mind is now entirely restored, thanks to the fund of resilience which I have in me ; my unruly desires are again under control, and I am leading a calm and dignified existence at the château of a beautiful woman friend, in the company of distinguished and important people." From the tone of this and other letters he appeared to think he owed his return to sanity entirely to himself. He believed himself to be wholly cured, and once more the vision of a new, splendid life surged up before him. " I am purged at last of all dross," he wrote from La Jonchère ; " my poetry will be more beautiful, my books more harmonious. One thing is certain : I have at present a genuine aversion to everything that is muddled and mean, to everything that smells frowsty and cheap." It was easy enough to write such words of assurance when under the influence of Cristina, nor was it difficult in her presence to feel safe from primitive sensuality.

Convinced of the success of his convalescence, Heinrich Heine left for Boulogne, " his best workroom," where he would write " a precious book, which shall bring joy to the world." He still felt he lacked the courage to face Paris, and he wrote to Mignet : " You will understand the reasons for this voluntary exile. You will see me return entirely cured and with my heart purified of its disfiguring stains." But the months of solitude he spent at Boulogne were less helpful to the state of his heart than the society life at La Jonchère. The calm of the seaside awoke the echoes of memory. Autumn came, with its dull days, grey sea, and low-flying clouds. During the long, sleepless nights his senses were tormented by thoughts of Mathilde, and soon the old bitterness came back. " I am condemned to love only what is lowest and most senseless . . . imagine how that must agonise a man of pride and spirit. . . ."

But he continued to fight for release from this sombre obsession. When he returned to Paris at the end of December, he left his quiet apartment and took rooms in the Rue Saint-Honoré so as to be in the centre of society life. But one meeting with Mathilde, which almost certainly did not take place by chance, put an end to the heroic struggle of months. He surrendered definitely and finally to his fate, and this time he knew that he was giving way to no passing temptation : Tannhäuser had returned once and for all to Madame Venus.

There followed then, little by little, the break with all that had been his life before the first meeting with Mathilde. For a time he tried in vain to reconcile his passion with his intellectual interests and his society engagements. But his jealousy interfered with all his efforts to retain his own liberty. In the end he made her break with her own circle and live with him. Since his return from Boulogne he had lived at No. 3 Cité Bergère, where his apartment seemed to him luxuriously comfortable. He was easily pleased, for his visitors speak of two rooms " as small as possible," meanly furnished with second-hand things. The tiny room which served him for study was practically empty, his library, as he confessed, consisting of one borrowed book. The Austrian poet Grillparzer, accustomed to the sumptuous apartments of Vienna, found the place horrible, and, like the respectable functionary he was, protested against " this slovenly *ménage*."

Nor was it the best setting for a beautiful woman ; but in that respect Mathilde was not difficult, for she had known none better. She quickly got used to such luxury as came her way, but she as easily did without the things to which she was not accustomed. Never once in her life did she own a private dressing-room.

For Heine the first period of his life with Mathilde awoke echoes of his younger years at home. But the girl did not know what a regular home life was ; she had grown up as carelessly as any self-sown flower by the roadside, idle when she could be, working when she had to work, as a child running wild about the countryside. She was probably the offspring of a peasant woman's liaison with some master's son ; her slender ankles and beautiful long-fingered hands betrayed an aristocratic strain. Her notions of housekeeping, as Weill said uncharitably, were so vague that she might have been brought up as a princess in a castle. It was Heine, therefore, who had to undertake the domestic arrangements. One day, when company was expected, a friend met him buying a chicken for dinner. The vagabond poet felt his domestic instincts revive. He triumphantly announced to his friend Detmold how he had just bought two easy chairs upholstered in red velvet, and then went on to say that at last he had a bed to himself, for really the July heat made the bed he shared with Mathilde insupportable. He decorated the walls with engravings given to him by his friends ; for example, a print of " The Reapers " by Robert, which he had praised enthusiastically in one of his criticisms of the Salon. But his means did not run to curtains or carpets.

All that Heine earned was spent on his housekeeping or on dresses for Mathilde. Money ran through the girl's fingers like water, and she never acquired the vaguest notion of its value ; she would give anything she had with her to the first person who begged from her in the street. She seems to have thought that Heine possessed some secret and mysterious source of wealth ; only very gradually did it dawn upon her that there was a connection between his work and the money they had to spend. One day, after she had undergone a rudimentary education, she came across her lover's name in a paper and was very proud of it, though she could not remember in what paper she had seen it. When she had been living with Heine for years, she took one of their friends aside and whispered the question whether it was really true that her Henri was a famous poet. To her Henri these little characteristic touches were a source of pleasure ; like Harun al Raschid, he rejoiced in his incognito, for he wished to be loved for himself, not as a poet, but as a man. He was assured of his intellectual advantage, but his masculine pride required constant confirmation. It seems almost as though he was haunted by some painful memory of his adolescence, a memory that remained, despite the countless successes of his amorous life.

It was not only the male in him, however, which found assurance in the company of Mathilde. She alone, the child-wife and great, strong girl whom he loved to call *sa petite*, was capable of rousing all the kindness which was in his nature. He regarded her with something more even than the sentimental tenderness which he felt for his mother—" the old hen," as he half insolently, half passionately called her in his letters—or for his sister Lotte, " the crystal doll." The man who seemed brimful of spite, whose biting irony spared no one, who could always find a wounding word even for those who had constantly helped him, this same man bestowed nothing but kindness on his peasant girl, expended it lavishly and weakly, without a fear that his weakness would be exploited or a thought of gratitude in return.

For fear was always at the bottom of his rancorous outbursts of hatred : " he had about him something of the wild beast perpetually on its guard, and in that respect he showed himself to be the descendant of a persecuted race," says Laube, who knew Heine's exaggerated mistrust better than almost anyone. " To most educated people he ascribed the worst intentions and the most subtly concocted intrigues." When Laube begged him to rid himself of this everlasting suspicion, Heine answered : " How can I change my skin, which comes from Palestine and which the Christians have tanned for eighteen hundred years ? " But Mathilde knew nothing of this tormented Heine ; she suspected it less even than his mother or sister. " Heine, c'est un très bon garçon, très bon enfant ; mais quant à l'esprit, il n'en a pas beaucoup," she said one day ; and all the years of their life in common did not suffice to shake this opinion of her lover. Towards the end of her life she still spoke of Heine's kindness, and recalled, with tears in her eyes, a thousand examples of his gentleness towards her ; she was, perhaps, the only creature with whom he left this tender impression.

Nevertheless, passion continued to rule in the little household, even after habit had staled the torment of desire. Mathilde was an exacting mistress, and the physical demands she made upon her lover were excessive. To such an extent did Heine himself become permeated with the atmosphere of animal sensuality that he did not hesitate to discuss with his friends the intimacies of his sexual life. The letters which he wrote during the first years of his liaison with Mathilde are packed with cynical libertinism in the style of a drunken student.

There were intervals, however, of relative lucidity, when he began to long for calm and solitude. " We are both very happy," he wrote; "that is to say, I never have a quarter of an hour's rest, day or night. . . . I have always thought that love is possession, and have always fought the poetic idea of renunciation; but platonic love has its good side too; it does not prevent us from dreaming during the day and sleeping at night, and, anyhow, it does not cost so much." He complained continually of his exhaustion: "I am as tired as a hunted bull, I won't say as a dog." The same note appears in his letters to Laube: "How I would like to be in some peaceful German fortress, with a sentry before the door to keep out my mistress and my other worries. I thirst passionately for silence."

But he was to seek silence in vain; for him there was to be no repose, no moderation. To the turbulence of his nights succeeded the turmoil of the day. When his "wild cat" was not screaming in duet with her parrot, or dancing and singing through the tiny apartment, she was plunged into moods of no less noisy despair, behaving as though her childish heart was filled with all the troubles of the world. At such times she would be shaken by hysterical fits of sobbing; she would throw herself on the ground, tear at her throat and bosom with her nails, with madness in her eyes. Then suddenly, and all the more suddenly if no attention had been paid to her, the great wench would sit up, the tears would subside, and her face break into smiles, her features would take on an expression of unexpected tenderness, and she would laugh with her high-pitched trilling laughter. "She cheers my life by the constant inconstancy of her caprice," said Heine. But there were times when this exhausting creature of violent changes weighed upon him more than he cared to say.

He was passing through a particularly difficult period; the struggle to make a living was becoming harder, and he felt more than ever hounded by his enemies.

It was towards the end of 1835 that the persecution of the group called "Young Germany" began. This group was little more than a loose federation of liberal writers, philosophers, and historians. It had no precise aim nor even a common ideal ; it was simply a group of thinkers in revolt against the dull political and social reaction which prevailed in Germany at that time. Varnhagen, who did not belong to the group, has left the clearest picture of that reaction : " We are ruled by constitutions which displease us. That is bad enough, but we shall see the results ; they will be worse. Nothing can be done about it, for those who understand the situation have no power and those who have the power lack all comprehension. Germany was not more shattered in spirit nor more stripped of intelligence in 1806 than she is to-day. We are living on the prestige of our strength and our spirit in former times."

Heine by no means realised the changes which had come to pass in Germany since his departure ; he knew only the Germany of 1830, as his friends remarked. Gutzkow, one of the most active members of " Young Germany," tried to enlighten Heine on the state of affairs : " Even in Paris you must have noticed that the attitude towards literature has changed much in the last ten or twenty years. The progressives are divided amongst themselves, and many of their members are going over to the party which claims to be right-thinking, patriotic, and respectable."

To awaken the masses from their heavy sleep, to put an end to the desertion from the ranks of those who believed in the humanitarian ideal, to reunite their scattered forces and shake the growing power of the Church and conventional morality, such was the programme of " Young Germany." Treitschke writes that " this radical movement had little direct effect in Germany, but it helped to undermine the foundations of the State, the Church, and the ruling classes, and thus to prepare the Revolution of 1848." Gutzkow and Wienbarg conceived the idea of starting a great weekly review to be called the *Deutsche Rundschau*, and addressed a manifesto to all the liberal elements in Germany asking for their collaboration.

The first effect of this project was to turn Wolfgang Menzel into a defender of patriotic interests, seeing that his own journal had, until then, held monopoly in literary criticism, and the new competition frightened him. He had been in close association with Gutzkow and on excellent terms with Heine, who, as editor-in-chief of the *Political Annals*, had invited him earlier to join him in Munich. Menzel was still in correspondence with Börne also. But as soon as he felt his position as " literary Pope of Stuttgart " to be threatened, he did not hesitate to attack his erstwhile friends ferociously. Until then he was not even anti-Semitic, for he had spoken only a short time previously in the Württemberg Chamber in favour of equality of political and civic rights for Jews. But suddenly, on perceiving that several eminent collaborators of the proposed review were Jews, he announced that " Young Germany is in reality nothing else than Young Palestine."

Strong in the assurance of support from ecclesiastical circles, and relying upon his good relations with the Government, Menzel—to quote Treitschke—" brandished his pistol at the chests of those university professors who had promised to collaborate in the *Deutsche Rundschau*. " University professors ? " he asked. " Are not the universities State institutions ? Have Christianity, morality, and marriage no longer any value in the Prussian State ? "

" Curious," wrote Heine later, " that it is always religion, always morality, always patriotism, which our enemies use to conceal their evil acts. What forces them to oppose us is never their own miserable interests, never professional jealousy nor their innate servility. No, ah, no ! they want to serve God, good morals, and the nation."

Menzel especially attacked Gutzkow's novel, *Wally the Sceptic*, writing that Gutzkow " had transplanted to Germany French licentiousness, which blasphemes against God in the arms of strumpets." This proved to be the line which enabled Menzel to rid himself of his rivals. Gutzkow and his publisher were arraigned before the court of Baden for blasphemy and indecency, and Gutzkow was condemned to ten weeks' imprisonment.

The Bundestag, always on the alert for manifestations of liberalism, hastened to follow up the alarm which Menzel had sounded. By a decree of December 10th, 1835, it forbade the publication of any work by a member of "Young Germany," and threatened their publishers with all the rigour of police measures. Heine's name headed the list of offenders.

At first Heine did not realise the importance of this decision, which he found the more absurd because he had not even replied to Gutzkow's invitation to collaborate, being fully occupied with his personal affairs. "I had more important matters in my head," he wrote to Campe. So far was he from imagining what it meant that, on receipt of the news, he wrote to his publisher saying : "I do not take the persecution of 'Young Germany' seriously at all. . . . Prussia would not dare to ban books which are not yet written ; ridicule would follow upon popular indignation." So far as he himself was concerned, he believed that, even if he was put on the list of proscribed authors, he would only have to send in an application to have the measure rescinded. He even thought to end the matter by making a declaration of ostensible submission in the form of a hypocritical appeal which he sent to the Bundestag. So accustomed was he to underestimate the intelligence of others that he felt sure his clumsy ruse would succeed, and that the Bund would be touched by his childish letter and repent of its misdeeds. "Thirty-six handkerchiefs will be wet with the tears of the Bund," he laughed. But when he found that the manœuvre had had no effect he was up in arms at once.

He sent Campe a book in which there were as few allusions as possible to political or social matters. In this book, *Florentine Nights*, he raised a sort of monument to his affection for Princess Belgiojoso. He did so, perhaps, to salve his uneasy conscience. But he was not altogether at home in *belles-lettres*. He wrote to Lewald saying : "You will see that if I am forbidden to write of politics or religion, I shall still be able to pay my way by writing pure literature. Frankly, this form of writing does not amuse me much ; I find little pleasure in it." But, though he avoided anything in the nature of direct provocation, he did not make the concessions to which other members of "Young Germany"—

Heinrich Laube for example—descended. He flatly refused to submit his new book to the censor, especially to the Prussian censor. " One thing is settled as regards myself," he wrote to Campe. " I will not hand over the German Press to Prussia ; I will not sell my honour for the royalties of a book. . . . In your letter before the last you yourself reproached me for having given way in humiliating fashion, now to-day it is you who advise me to adopt such a shameful attitude."

He still refrained from giving public expression to his revolt, for he still awaited hopefully a favourable decision by the Bundestag. In the meantime he vented his fury on Menzel, " that foul hypocrite." " If ropes could be written, he would have been hung long ago." He tried to induce him to fight a duel, but Menzel was quite content to refuse and be called a coward. In the preface to his new book, the third volume of the *Salon* which appeared separately under the title *Ueber den Denunzianten*, Heine settled his account with Menzel. But the preface was more than a personal quarrel satisfied by firing all the poisoned arrows which he had at his command. It was also a furious attack on all those " guardians of the German spirit " who tried to destroy their enemies by calling them Jews and Frenchmen. " Perhaps there are a few sincere Francophobes amongst these people who so miserably fail to understand our sympathy for France and make such crazy accusations against us. But most of them are rascals—shameless, dishonest, cowardly rascals—who deliberately cultivate a hatred they do not feel. They themselves lack every virtue the German people possess, but they don the vices of that people so as to give themselves the appearance of being patriotic, the better to be able to insult in safe disguise those who are the real friends of the nation. . . . Amongst the masses, hatred of France is synonymous with love of country : by cleverly exploiting this sentiment they win over to their side the mob, when all they really want to do is to attack those young writers who are trying to bring about friendship between France and Germany. There was certainly a time when such hatred was of service to the State, when it was a question of overthrowing a foreign domination : but to-day the danger lies no longer in the west ; France no longer threatens our independence. The Frenchmen of to-day are not the Frenchmen of yesterday. In the kingdom of the mind they are our brothers, whilst in the material sphere their interests coincide more and more with our own. To-day France is our natural ally. He who does not understand this writes himself down a fool ; but he who understands it and acts against it is a traitor."

In the preface to his book *Französische Zustände* Heine had already foretold that the future federation of Europe could only be realised through an alliance between France and Germany. He dreamed of that same commonwealth of peoples which so many others after him were to visualise. "If we can only make the masses understand what is happening, they will no longer allow themselves to be poisoned by writers in the pay of the aristocracy : the great *entente* between the peoples, the holy alliance of nations, will be realised, and we shall no longer need permanent armies composed of thousands of assassins ; we shall be able to beat their swords into ploughshares ; we shall have peace, prosperity, and liberty. . . ."

Heine boasted in a letter to Laube that "the thieves of to-day have little hold upon those who know the watchword of the future." But to be right about the distant future did not help him to solve the difficulties of the immediate present. The ban imposed by the Bundestag closed the columns of the newspapers to him and deprived him of the proceeds from the sale of his books. Campe was frightened, for the edict of the Bundestag had mentioned him by name, and throughout Germany he looked for a censor who would allow the publication of a new book by Heine. Life with Mathilde was expensive, too. At the same time he seems to have fallen into trouble over another "thorny affair." Whether this affair was due to some obligation lightly undertaken for a friend, or whether it was some piece of blackmail resulting from the dubious company he kept, is not known, but in any case it caused him serious concern.

In the midst of all this worry he again fell ill. "Contrary to custom, it is not an imaginary illness this time but a very real one." He developed all the symptoms of the terrible cholera epidemic which had swept Paris in 1832, but which he had at the time escaped. When he recovered, he contracted jaundice, and the doctors sent him to the south of France. But the noise of Marseilles racked his frayed nerves. "Marseilles is Hamburg translated into French, and I cannot abide Hamburg now, even in the best translation." He retired to Aix-en-Provence, where, instead of the sunshine of the Midi, he found snow and the mistral.

The situation was desperate. "I am more sick in soul than in body ; the jaundice now is in my heart," he wrote to Princess Belgiojoso. "Should I not make an ignoble peace with the authorities across the Rhine, in order to be able to escape from these worries, this exile, and this irksome want which is even worse than complete penury ? "

Pursued by trouble, with nerves on edge, he turned once more to Salomon Heine. His uncle owed him a very real debt of gratitude. He had already lost one son during his journey to Rome ; in 1832 he had been very near to losing the other when he was stricken with cholera in Paris. It was Heinrich Heine who had nursed his cousin Carl, remaining by his side to do so in the plague-stricken city from which all who could had fled. But once again Heine spoilt everything by one of those tactless letters which he knew too well how to write. Applying to Salomon Heine in such circumstances, he must needs strike him at his most sensitive point, his pride as a self-made man, by calmly telling him that his best title to public esteem lay in the fact that he bore the same name as Heinrich Heine !

That his uncle's reply was a flat negative is not surprising, but he appears to have found some other way also of avenging his wounded dignity upon his vainglorious nephew. Anyhow, he succeeded in making him furious, for later Heine wrote : "He has committed a grave injustice against me, an action which has fatally damaged my honour in Paris and even my material circumstances." Not for very many years did Salomon Heine forgive this blow to his self-love ; forget it he never did. On the rare occasions on which he wrote to his nephew he continued until his death to sign himself: " Salomon Heine, the man who bears your name."

In his desperate situation, after having knocked in vain at so many doors, Heine made appeal to his old friend Moser, asking him to lend him four hundred francs, adding with charming frankness : " My financial affairs are now in such a bad way that nobody but a madman or a friend would lend me money." Princess Belgiojoso also intervened on his behalf. She knew that, amongst her exiled Italian friends, several had appealed to the generosity of the French State, preferring the aid of a foreign Government which was liberal to the shame of giving way to the reactionaries of their own country. She had already once persuaded Mignet to intervene on behalf of Augustin Thierry, and she now used all her woman's wiles to get him to interest Thiers on behalf of Heine.

Whilst awaiting the outcome of these efforts Heine signed a contract with Campe by which he engaged himself to hand over to him all he wrote during the next eleven years. For this the publisher paid him the sum of 20,000 francs, which, as Heine confessed to his brother, he urgently needed if he was to keep out of the debtors' prison. He was in a precarious situation which his illness did nothing to alleviate ; he was unable to work, unable to do anything else than await the signature of the contract and the arrival of the money, as a condemned man awaits his reprieve. The influence of the Princess was great. Thanks to her good offices, Heine obtained from the French Government an annual grant of 4,800 francs drawn from the secret funds. His position began to be a little better, but the hard time he had been through left his nerves on edge for months.

His life with Mathilde continued to be a source of constant agitation. Jealously he watched her every step, every burst of laughter, every look she gave another ; and when a day passed without providing even an imaginary cause for criticism, then he dreamt of it at night. A visitor tells how he went walking one day on the boulevards with Heine, while Mathilde went in front on the arm of their friend Moritz. Heine followed the couple with his eyes uneasily, and every two minutes would exclaim : " Where are they, then? Where are Moritz and Mathilde ? " At length his friend burst out laughing and said : " I believe Heine is jealous, even on the open street by daylight." It was scarcely an exaggeration.

About the same time—April 1837—Heine, Mathilde, and their friend Detmold were dining together in the restaurant " Bœuf à la mode." At the next table were some students who had drunk a little too much and kept on casting glances at Mathilde. The good-looking girl was not unwilling to be admired. She laughed her best, and doubtless looked to see the effect she was making. Certainly she did not notice the effect she was having upon her Henri until one of the students called across the table to her, and promptly had his ears boxed. The scene in the restaurant was followed by a duel in the Bois de Boulogne, but Heine's second, the Marquis de Custine, brought about a reconciliation without a shot being fired.

Despite this primitive display of jealousy, which years of life together did nothing to diminish, Heine showed no consideration at all for Mathilde's own feelings and continued to claim full liberty for himself. Grillparzer noted the presence of " two grisettes " in the tiny apartment even at the beginning of their union. This would seem to confirm the statement of Alexandre Weill, not always the most reliable of witnesses, that Mathilde tolerated her lover's other mistresses in her house. Weill explained this by saying that she would only allow women to be there who were less beautiful that herself, and that any appearance of personal superiority in another woman she found insupportable. She knew her own power over Heine. Either from prudence or indolence, she refrained from trying to penetrate into his intellectual world. One day she worried a friend who had spoken enthusiastically of the *Reisebilder* to get her a copy in the French translation. But, after glancing at it, she turned pale and began to tremble, and piteously begged her lover never again to address such tender words to other women. Nevertheless, with her childish faculty for ignoring all that was disagreeable to her, she took care not to try to keep him to his promise. She confined herself to exercising her primitive diplomacy in the field of more immediate dangers.

Thus she came day by day to steal a little more of his life from him—imperceptibly, with a sort of method concealed behind the uncertainty of her whims. At first she had been accustomed to spend the summer—her "grass widowhood"—at home with her mother. But little by little Heine gave way to her importunities and they separated less and less. His periods of repose were spoilt by "the wildness of this dearly beloved person." But as soon as Mathilde was no longer there to plague him he took his revenge with boyish enthusiasm. When she fell ill one day he became terribly upset, had her taken to a nursing home, and surrounded her with attention. But as soon as he had left the home in the evenings, he would hurry off to a masked ball and stay there until tired out at five in the morning. Or else he would go to the theatre "for his own enjoyment," as he said, not to one of the light entertainments which Mathilde's restlessness used to impose upon him. "I am enjoying complete freedom, abusing it even," he wrote to a friend.

It was an uneasy, unfruitful period in his life. He grew fat, and his quick mind no longer showed in his coarsened features; "the beautiful rhyme of his lips," as Gautier called it, developed a sensual heaviness. When he caught sight of himself one morning in a mirror he exclaimed in alarm: "I look exactly as my poor father did when he ceased to be good-looking." His neck grew thick, and, with his broad shoulders and heavy arms, which seemed to indicate iron muscles, he appeared to those who did not know him "more like an athlete than a poet." He was only too glad to encourage this illusion of good health himself, for his disease began to show itself in alarming fashion. "My left hand grows thinner daily and one can see it dying," he wrote in July 1837. Two months later a malady of the eyes began to terrify him. It grew worse so rapidly that he was obliged to shorten his holidays and return to Paris. The right eye was completely blind, and with the left he could only see the vague outline of things. His physician in Paris, Dr. Sichel, applied the usual treatment of the period which chiefly consisted of frequent blood-letting. The evidence of the terrible disease which had been contracted at Göttingen escaped the doctor, even though the dilation of the pupil of the eye, which to-day is a recognised symptom, was very marked : " The pupil of the right eye was so dilated that it almost covered the entire iris." A terrible fear of becoming totally blind took possession of Heine. He kept strictly to the prescriptions of his doctor ; but when, after a few months, his eye trouble got somewhat better, he again began to lead his former dissipated life. Something had changed in him, however ; " black care of the future poisons my days," he wrote. Vaguely he felt that the appalling sexual slavery which chained him to Mathilde was ruining him body and soul. " This liason will come to a bad end. It is as well to know it in advance, so that the blow, when it comes, does not crush me altogether."

But, just as he began to free himself from this erotic stranglehold, another and a new sentiment took possession of him in the shape of pity for so much inexperience and incapacity. This feeling of responsibility towards a feeble improvident being was to become in him the strongest tie of all. One day, when on a visit to Mathilde's village home, her old mother brought out of a chest a tiny child's chemise. Tears mounted to Heine's eyes as he took the small thing in his hands. He carried it back with him to Paris, spread it on his table, and sat for a long time caressing this souvenir of his mistress's childhood.

In the first stages of their love he had been able to do without his friends, but as the years passed he came to miss them more and more and to feel an increasing need of intellectual company. His *ménage* with Mathilde was accepted as the normal thing by Bohemian Paris. His friends Théophile Gautier and Alphonse Royer lived similar lives, and the three couples often met in the Café Montmartre, where the three high-spirited women attracted much attention. But Parisian society which had so graciously welcomed Heine, could not accept Mathilde, with her all too visible signs of humble origin and her irregular social position. Heine speaks of this ostracism in his essay on the French stage, in which the following passage is scarcely to be explained except by the humiliation of some personal experience : " The doors of all French *salons* stand open to the most vicious of Messalinas, on condition that her husband trots patiently behind her like an animal. But the young girl who throws herself into the arms of a lover, madly generous and ready for any sacrifice, is banished for ever from good society. Still, it happens rarely enough, for, in this country, girls never love, or, if they do fall in love, they try to get married as quickly as possible, in order to enjoy the liberty which convention only allows to married women." There follows a general observation on the difference between established convention in France and in Germany. " In Germany, as also in England and the other Germanic countries, we allow girls the fullest possible freedom, whereas married women remain under the strict and anxious regard of their husbands. Here in France it is the opposite. . . . We Germans, and our Germanic neighbours, pay the homage of our love to single women : it is to their charms alone that our poets sing. But amongst the French, love is addressed only to married women, in art as in life."

The only persons of his class who received Mathilde were Germans visiting Paris. Heine avoided the *émigrés* who lived there as much as possible, for there were Austrian Government spies amongst them, journalists who enquired into his private affairs and disorted his words, and beggars who took his money and then slandered him. " But the suit you gave him was still in good condition," said Mathilde in astonishment when she discovered one day that a young German was speaking ill of her Henri after having accepted his presents.

Many German visitors became friendly with Heine. Heinrich Laube, the future director of the Burg Theatre in

Vienna, spent much time in France, and it was through him that Heine made the acquaintance of Richard Wagner, who arrived in Paris in 1839, accompanied by his wife Minna and his dog, a great Dane. Wagner was then scarcely twenty-six, and was still in the modest early stages of his career. With his first opera, *Liebesverbot*, he had met with nothing but rebuff; he was still seeking a producer who would have the courage to take *Rienzi*. Paris, which Wagner had envisaged as the "cultural centre of European grand opera," brought him nothing but trouble and disappointment. In the straitened circumstances and isolation of his life in Paris, Wagner found much pleasure in Heine's company. Himself a great conversationalist, he liked to pit his wits against such a brilliant companion. But he owed more than pleasant companionship to Heine. No doubt he was already familiar with the legend of Tannhäuser, but the use Heine had made of it in the famous poem in *Elementargeister* attracted Wagner's attention once more.

In the first volume of his *Salon*, published in 1834, Heine had inserted a piece entitled "The Memoirs of Monsieur de Schnabelowopski." In this story Heine devotes a whole chapter to describing a play called *The Flying Dutchman*, which his hero sees in an Amsterdam theatre. The beauty of the story made a great impression on Wagner. In his autobiographical sketch, published in 1842, Wagner wrote: "This powerful dramatic theme invented by Heine, the story of the redemption of the wandering Jew of the ocean, inspired me to use the legend as a subject for an opera. I arranged matters with Heine himself, and prepared the libretto. . . ." Thanks to an introduction from Meyerbeer, Wagner succeeded in interesting Pillet, the director of the Paris Grand Opera. Pillet became so enthusiastic that he at once bought the author's rights for the scenario from Wagner for the sum of five hundred francs on account, and entrusted the preparation of the text to Henri Revoil and Paul Foucher . . . but the music he entrusted to Dietsch.

The serious disappointment which Wagner felt at this result was alleviated by the five hundred francs, which enabled him to leave his miserable rooms in the Rue du Helder and install himself at Meudon. There, free from immediate material cares, he was able to work throughout the winter of 1841–1842 on *The Flying Dutchman.*

When the opera of Dietsch was performed in 1842, Heine claimed his share of the authorship in an anonymous account of it written for the *Augsburger Allgemeine Zeitung* : " *The Flying Dutchman* of Dietsch has proved a dismal failure. I have only seen the libretto, and I found out, to my disgust, that the beautiful story which a German writer (Heinrich Heine) had supplied, ready-made for the theatre, had been massacred in the French text."

Many years later, when he had reached maturity, it pleased Wagner to repudiate his past. He refused to admit that Heine was the originator of the story. In 1871, when editing a collection of his works, he even went so far as to change the passage that referred to *The Flying Dutchman* in his autobiographical sketch, replacing the words " Originated by Heine " with " Copied by Heine from a Dutch play of the same name." But all the efforts of scholars to trace this Dutch drama have been in vain. The story of *The Flying Dutchman* told by Heine in "The Memoirs of Monsieur de Schnabelowopski " was certainly born in the poet's imagination.

But at the period in question Wagner did not foresee his recantations. The presence in Paris of their mutual friend Laube brought about frequent meetings between Heine and Wagner. " The conversation between these two men was the most brilliant I have ever heard in my life," wrote the painter Friedrich Pecht, who about this time painted a portrait of Heine, and who has left a glowing account of a dinner he attended at Brocci's in company with the three couples. " The beautiful Frenchwoman," says Pecht of Mathilde, " at first sight eclipsed the two German women. Light-hearted, naïve, charming, and as ignorant as a child, she far outshone Frau Laube, who was very witty but a little faded, and Frau Wagner, so good-natured, but rather domestic. And yet, for all her full figure and her satin complexion, she was no more than a feast for the eye, although a glorious one, and she can never in her life have got beyond being an *enfant terrible*, whose laugh alone sufficed to spread joy around her."

Heine began to realise that the charm of the *enfant terrible*, this appeal of blissful ignorance, were obstacles to his own passage through the world. During the winter of 1839 he decided that Mathilde should be given at least the elements of the education she so completely lacked. Since she herself was wholly without initiative, and, in the ordinary affairs of life, quite incapable of applying herself to any serious occupation, he just simply sent her to a girls' school.

This big, jolly young woman was a strange sight amongst the little pupils, but Mathilde played her part as though it was an amusing adventure. She displayed her newly acquired knowledge with childish pride, and her joy knew no bounds when she discovered that she knew the names of the Kings of ancient Egypt better than her great Henri. Intellectually she was of the same age as the little girls around her. At the school ball she danced with the same abandon as in some low *bal masqué*. But these efforts to raise Mathilde to the level of his own former life only succeeded in making Heine realise more clearly all that his mad passion had caused him to lose. A change was coming, although he would not yet admit it to himself.

This winter of 1839–1840, in which he rejoiced in a period of convalescence after his eye trouble, saw a painful awakening of his conscience. It seemed almost as if the period of semi-blindness through which he had passed had served to restore his perspective and to shake his senses free from their enslavement. The outward show of good humour he displayed during this period was perhaps only one of his customary reactions to inner distress. It was in reality a troubled and indecisive period, and one in which he still avoided any rigorous self-examination. It was then that he undertook the most ill-advised of all his literary battles by writing *Das Buch Börne*. The fight against Menzel, and the blind hatred inspired by nationalism, was succeeded by a fight against another form of intellectual blindness—that of Jacobin intransigence. Attacked at the same time by the Right and the Left, Heine sought to justify the middle course which he had adopted.

But the disquiet which filled him led him to exaggerate the importance of defending his own position and to carry the war into the field of personalities once again. He later admitted that all the objectionable part of the book referring to his opponent's private life had not existed in his original version, but had been added hastily to the proofs "in an hour of weakness and not without provocation."

In the spring of 1840, after a long interval, his unhappiness again found expression in poetry. During all the years that sensual satiety had taken possession of him he had sought in vain to find one single sentiment which lent itself to lyrical treatment. Now and then he had succeeded in putting into verse some passing mood induced by an amorous adventure, but his passion for Mathilde awoke in him no creative note. "How strange it is," he said, "that overwhelming love writes no verse; it scarcely permits you to write prose." And again, in October 1839, he remarked: "I have not much confidence in my own poetry—I mean that which is written in verse." He tried to explain this incapacity on the grounds of inner evolution and the general tendency of the period. "My age, perhaps indeed the whole period in which we are living, is no longer congenial to poetry, and demands prose for its expression." But this pleading of poetic sterility was merely an excuse for not examining himself too closely. Perhaps, too, he was ashamed of admitting that those who had predicted the consequences of his liaison with Mathilde were right. As soon, however, as he did arrive at the realisation of his own tragedy, he again found his old power of creative expression.

The impressions he had received in Mathilde's native village—the old mother bewailing the loss of her child far away—form the theme of the lament of Ceres in the poem "Unterwelt," which is his first admission of his defeat. In this poem, a kind of epilogue to his passion, as "Der Tannhäuser" had been the prelude, he describes the inferno of his life with Mathilde :

Stets vergeblich, stets nach Frieden
Ring ich. Hier im Schatten reich
Kein Verdammter ist mir gleich.

" I always strive for peace, always in vain. Here in the realm of shadows none of the damned is my equal."

He was still able to mock at grief ; but bitterness pierces through the thin cloak of the mythological setting and finds an expression entirely personal to himself in the two last stanzas, which were not added until two years later.

Zuweilen dünkt es mich, als trübe
Geheime Sehnsucht deinen Blick—
Ich kenn 'es wohl, dein Missgeschick :
Verfehltes Leben, verfehlte Liebe !

Du nickst so traurig ! Wiedergeben
Kann ich dir nicht die Jugendzeit—
Unheilbar ist dein Herzeleid :
Verfehlte Liebe, verfehltes Leben !

" At times it seems to me as though secret longing dimmed your eyes. I know it well, your unhappy fate : a life that has failed, and love that has failed !

" You nod so sadly ! I cannot give you back the days of your youth. Your stricken heart is incurable : a life that has failed and love that has failed."

The poems which fell from his pen in that year of 1840 are overflowing with the bitterness of remorse, and such laughter as there is, is very near to weeping.

Der Stern erstrahlte so munter,
Da fiel er vom Himmel herunter,
Du fragst mich Kind was Liebe ist ?
Ein Stern in einem Haufen Mist.

" The star shone so merrily, and then it fell from heaven. You ask me, child, what love is ? A star upon a dunghill."

The rosy blush of dawn had faded, and the years spent with Mathilde appeared to him stark naked in their truth. But he turned the accusing finger against himself.

Für eine Grille—keckes Wagen!—
Hab' ich das Leben eingesetzt;
Und nun das Spiel verloren geht,
Mein Herz, du darfst dich nicht beklagen.

Die Sachsen sagen: " Minschenwille
Ist Minschenhimmelryk."—Ich gab
Das Leben hin, jedoch ich hab'
Verwirklicht meines Herzens Grille!

" For a caprice (the wanton!) I offered my life. And now that the game is being lost, my heart, you must not complain.

" In Saxony they say, ' Man's will is his heaven.' I gave my life, but I have made real my heart's caprice."

Never had Heine been farther from Mathilde, or nearer to ridding himself of the stranglehold of their passion, than during the summer of 1841, when he wrote those lines at Cauterets. They make it clear that when he pleaded the unsuitability of the age as the reason for the drying up of his poetic springs it was nothing more than a pretext to cover his own moral cowardice. But a change had now come over him; suddenly he found his tongue again, and great schemes filled his mind. It was in the solitude of the Pyrenees that he wrote *Atta Troll*, the last free song of romanticism. The poem was also an answer to his opponents, and a denunciation of their pettifogging short-sightedness and their servility before the fashion of the day. But the whole tone of this reply is far superior to that of his book on Börne. "Jealous incompetence, after a thousand years of reflection, at last has found its great weapon against the full expression of genius," he wrote in the preface. " It has found the antitheses to talent and character."

Conceived as " a protest against the plebiscites of the orators of the moment," *Atta Troll* is also a criticism of the poet Heine himself, at once a farewell to a stage in his own poetic development as well as to a general form of artistic expression which, in his opinion, had had its day. The unfrocked romanticist, as he called himself, wrote in *Atta Troll* the epitaph to German lyrical poetry. Romanticism, with all its symbols and tendencies, was no longer in accord with the pressure created by the more profound ideas then struggling for expression, nor with the requirements of the new world which was taking shape. Heine wished to close the old lyrical German school and inaugurate the new one which should replace it. Later he said that he had realised his intention. In *Atta Troll* he placed himself at the cross-roads facing the avenue to the future, and in the history of his creative art it is his most important period. In later years he spoke of it as the happiest period of his life ; he felt that he was escaping both from a degrading passion and from an outworn form of art.

But, just at the moment when he felt himself capable of repairing the early faults of his " frustrated life," the sequel to that earlier period, which had produced *Das Buch Börne*, fell upon him with disastrous force.

The publication of the attack on Börne had aroused a storm of protest in Germany. Heine's best friends abandoned him and his enemies saw themselves justified. Even Gutzkow, who never ceased to proclaim himself a brother-in-arms of Heine, went over to the indignant partisans of Börne. Instead of annihilating Börne for ever, as he had intended, Heine only succeeded in reviving him. " People do not look upon Börne as a writer, but as a holy symbol of German liberty," wrote Campe to Heine, with reference to the reception of the book in Germany. He added with characteristic bluntness : " Even Börne's old political opponents have gone over to his side, for they respect in him his honest, sincere, and incorruptible character. . . . Your book has produced exactly the opposite effect to that which you intended. Do you fully realise the extent of your mistake ? There are people who commit suicide, who give up their life of their own free will, but a literary suicide is something new." It was above all the disgraceful insinuations concerning Mme. Strauss, the mistress of Börne, and against her husband, which roused sympathy for the victims and indignation against Heine.

The neglected husband of the energetic Jeannette Wohl-Strauss found himself suddenly fulfilling the rôle of martyr. His indignant protagonists pressed him to assume the rôle of hero, a part which he seemed little disposed to play, since he hesitated so long before demanding satisfaction for his wounded honour. Then one afternoon in June 1841 he encountered Heine in the Rue Richelieu. Heine, short-sighted and with his head in the clouds as usual, passed by without noticing him. No doubt it was the expression of mocking indifference on the poet's full face which aroused the fury of Strauss, who ran after him uttering abusive words. There were no witnesses to this street scene, and the accounts of the two men contradict each other at every point. According to Heine, " the incident reduced itself to a few words babbled out tremblingly by this individual," to which Heine had replied, smiling, that Herr Strauss knew where he lived if he had anything to say to him, and that he would be able to await him there, since he had already waited a full twelve months. Strauss alleged that the scene ended by his smacking Heine's face. This account, however, which was published in the German Press, seems highly improbable, not only because Heine was hardly the man to accept an insult and then go quietly home, but also for another reason. Strauss gave the names of three eye-witnesses, who were later obliged to admit that they had not been present. The incident at least serves to show the violence of the indignation which Heine had aroused against himself, since three respectable men were induced to bear false witness against him.

The news which reached Heine in the solitude of Cauterets concerning the campaign being waged against him came like an echo of the troublous times which he had thought were over. He returned to Paris to accept the challenge of Strauss. He instructed his friends, Théophile Gautier and

Alphonse Royer, to demand that the duel should be with pistols ; Strauss, as the offended party and challenger, claimed the right to choose the weapons and insisted on fighting with swords. But Heine knew that he must seize this opportunity to prove his courage and put an end once and for all to any accusations of personal cowardice. The negotiations concerning these details dragged on ; Strauss probably felt conscious of the absurdity of paying with his life for an insult to his wife and himself which nothing could erase from the book in which it was written. Friends offered to fight for him in his place, and tried to provoke Heine to this end. But those days in which he seemed to be facing death had not robbed Heine of his good humour, for he replied : " If you are tired of life, you need only to go and hang yourself."

The obstinacy with which he insisted on the use of firearms was perhaps inspired by more than mere gambler's courage. There seems also to have been in it a desire to leave the fate of his " frustrated life " to chance—or to some supreme power which would relieve him from the responsibility of deciding his future for himself. He appears to have expected a fatal result to the duel, perhaps even to have secretly hoped for it. For, just at the time when he felt himself most liberated from Mathilde, he was allowing himself to be persuaded to tie himself definitely to her. Friends, both real and false, spoke to him of his duty towards the woman, so alone and helpless in the world. He let himself be persuaded ; after all, to-morrow he might no longer be there to dry her childish tears. . . .

On August 31st, Heinrich Heine was married to Mathilde, and in a church, since that was the only kind of marriage which meant anything to her. As a Protestant marrying a Catholic, he had to sign a declaration that any children resulting from the marriage would be raised in the Catholic faith. He signed the paper with a wry smile, for he knew already that he would never be a father. The day of the ceremony was one of tropical heat ; the sun beat down mercilessly upon the sweltering city, and even in the dark church the air was parched and suffocating. "Meine Frau," Mathilde kept repeating, in her childish voice, one of the rare words which she had picked up from her Henri and which now acquired for her its real significance. Heine wiped the perspiration from his face and tried with his customary sallies to shock the solemnity of the participants in the ceremony. "I have made my will and left everything to my wife, but naturally on one condition—that she marries again immediately after my death. In that way I shall be sure that at least one man will regret my passing." Mathilde joined in the laughter, but nevertheless, when she replied, it was very earnestly : "Joke away if you like, but you know very well that I shall never desert you, either in life or in death, and that if you were to die to-morrow I should never marry again."

At seven in the morning on September 7th the duel with Strauss took place. It seemed as if the heavens had opened, and a torrent of rain poured down from a leaden sky until the roads in the valley of Saint-Germain were deep in mud. Heine, as usual, had a jest ready for the occasion, and muttered to his companion as they trudged along : "How filthy is the road of honour !" Both the duellists behaved in a way which would have roused jealousy in the hearts of the students of Göttingen. Strauss aimed with a steady hand, and his bullet grazed Heine's hip, so that, although the bone was not affected, his thigh swelled up and blackened. Heine himself simply fired in the air.

After a few days in bed Heine completely recovered. Destiny had decided for him that his life should be bound for ever to that of Mathilde.

He was perhaps glad to have to struggle no more for his freedom. Nevertheless, he said to his little friend Weill, who trotted after him like a faithful dog which was inclined to snarl, "That harpy Frau Wohl has managed to avenge herself all the same."

CHAPTER IX

THE POWERS OF THE FUTURE

"The second act is European; the world revolution, the great duel between those who possess nothing and the aristocracy of property-holders; and there it will no longer be a question of nationality or of religion, there will be only one Fatherland, the earth, and only one Faith, man's happiness on earth."

(*Lutèce.*)

ONE DAY in October 1843 a traveller sat huddled in the corner of a stage coach. The German winter was cold, gusts of wind stirred the damp mist, and the traveller shivered. He had lived so long in Paris, that he had forgotten to clothe himself suitably for the rougher climate of his native land. His small coat reached scarcely to his knees; he shivered again, and envied his travelling companions, all warmly ensconced in their thick winter greatcoats.

More than twelve years had passed since Heinrich Heine had seen his Fatherland. He was so deeply rooted in Paris, especially since his marriage, that he could not envisage settling permanently elsewhere. "Never, never shall I return to live in Germany," he wrote to his brother.

Nevertheless, although he was so thoroughly at home in France, and despite the unhappy memories of his own country, he had begun to feel homesick. "When I think at night of Germany, then sleep deserts me," he had said, in a poem written just before his departure. And yet he was revolted and alarmed to such an extent by the political state of the country that, before setting out for Hamburg, he had recommended the utmost discretion to his family, lest the authorities of the various German States which he must traverse should learn of his presence. He was tormented by a desire to see his mother again.

Nach Deutschland lechzt' ich nicht so sehr,
Wenn nicht die Mutter dorten wär!
Das Vaterland wird nie verderben,
Jedoch die alte Frau kann sterben.

"I would not thirst so much for Germany if my mother were not there! The Fatherland will never fade, but the old woman may die."

During all the years he had dwelt far from her he had written regularly, and awaited her own letters with impatience. Every detail of the old lady's peaceful life interested him; he read everything she had to say about her relations with her other children, with her friends, and even with her servants. And she on her side had followed all her son's work, asked endless questions about his literary projects, and complained if the news he gave her was not detailed enough. In all his dealings with his mother, Heine remained a small child in need of advice and consolation. Often his letters were written hastily, and contained only bald accounts of his doings. But others were long, and bear witness to the close communion of ideas between Betty Heine and her son. He did not hesitate to tell her all his worries, great and small, his financial troubles, and the fluctuations of his health. He even told her the whole truth about his most intimate affairs, and about his life with Mathilde. In all this correspondence there is no trace of any kindly condescension on the part of a son writing to a mother whom he knows to be on a different intellectual level. When he wrote to her, he seemed not to remember that he was a man, and that he should therefore seek to spare the feelings of a woman no longer young. On the contrary he went into all the details of his love for Mathilde, with all its nervous storms. To the good, conventional old Jewess who had never known the complications of a wayward heart, he related all the ups and downs of his passionate attachment to the violent, capricious Frenchwoman. He even confided to her his fear that one day his love might die and leave him with nothing but the agony of having to put up for the rest of his days with his wife's unbearable character.

Heine often concealed the warm sincerity of his devotion for his mother under a mask of banter and crudity. " And you, you darling old cat, how are you ? " he wrote just before his arrival. " If you die before I have a chance of seeing you again, I shall blow out my brains. Remember that, if ever you want to exchange your present apartment for a worse lodging-place ! Keep it well in mind, then you will not force me to commit such an imbecility."

He had a terrible shock when he read in the newspapers of the great fire of Hamburg in May 1842. For twenty-four hours he was without news of his relatives, and he nearly went out of his mind. Even the unimaginative Mathilde caught the contagion of his terrified anxiety, and became " ill with fear."

Betty Heine had indeed been in danger when the great city was devoured by the flames. For three and a half days a tempest of fire swept across the town, and, as once at Pompeii, a rain of sparks fell from a blood-red sky. Enormous vats of spirits had burst with the heat, throwing great columns of alcohol into the air, which fell again to form dancing blue streams of fire in the streets. In the midst of the ruin the tolling of the great bell had brought the central tower of the cathedral crashing down.

When Betty Heine's apartment became threatened, she took shelter in her daughter's house farther from the centre. But, when she heard that the fire was actually approaching her own home, her only thought was to save the papers of her Harry—as she always called him—which were hidden in a box in her bedroom wardrobe. Only with great difficulty, and by promising to go herself, was Lotte able to dissuade the old lady from making the risky expedition across the city. When Lotte arrived at her mother's house she found two rough-looking individuals seated in the living-room before a bottle of wine. All the riff-raff of the water-front had profited by the general disorder to enter and pillage the abandoned houses. Without hesitating, Lotte walked past the unwelcome visitors, one of whom followed her with an axe in his hand. The courageous young woman had already found the box, and quickly gave the order to open it. The man obeyed, hoping to find valuables inside it, and Lotte, profiting by his surprise and disappointment, seized the papers and escaped from the room. But just then a thick cloud of smoke blew into the house, and sparks landed on her clothes. She fainted, and was picked up by a fireman, but, when she came to again, the precious packet was missing. In spite of her distress, Betty Heine's first thought was to write to her son to tell him they were all safe ; she even took the trouble to find stamps for the letter and thereby save him the few pence of extra postage—a touching piece of maternal solicitude which moved Heine to tears.

The fire warned him to postpone his projected visit no longer than necessary. First he prepared his mother for the change in his appearance, telling her not to let it frighten her. For his disease had made great headway during the previous year ; half his face was paralysed, and his eyes bore the characteristic symptoms. Instead of the lithe and slender figure which his mother remembered, there was now a man of heavy corpulence. His complexion, too, had changed ; there was a high colour in his cheeks which would have led one to think him in good health but for the dreadful rigidity of his facial muscles. And in the look which came from under his red and swollen eyelids there no longer shone any mischievous or day-dreaming glance.

The twelve years had much aged his mother also, as Heine realised sorrowfully when he saw her. Time, worry, and the shock of the fire seemed to have reduced her stature, and her self-control had given way to perpetual nervousness and irritability. Her life was further complicated by the pride which still dwelt in her small body. Since the fire destroyed her comfortable house she had taken to living in two small rooms, for she had not been insured, and her means did not permit of more. " What misery," Heine had exclaimed, though he himself could not claim to be spoilt in this respect.

The old lady had given up her former friends; since she could no longer receive them in the manner to which she had been accustomed, she lived shut away, and quite alone.

Heine found that his sister also had a faded look, although, with her long hair framing her face and falling in ringlets to her shoulders, she still had an air of distant youth even though she was about to become a grandmother.

The head of the family, Salomon Heine, was very ill, but, despite his suffering, was still engrossed in his business, forcing himself to work by the exercise of the same indomitable will-power which had never spared either himself or others. His nephew managed from time to time to amuse the morose old man by his witty sallies. Heinrich, in fact, went to great pains to win the favour of his family circle; he attended all the receptions with good humour, even to the elaborate supper and dance given by his niece Madame de Voss, Lotte's eldest daughter, who had married a Dutchman and "lived like a princess, in comfortable, solid luxury."

"I am being very amiable and friendly," Heine wrote to Mathilde, when giving her an account of these family gatherings. "What hard work it is to please people who have no interests. When I return I shall be as taciturn as possible in order to recover from such an effort to be agreeable."

For once Hamburg was not for him a city of hate and humiliation. He found repose amongst his relatives, and relief at being able to lead his own life for once. One thing alone worried him—anxiety as to what Mathilde was doing in his absence. On leaving Paris he had sent her to board with Madame Darte, at Chaillot, in the same girls' school in which she had received her education. He had repeatedly impressed upon the headmistress that he was leaving all that was dear to him in her sole charge, but, as soon as he was out of sight, he felt that he had not said enough, and that the precautions he had taken were insufficient. "To leave her alone in Paris, in that awful sink of iniquity," was a great decision. It worried him day and night. "I feel I shall go mad when my thoughts take the road to Chaillot," he wrote. What mischief was Mathilde not capable of committing ; to what temptations might she not succumb ? His letters to her were written in the tone of a strict parent addressing a child of twelve ; they contain little else than counsels of good behaviour. She must not go out much ; must not see this man or speak to that woman ; she should try to improve her handwriting ; she ought to begin to learn German. No, she should not do that ; she shall have lessons in it as soon as he returns. Even the traditional parental threat was not lacking, for once he wrote : " Do not forget that my eye is always upon you ; I know everything you do, and what I do not know I shall certainly hear when I return." But, in spite of all his entreaties, Mathilde did not write him a line during all his absence. This selfish indolence on her part drove him to despair, but drew from him no word of anger.

At last he could bear it no longer, and made ready to leave Hamburg, only postponing his departure to conclude a contract with Campe which should provide for Mathilde's future. To obtain this material security for her who was as unarmed as a child in the presence of life, he placed himself entirely in Campe's hands, selling him the whole of his future literary output for an annuity of 2,400 francs, which should pass to Mathilde after his death. Then he packed hurriedly and left, without staying to say good-bye to his uncle, forgetting even his passports and his note-books—all because of Mathilde's silence.

Nevertheless his short stay brought him more than family reunions and a contract with his publisher. As soon as he was settled again in Paris, he perceived that the renewal of contact with his own country had provided more inspiration than he realised at the time. The simple fact of having been once more surrounded by those who spoke the language in which he wrote, enlivened his style. The constant use of French had affected his conversation ; his mastery of literary German remained, but his friends had noticed that in talking he occasionally hesitated over a word.

" Verse comes to me much more easily when I breathe

the air of Germany," he wrote to Campe. And with this conviction in his mind he set to work at once, and, in the space of three months, had finished his satirical poem : *Deutschland : ein Wintermärchen.*

The impulse which made him write this winter's tale was not due entirely to his trip to Germany. It was partly a natural evolution by which Heine kept step with the dominating tendency of the period. *Deutschland* is in a sense the sequel to *Atta Troll.* After his farewell to romanticism, as a stage in literature which had passed, there had to be a plan for the new poetic style which was bound to follow.

At the time of Heine's departure in 1830 Germany was still under the undisputed spell of romanticism ; when he paid his visit to Hamburg, romanticism still survived tenaciously, as literary forms do survive the causes that produce them. Nevertheless a new spirit was abroad, and a new generation had grown up—born in that same year of 1830, begotten by the Revolution of July when France had once more proclaimed herself the mouthpiece of liberty and progress. They were born also of the disillusionment of a people who had waited in vain for an improvement in political conditions, and for the realisation of the promises made in 1815. Treitschke writes : "The boastful self-sufficiency of the ultra-nationalists was unable to survive so many disappointed hopes ; a reaction was inevitable, and, with our people who move heavily when they move at all, such changes almost always materialise in a violent outburst of brute force."

The contrast between a Germany divided into States under absolutist regimes and the western democracies, between the liberal development of France and the total suppression of civil liberties in the States that were members of the Bund, had ended by effacing even the memory of the xenophobia which had followed the wars of liberation. All that was liberal in Germany was engulfed in a wave of cosmopolitanism. A radicalism arose—stamped with international ideas, and possessed by the dream of a universal democracy.

The growing discontent was countered by more violently repressive measures on the part of the reactionaries. Metternich skilfully used the nightmare bogey of revolution in order to extort exceptional measures from even the most lenient of the German rulers. Germany fell into the grip of a police terror, accompanied by harsh sentences of imprisonment, and by edicts from the Bund which declared any criticism whatever of the existing regime to be high treason. This hand-to-hand struggle, between liberals and radicals on one side and the ruling powers on the other, aroused passions throughout the country. Heroism was in the air, and men's minds were caught up in a wave of emotional enthusiasm. The intellectuals threw themselves passionately into the fight. The æsthetic sentiments which were at the root of romanticism no longer appeared to them acceptable ; the idea of beauty was eclipsed by the idea of justice, and all creative activity which was not designed to take immediate effect seemed to the apostles of radicalism to be treason against the cause of liberty. To take refuge in the past became a cult of individualism no longer to be tolerated. Writers and poets sounded the tocsin for a rally to the common cause, and preached solidarity with the masses. German literature was carried away by the " lyricism of the hour," and the poetry of the day was the poetry of action.

Some few individuals stood out from amongst the crowd of journalist-poets which suddenly appeared, and these acquired celebrity far in excess of their literary merits by reason of their close connection with the movement in fashion.

Foremost of these was Georg Herwegh, " the iron skylark," a young Swabian who boasted of having deserted from his regiment : " I exchanged the flag of the King who oppressed me in order to serve for nothing under the flag of the people." During his passage through Germany, in 1842, he had a triumphal reception such as had fallen to no other German poet. His popularity went to his head. He had come to think of himself as the nation's genius, called upon to lead it to freedom.

Hoffmann von Fallersleben was a good type of liberal

German whose gift for facile, musical rhyme was employed to clothe his simple, vigorous sentiments. His poems had the same vogue as popular songs—some were adopted in the Protestant hymn books, others became national songs : his " Deutschland über Alles " is an excellent and striking example of German dynamism. Had he been born a generation earlier, Hoffmann von Fallersleben would have been a Körner or a Schenkendorf, an official herald of national reconstruction. But as victim under the yoke of reaction, relieved in 1844 of his Chair at Breslau University, he became a radical agitator. He, too, travelled in triumph through the country, apostrophising the masses in ringing poems which told of his own tribulations. Others also there were who aspired to combine the rôle of poet with that of man of action, and who in a brief space ended either as exiles, or as state officials who had bowed the knee to authority.

Heine had been amongst the first to proclaim the community of interest between literature and the problems of the day. He it was who invented the word *Zeitbild* to describe poetry which mirrored current history. In his poem " Tendency " he showed the mission of a modern poet.

Girre nicht mehr wie ein Werther,
Welcher nur für Lotten glüht—
Was die Glocke hat geschlagen
Sollst du deinem Volke sagen,
Rede Dolche, rede Schwerter !

" Do not coo any more like Werther, who only glowed for Lotte. What the bell has tolled forth, say it to your people. Talk daggers, talk swords ! "

But in the last stanza of the same poem he shows that he had not much faith that his compatriots would keep up their courage, and he concludes with the sarcastic advice :

Aber halte deine Dichtung
Nur so allgemein als möglich.

" But, in your verse, keep to generalities as much as possible."

In the winter of 1841 he too acclaimed Herwegh "the skylark of the German springtime." But his critical eye had already noted the young poet's boundless faculty for illusion, his shallow optimism, and his personal vanity. Connoisseur as he was of German psychology, he wrote of Herwegh :

. . . Nur in deinem Gedichte
Lebt jener Lenz, den du besingst.

"Only in your poems does the spring exist of which you sing."

Heine's scepticism was soon justified by events. When Herwegh, intoxicated by his triumphal journey through Germany in 1842, requested an audience of King Friedrich Wilhelm IV, to present to him the demands of his people, he became so embarrassed when confronted with the King that he was dismissed with a few paternal words of advice. Only later, when the news of his absurd audience had leaked out in the Press, did Herwegh regain courage. Then, in an attempt to save his badly damaged reputation, he wrote an open letter to the King which was as clumsy as it was insolent, and which earned him his prompt expulsion from Prussia. "It is you, the wandering knight of former days, who, in imitation of the great Don Quixote de la Mancha, address letters to tyrants in the style of an impertinent schoolboy!" It was thus that Heine mocked Herwegh, when he made a rich marriage later on, and had disappeared from the scene of activity to enjoy an idle, comfortable existence.

Dingelstedt, another poet who enjoyed a temporary success in similar circumstances, inspired Heine with no more confidence than the others. When he came to Paris, Heine wrote of him, in a satirical poem, that "it is only in the depths of his soul that a real German cherishes liberty." In this case also he was not deceived, for Dingelstedt soon bartered his cosmopolitan convictions for the post of Royal Librarian in Stuttgart, and the title of Court Counsellor.

Heine did not believe in the international convictions of

the German writers of the day. He suspected that these new radicals were simply the successors of the " Old Germans " of a few years previously. He warned his French friends against those German democrats who, in their private meetings, demanded Alsace even at the risk of a war. " A poet should not play the patriot, he is by nature a cosmopolitan," he repeated constantly to the circle of young Germans around him.

In the preface to *Deutschland* he clearly defined his attitude towards these " Pharisees of nationalism " : " Calm yourselves, I too love my Fatherland, as you do. . . . I am a friend of the French as I am the friend of all who are decent and intelligent, and because, personally, I am neither stupid enough nor wicked enough to wish that my Germans and the French, the two chosen peoples of humanity, should break each other's necks to profit England and Russia, and to please the profiteers and priests of the world. Obviously I do not find it as easy as you do to annex Alsace and Lorraine to Germany, for the inhabitants of those parts prefer to stay with France, on account of the rights they have acquired by the French Revolution and because of French equality before the law and their free institutions, which please their bourgeois souls."

This *Deutschland* is an astonishing piece of work in which many different themes are strung upon the thread of the poet's fancy. Enchanting legends, unearthed from the beginnings of history, jostle with ironical diatribes against Prussian militarism : " still the same pedants as ever ; their every gesture a right angle and their faces frozen stiff as ever in icy arrogance." There is dialogue in the piece, both humorous and sentimental, and again mixed up with jets of burning satire, as when he apostrophises the royal eagle of Prussia as an ugly bird whose tail feathers he would like to pluck and whose claws should be clipped. This easy-flowing work in which gems of poetry are mixed up with scabrous descriptive passages, ends in a magnificent piece of verse—the vision of a walk at night through Cologne, in which a masked man follows Heine like a shadow, bearing a lictor's axe. To the poet's question, he replies : " I am the action of your thought."

But the essence of the book is its satire—satire of unprecedented violence, such as German literature had never known. One can well understand that Heine referred to " his father Aristophanes " in order to justify his audacity. It is the expression of his disgust with a Germany which could not make up its mind to choose between absolutism and democracy, between the past and the present ; " a knight-errantry of blockheads," detestable mixture of Gothic stupidity and modern lies ; a theatrical parody of the past to which Heine declared he would prefer the real Middle Ages.

At the time of his visit to Hamburg, the " year of conditional truce with the Press " ended, and was replaced by a " state of siege." At the beginning of 1843 a special jurisdiction was established for Prussia by the King, with a special censor's office. In Bavaria reaction had for some time been the order of the day, and included measures which were as rigorous as they were absurd. The pseudo-liberalism of Louis I appeared in its true colours, and betrayed his pathological vanity to the full. He would no longer tolerate the slightest breath of criticism, and did not hesitate to cast his oldest friends into prison, or to oblige them to do penance for the offence to his august person by kneeling before a picture which represented His Majesty in full panoply of State.

It was the violence of this reaction and its abominably offensive attitude towards individuals which encouraged Heine to attack the reigning sovereigns in person. His satire was directed in a series of poems upon Friedrich Wilhelm IV, the amphibious nonentity, neither flesh nor fish. Of this " New Alexander," he wrote :

Ich bin nicht schlecht, ich bin nicht gut,
Nicht dumm und nicht gescheute,
Und wenn ich gestern vorwärts ging,
So geh' ich rückwärts heute.

" I am not bad, I am not good, not stupid, and not

clever. And if I moved forwards yesterday, I move backwards to-day."

Still more cruel are " the songs in honour of Louis I," the audacity and biting humour of which exceeded anything that had ever been written in Germany against the sacred person of a wearer of a crown. In this respect Heine differed from the other liberals in revolt. Certainly he was safe in Paris when he shot his poisoned arrows, but neither more nor less than other German exiles. In any case he was less protected than was Herwegh by his newly acquired Swiss nationality.

When he thus threw himself into the political fight his contemporaries believed that he had protected himself by adopting French nationality. An announcement in the *Kölnische Zeitung* of November 12th, 1843, which appeared to be officially inspired, certified that Heine had acquired French naturalisation papers and was no longer a Prussian citizen. In actual fact Heine had begun to take steps to this end in 1842, at the time when reactionary activity was redoubled in Germany and a conservative Government, which looked with small favour on radicals, had been established in France. The result was that the French Minister in Prussia, the Comte de Bresson, in November 1842 had addressed the following letter to Bülow, Prussian Minister of Foreign Affairs : " Monsieur Heine, man of letters, born in Düsseldorf, has declared himself desirous of becoming a French citizen. This foreigner appears to have been expelled from the Kingdom of Prussia about ten years ago. The Garde des Sceaux, before admitting the request which has been made to him, would be glad to learn the reason for the expulsion, and to know what is M. Heine's present position with regard to the Prussian Government, and what would be the consequences should French naturalisation be accorded to him."

It appears that the French Government took an exaggerated view of the importance of Heine's political rôle in Germany. The statement regarding his expulsion was false, and, since the information obviously did not come from

Heine himself, one is led to believe that the attitude adopted by the French authorities was due to the insistence of foreign Governments, especially that of Austria, which was constantly warning France against "this detestable writer," as Metternich called him. However the French authorities did not share the panic felt by absolutist Governments for agitators. On the contrary they were convinced that the German exiles could scarcely prove an element of unrest in the country which had sheltered them. A circular addressed by the Minister of the Interior, in 1832, to the Prefects of the Departments of Moselle, Bas-Rhin, and Haut-Rhin, made this clear. It requested that the German *émigrés* should be treated as well as possible, and pointed out that the comparison which they would be obliged to make between the unhappy state of affairs in their own country and conditions of life in their new home could only be in favour of France.

But Heine's case might well have seemed particularly serious, especially to such a conservative Minister as Guizot, and it was doubtless with astonishment that the reply signed by the Prussian Minister, Graf von Arnim, was received. "We possess insufficient documentation to establish with certainty whether the man of letters, Heinrich Heine, has ever enjoyed rights of citizenship in this country. In any case there is no record of measures having been taken against him."

Heine therefore proceeded with his request for naturalisation, as is shown by a letter from the Préfet de la Seine to the Mairie of the 3rd Arrondissement, dated June 26th, 1843, in which his application is judged insufficient because there is no certificate of birth affixed. Whether he was unable to produce the document, or whether he gave up the idea for some other reason, Heine never became a French citizen.

Towards the end of his life he gave the following explanation: "I took the precaution of going through the formalities which, whilst placing me under no obligation, made it possible for me to obtain naturalisation quickly should the necessity arise. But I was never able to bring myself actually to perform the deed. It would have been an awful thought, a mad thought, were I forced to say that I was a German poet, but a naturalised Frenchman. I should have seemed to myself like one of those two-headed monsters they show in fairs." This was written at a time when nothing was left to induce him to conceal the truth, and he certainly had no hope of obtaining advantages in Germany.

This step towards naturalisation, which was undertaken only to be abandoned, seems characteristic of the ebb and flow of Heine's courage. At first, prudence counsels him to make concessions. Then, at the last minute, his independence asserts itself and drives him to throw caution to the winds. In that mood he would run any risk, as if determined to make amends for earlier weakness.

When, at the beginning of 1840, he again began to write regularly for the *Augsburger Allgemeine Zeitung*, he was still the pet aversion of the Austrian Government. Metternich boasted to the Prussian Ambassador that he had received a "letter from the famous Heine . . . which amounts to complete surrender on the part of this detestable writer." But in 1836, when he said this, Metternich was either referring to the petition which Heine had made to the Bundestag at the time of the suppression of "Young Germany" (which seems probable from the text given by von Maltzan), or else the surrender was not as complete as Metternich liked to think. In any case he surrounded Heine with spies, who regularly sent him long reports about his life in Paris. Metternich had in his pay a German from Berlin, named Adalbert von Bornstedt, who had begun by writing violent attacks on the Prussian Government in the French Press, but had speedily made his peace with that Government, and on such terms that he was allowed to start a German paper in Paris and to import it into Prussia. "A super-liar," said Heine of this man; "obliged to leave Berlin for dubious reasons, and accused of theft in Algiers, where he was publicly disgraced; in short, a creature as ignoble as his writing is poor." But, with the usual cunning of his type, Adalbert von Bornstedt succeeded in obtaining the entrée to the French newspapers, and he attacked Heine in *Commerce* almost as soon as he resumed his writing as correspondent for the *Augsburger Allgemeine Zeitung.*

But this time Vienna did not wax indignant because Heine " dragged the French Government through the mud," as it had done through the mouth of Gentz in 1832. The arrival in power of Thiers had roused Metternich to the pitch of violent anger ; Thiers, " that creature wretched from every point of view," as he called him in his confidential letters, " the very personification of the revolution of 1830."

Heine parried the first attack by an article published in *Le Constitutionel.* It was followed by a second attack from the same quarter, announcing that he had sold himself to the French Government for 100,000 francs. Heine was in fact receiving the annual grant of 4,800 francs which Princess Belgiojoso had obtained for him some years earlier, before he had recommenced his journalistic activities. But the French Government appeared to take little interest in what he wrote. Later Heine said, " The French grant was nothing more than a gesture of national generosity, of political fraternity, which is shown in this country in finer fashion than Christian charity ever was."

When Guizot succeeded Thiers in office, he too seemed unconcerned about the articles written by Heine. Heine relates that he only saw Guizot once—when he went to thank him for having maintained the grant in spite of his radical opinions. Guizot on that occasion replied, with a smile, that he " was not the man to refuse a crust of bread to a German poet living in exile." This account accords with the fact that, when the articles appeared in book form, under the title *Lutèce*, Heine sent copies of it to both Thiers and Guizot, on the assumption that they had not seen the articles.

Shortly before the publication of *Lutèce* a rumour appeared in the French Press " that Heine had ridiculed Guizot " in the book. Michel Lévy drew the author's attention to it, and Heine, in a letter sent with the copy of the book, requested Guizot to assure himself that the insinuations were nothing but malicious falsehoods.

Heine once said of these two statesmen : " I liked Thiers

better than his rival Guizot, but because of his personality, not of his attitude of mind. Thiers saw things in the light of a narrow nationalism, whereas Guizot's cosmopolitan way of thinking was similar to my own." In any case, neither Thiers nor Guizot is the central figure of *Lutèce*, which, although a collection of articles written as day-to-day journalism, is a studied piece of work giving the deeper and more intimate reasons for the events related. " The hero of my book is the social movement which Thiers had unloosed when he set Germany going with his bugle blast, and which Guizot tried in vain to stem."

Heine's interest in the social movement had been strong in him since the days of his youth. During his stay in Paris it had developed rapidly, until at the time he was correspondent for the *Augsburger Allgemeine Zeitung*, it had become a passion with him. It has been seen that he was at first attracted by Saint-Simonism. He remained in contact with Enfantin, the head of that sect, even after he had gone to Egypt. He also had connections with the remnant of the party, " the partisans of which may be seen wandering through life under strange labels." But he realised that their doctrine would not suffice to solve the problems of the day, which appeared to him to become more and more acute. He became interested in Fourier, whom he met in Paris. He often saw him, clad in his shabby old grey redingote, hurrying past under the arcades of the Palais Royal, his pockets stuffed with bread and a bottle of wine which he had bought for himself. " How is it possible," said Heine, to a German friend, " that men like Fourier, true benefactors of humanity, should in France be obliged to live in such penury ? " And his friend answered: " It certainly does little honour to the country of intelligence, and it could not happen in Germany. In our country the Government would take men who had such principles as his under their special protection, and would provide them with free board and lodging for the rest of their lives."

Heine attended the great banquets which were organised by the followers of Fourier, particularly on his birthday, April 7th. Hundreds of people would be grouped around the long tables set up in the largest room of some popular dance-hall. They were chiefly people drawn from the well-to-do classes, amongst them some hundred women, to whose emancipation a special toast was drunk. Over the chairman's table a great white flag floated, and there would be a table for the children, dressed all in white and wearing crowns of flowers in accordance with the Master's wishes. For them the kingdom of peace and happiness had already arrived—the kingdom for which their fathers still fought and suffered. And, when the toast was drunk, the great voice of the worker-poet Boissy would boom through the hall : " To Fourier ; to the revealer of man's social destiny ! To the great genius who has known how to combine order with freedom—to transform duty and labour into pleasure."

One night, in 1847, on leaving one of these late gatherings which he persisted in attending despite his poor state of health, Heine passed a man whom the guttering gas-lamps of the Rue St-Honoré revealed as having a round vivacious face, with eyes hidden behind blue spectacles. " Were you there too ? " some passer-by asked this man—and Heine paused to hear the reply. " No," answered the man in blue spectacles, " I only stopped because I saw a crowd. Ah ! It is always the same tune with these followers of cults ! Blessed be Jesus Christ, who has saved us from our sins ; blessed be Saint-Simon, who has taught us to understand life ; blessed be Fourier, who has revealed the social laws to us ! It is farcical ! When will someone shout : Blessed be common sense, that worships nobody ? "

" Who is it ? " asked young Meissner of Heine as they moved on.

" Amongst men he is known as M. Prud'hon. But really it is a demon. I am always refreshed in my soul when I see someone like that. One word from him does me good, after so much fine talk and tepid speeches. He is right ; he is entirely right."

" Yes, but what sort of a man is he ? " asked Meissner impatiently, with youthful curiosity.

" You keep saying ' man,' " Heine replied. " I have told

you that it is not a man, in spite of its blue spectacles. It is the principle of destructive criticism in the guise of a political philosopher, who is, in addition, endowed with a poet's power of expression. Victor Hugo appears to have surrendered his genius of antithetical statement to him, and Alexandre Dumas has lent him his imagination. His works, or, to use the jargon of the police, his subversive writings, are read like novels. They are passed from hand to hand here in France ; people are amused by them, and do not see that, as the pages are turned, dragons' teeth drop out which will one day produce a blessed harvest." A malicious smile played about Heine's lips—the smile of one who sees far into the future ; the sort of smile his friends called destructive.

Heine had perceived for a long time that the theoreticians of Socialism were only the forerunners of a movement of far wider scope. " For the followers of Saint-Simon and Fourier the social problem is a question of gradualism," wrote Heine, in July 1843. " They are not urged on by any demoniac necessity, they are not the predestined instruments by which the supreme Will of Mankind will realise its mighty intentions. Sooner or later the scattered family of Saint-Simon and the general staff of Fourier will merge into the growing army of the Communists, lending their formulæ to brute force, and playing a rôle similar to that of the Fathers of the Church." " The Communists are the only party in France worthy of close attention," he said at another time. He fully realised that France was still well protected by her bourgeois spirit, which, in *Lutèce*, he described as conservative, " not from any innate tendency, but from reasons of external necessity." " Fear is here the supporting pillar of everything." But he saw, rising from the depths of society, the ranks of the discontented who were in opposition to " the enthusiasts of calm possession." He had no illusions as to the meagre importance at that time, between 1840 and 1843, of the plottings of secret societies, groups of foreign workers, and other sparse and scattered cells of the movement. But he felt that Communist propaganda possessed a language which every people could understand : " The elements of this universal tongue are as plain and simple as hunger or envy or death. They are quickly learnt."

When Heine combated the rousing of the spirit of bellicosity, personified in France by the nationalism of Thiers, as he combated the same spirit in Germany, he saw, not only the danger of the immediate conflict, but the even greater peril of the future : " What would have been the end of the movement for which Paris was giving the signal ? It would have been war, the most horrible and destructive of wars, which would have summoned to ruin on the battlefield the noblest peoples of civilisation. I speak of Germany and France. But that would have been but the first act of the great drama, almost a prelude. The second act is European, the great duel between those who possess nothing and the privileged aristocracy of the possessors." And again : " As soon as the terrible wheel had begun to turn we should have seen an antagonist arise who would have proved the most formidable of all the opponents who have ever attacked the existing order of society. At present he still hides his identity, living, like a poverty-stricken *prétendant*, in the basements of society where, between death and mildew, the new life is germinating. Communism is the secret name of this terrible antagonist, which offers the rule of the proletariat with all its consequences in place of the rule of the present bourgeoisie. The duel will be breathless ! How will it end ? Only the gods and goddesses who know the future can predict that. We know only one thing : that Communism, although little spoken of to-day and though still remaining dormant on its miserable bed of straw in the recesses of garrets, is none the less the sombre hero destined to a great, if temporary, rôle in the modern tragedy."

When Heine wrote the dedication of *Lutèce* to Prince Pückler-Muskau in 1854, he announced with pride that he had been one of the first to see the danger which menaced society. " I have spoken often and with precision of the demons which lurk in the lowest depths of society, ready to pounce from their dark hiding-places as soon as their hour strikes. It had become the custom to regard these monsters, to whom the future belongs, through the wrong end of a telescope, and, viewed in this manner, they appeared to behave like crazy fleas. But, when I showed them in life size, I revealed their resemblance to the most terrifying crocodiles which ever crawled from out the mud."

In the second half of 1843, Heine found himself obliged to give up his post as political correspondent for the *Augsburger Allgemeine Zeitung*. He found himself in disagreement with Guizot's policy, and feared to provoke him by his criticism, and thus bring about his expulsion from France. But, a few months after he had written his last warning against Communism, he came into contact with the man who was to give that movement its bible, and provide it with its momentum—Karl Marx.

Heine made the acquaintance of Marx soon after his own return from Germany, in December 1843, one month after the arrival of Marx in Paris. Karl Marx was then barely twenty-six years old, and was still enjoying his honeymoon, having only a few months earlier married the beautiful girl to whom he had been engaged for seven years. He had come to Paris to study economic and social questions, with which he was still unfamiliar.

Marx was descended on both sides from a long line of rabbis. His father had been the first to break with the family tradition, and had been a lawyer in Trèves. The anti-Semitic wave had then been so strong that the first of the family to attempt to emancipate himself from its traditional vocation had at the same time been obliged to renounce the religion of his ancestors. His father and all his family became converted to Christianity almost before Karl Marx had reached school age. The boy showed great talent, and did brilliantly in his studies, but he made no friends. His aggressive pride and general intransigence of character created something like a vacuum around him. But his solitary existence did not darken his adolescence ; he was scarcely eighteen when he proved his influence over his fellows. Almost immediately after leaving school the rabbi's grandson became engaged to " the prettiest girl in the town," as he used to say later, with a little show of vanity. His future wife was Jenny von Westphalen, daughter of a high Government official, and member of one of the chief aristocratic families of the country.

First a student of law at Bonn University, then later at Berlin, where the powerful influence of Hegel proved of greater attraction to him than his legal studies, Karl Marx had at first aspired to the peaceful career of a savant, to a chair in a university, and, above all, to " the search for the idea in reality itself." The death of his father made it necessary for him to earn his own living, and obliged him to terminate his already unduly prolonged studies at the university. In 1842 he joined the editorial staff of the *Rheinische Zeitung*, newly founded at Cologne by a group of rich industrialists. Even then his work was distinguished by his self-assurance and the vehemence of his style, so that the youngest of the paper's contributors soon came to fill the chief place in it. By the end of the year he was editor-in-chief. His violent criticism of the Rhenish Diet attracted the attention of the Prussian Government, which did him the honour of sending a special censor to Cologne to watch over such a formidable adversary. When reaction finally obtained the upper hand in Prussia, and the " year of truce with the Press " was ended by royal decree, the *Rheinische Zeitung* was the first victim to fall. It was suppressed in the spring of 1843.

His experiences as a journalist had shown Marx that his knowledge of philosophical and juridical questions, extensive though it was, was not sufficient to enable him to propound solutions for the problems of the hour. He realised also that the new industrial civilisation then evolving required to be studied more deeply than was possible in Germany, where its development was hardly perceptible. For this reason he chose Paris as the field for his studies. Heine and Marx were brought together by their collaboration in the *Deutsch-Französische Jahrbucher*, which Arnold Ruge intended to publish in Paris.

Heine was at once profoundly impressed by the personality of Marx. The physique of the young savant and journalist was quite unlike that of the usual man of letters. His thick-set body and broad shoulders bore upon them a square head crowned by a mop of abundant black hair. Hair grew on his cheeks, and in little tufts in his nose and ears and on his wrists. He seemed like Pan or some other mythological creature. Only his cold and piercing look denoted the man of learning who possessed a judgment which was pitiless in its logic. At bottom an invincible need for domination, a thirst for immediate action, prevailed even over his strong inclination for study.

From their first meeting hardly a day passed on which Heine did not visit the humble apartment of Marx and his wife. Often he would fish out from his pocket a piece of paper on which he had just written a poem, and which he wished to submit to Marx's judgment first. The two men would sit for hours arguing about a poem of eight lines, trying to give a fastidious piece of work the necessary note of spontaneity. " Give up these everlasting complaints about love," Marx advised ; " show these poets how they ought to act ; show them how to use a whip." " It was I and Marx who introduced Heine to political satire," said Ruge later. But it was not true. Marx only strengthened a tendency which Heine had already possessed before their meeting.

In the first and only number of the *Deutsch-Französische Jahrbucher*, which was published in February 1844, and in which Heine's impudent " Hymns in Praise of Louis I of Bavaria " appeared, Marx wrote : " Oppression must be rendered still more oppressive by making the people realise their oppression. The shame of the deed must be made still more shameful by crying it aloud from the house-tops." But Heine was not the only one who came under his influence. In the same article Marx again took up the theme expounded by Heine in his book, *Zur Geschichte der Religion und Philosophie in Deutschland.* " The philosophy of Germany is the prolongation of her history. . . . What Germany merely thought, other nations actually did in politics. Germany represented the theoretical conscience of the nations. In Germany abstraction and high-minded thinking have always walked hand-in-hand with meanness and servility in the field of action."

The relations between Marx and his wife and Heine rapidly grew closer during the year 1844. Where Marx himself was unable to show enough sympathy for the poet's exaggerated sensibility, his wife was always ready to listen to the outpourings of his woes and worries. But, as their daughter wrote later, "It was not always to ask help that Heine visited my parents, sometimes he brought it." On one occasion when Heine dropped in upon the young couple he found them in the depths of despair, terrified for the life of their baby. Their first-born, Jenny, was then only a few months old, and Heine arrived to find her in a fit of violent convulsions. The household was gathered round the child's cradle ; the inexperienced young parents, and a girl who used to help them in the household, were equally helpless to do anything but watch with horror the stiffening of the tiny limbs. "You must put the child into a hot bath," Heine immediately said, with sudden authority. Then, seeing them all paralysed with fright, he himself took up the little body, with infinite care, and laid it in the warm water, bending low to watch, with his short-sighted eyes, the miraculous effect of his cure. In later years Marx often repeated to his eldest daughter, "It was Heine who saved your life" ; and his children grew up with this picture of Heine as rescuer in their minds.

During the second half of 1844, Heine and Marx collaborated in the publication of the paper *Vorwärts*. Serious differences had arisen between Ruge and Marx on account of the latter's growing Communist tendency, and it was this disagreement that brought about the premature end of the *Deutsch-Französische Jahrbucher*.

Vorwärts was a weekly paper published in Paris in the German language. Before the leftward tendency became so conspicuous it had led a calm and uneventful existence. It had been founded in 1844 by a German journalist named Henri Börnstein, with the financial aid of Meyerbeer, and it included amongst its staff the notorious Austrian spy and *agent provocateur*, Adalbert von Bornstedt. But, at the time in question, neither Heine, nor Marx, nor the young and enthusiastic Bernays, who became its editor-in-chief, had any suspicion of the rôle Bornstedt was playing.

It was in *Vorwärts* that Heine published his "Silesian Weavers," which showed the influence of Marx in a growing sympathy with the claims of the workers. In June 1844, the weavers of Silesia had risen in revolt against the starvation wages and sordid misery of the life inflicted upon them by their exploiters. They had attacked the factories, smashing the machines and breaking everything upon which they could lay their hands. One after another the surrounding villages became possessed of this fever of destruction. Over and above the din of doors being broken down, of windows smashed to atoms, and the wrecking of machines, rose the improvised song of the excited mob, the "Judgment of Blood," which cursed the exploiters of the poor as devils from hell. Prussian troops were hurriedly despatched to the scene, and soon suppressed in bloody fashion the rioting of the hungry wretches. "Order was restored," and misery again lay heavy upon the Silesian villages.

The *émigrés* had followed the course of these events with indignation, and on Heine, with his pronounced sense of social justice, their effect was immense. To the clumsy song which had been born in the heat of bloody conflict he lent the inspiration of his own anger, and he transformed the hot, stammered curses of the weavers into expressions of biblical power.

Deutschland, wir weben dein Leichentuch.
Wir weben hinein den dreifachen Fluch.
Wir weben, wir weben!
. . . *Ein Fluch dem König, dem König der Reichen,*
Den unser Elend nicht konnte erweichen,
Der den letzten Groschen von uns erpresst,
Und uns wie Hunde erschiessen lässt . . .
Wir weben, wir weben!
Ein Fluch dem falschen Vaterlande

Wo nur gedeihen Schmach und Schande,
Wo jede Blume früh geknickt,
Wo Fäulnis und Moder den Wurm erquickt
Wir weben, wir weben!

" Germany, we are weaving your shroud. We are weaving the triple curse into it. We are weaving, weaving!

" . . . One curse for the King, the King of the rich, whom our wretchedness could not move to pity, who squeezed the last penny out of us, and had us shot like dogs. . . . We are weaving, weaving!

" A curse on the false fatherland where only shame and humiliation thrive, where every flower is broken before its time, where the worm rejoices over rot and decay. We are weaving, weaving!"

Nevertheless although he followed Marx closely along the road of social revolution, Heine was not won over to the Communist faith, to which Marx was ever more clearly tending. The doctrine had great attraction for Heine, but the apprehension which had been perceptible in *Lutèce*, written before he had met Marx, was not allayed by Marx's dialectics and the inexorable logic of his conclusions.

Marx realised quite well that Heine lacked enthusiasm for the new religion, even though he accepted its logic and it appealed to his sense of justice. But the usually imperious and uncompromising Marx overlooked this weakness in his friend. " One cannot judge poets by the standards applied to ordinary people," he would say; " one must just let them follow their own bent, they are made that way."

The relations between Marx and Heine were abruptly terminated in January 1845. At the request of the Prussian Government the French authorities forbade the publication of *Vorwärts*. Bernays, the editor-in-chief, was arrested and the other members of the staff expelled from France. Heine alone was left unmolested. On account of his numerous friends in France, Guizot had not dared to treat him with the same severity as the others.

The separation from Marx was a blow which Heine felt acutely. Marx had awakened a conflict in his mind which remained unsolved almost until the end of his life. Heine explains his attitude towards Communism in the preface to the French edition of *Lutèce*, which was written in March 1855 : " I made this admission, that the future belongs to Communism, in an agony and fear which, alas, was not feigned. I think with horror of the time when these gloomy iconoclasts will arrive in power. Their horny hands will mercilessly smash the marble statues of beauty . . . my *Book of Songs* will be used by the grocer to make paper-bags to hold coffee or snuff for the old women of the future. I foresee all this, and, alas, I am seized with unutterable sadness at the thought of the ruin with which the conquering proletariat threatens my poems, which will surely perish together with all the old romantic world. And yet I frankly admit that this same Communism, so hostile to my interests and to my inclinations, exercises a charm upon me before which I am powerless. A terrible syllogism holds me in its grip, and, if I am unable to refute the premise ' that every man has the right to eat,' then I am forced to submit to all its consequences. From much thinking about it I am like to lose my reason ; I see all the demons of truth dancing triumphantly around me, and at length the generosity of despair takes possession of my heart and I cry : ' For long this old society has been judged and condemned, let justice be done ! Let this old world be smashed in which innocence is long since dead, where egoism prospers and man battens upon man ! Let these whited sepulchres be destroyed from top to bottom, these caverns of falsehood and iniquity. And blessed be the grocer who shall one day use the pages of my poems as paper-bags for the coffee and snuff of poor old women, who, in this present world of injustice, too often have to go without that solace ! *Fiat justitia pereat mundus !* ' "

CHAPTER X

FAMILY CONFLICTS

Ach! Blutsfreunde sind es eben,
Welche mir den Tod gegeben.

"WHAT IS HAPPENING? Are you ill? Is the devil tormenting you? Or am I mad myself?" wrote Heine to Campe at the beginning of July 1844, when repeated letters had brought no reply from the publisher. "I do not think I can stay here; I think I shall run up to Hamburg." And by the end of the month he was on his way to Germany. This time he took Mathilde with him, remembering the agonies he had endured at the first separation. With them also went Mathilde's parrot, Cocotte, from which she never separated. The journey by sea from Le Havre to Hamburg was made to the unceasing accompaniment of Mathilde's chatter and the squawking of the bird. On disembarking at Hamburg, Mathilde, who had great difficulty in finding room for her stout person in the narrow German cabs, accidentally dropped the wooden case which she was clutching in her hand. Moritz Embden, who had eyes for nothing but his brother-in-law's mysterious new wife, hastened to pick up the case without noticing what was in it. Thereupon the frightened bird took a vigorous nip at the stranger's fingers through the bars of the box, so that Moritz dropped it again with a yell of surprise. This brought Mathilde bursting from the cab to hurl herself in tears upon the improvised cage. The parrot squawked its loudest and the woman cried, but the general hullabaloo was dominated by Heinrich Heine's shouts of laughter.

Mathilde stared forth with round uncomprehending eyes at this strange new world—the world of her Henri. She understood no word of German. When a visitor called she welcomed them with the only two sentences she had picked up : " Guten Tag," and " Nehmen Sie Platz." Then she would rush from the room, screaming with laughter. Her husband's womenfolk looked quizzically at the fat Parisian, vulgar despite her beauty, careless and ignorant, but filled to the brim with the pride of one who had never before been out of her own country. The men of the family, on the other hand, regarded her somewhat differently. What struck them most was her marvellous complexion, the beauty of her large liquid eyes, and her infectious laugh. But her gaiety quickly evaporated, and she soon became annoyed by the stares of the curious. She was unaccustomed to the ways of these people, and disliked them, and she missed the light amusement to which she was accustomed in Paris. She was not used to adapting herself to her surroundings, and, as soon as the charm of novelty had faded, her abominable temper became all too evident. When the news came that her mother was ill, she hailed the unexpected excuse for returning home almost with joy. She left as soon as it could possibly be arranged, still clutching the parrot's travelling cage tightly in her hand.

Her departure made it clear to Heine that he would have to choose between Mathilde and living in Germany without her. Just at that time the doctors were urging him to regain his strength by spending some time at the seaside. They impressed upon him that he must take great care of his health ; his eye trouble had returned more acutely than ever. For several weeks he had been totally blind, and even when vision returned to some extent he was unable to use his eyes for reading. The slightest effort was followed by appalling headaches. He had no need of the doctors' warnings in order to feel alarmed, he knew very well how grave his condition was. Indeed his visit to Hamburg was made for no other purpose than to arrange for Mathilde's future in the event of her being left alone in the world. He had hopes that Salomon Heine would partly relieve his anxiety on this score. Salomon was dying, and illness had by no means sweetened his temper. He was far from content with his nephew's audacity in mocking highly respectable people so outrageously, and even ridiculing the sacred persons of reigning families. " Listen," he growled to Heinrich one day. " I do not understand how you can dare to write the things you do against the King of Bavaria. What are you compared with him anyhow ? A good-for-nothing, that's all you are—just a good-for-nothing." The old man spat out the words contemptuously. " You may be right, uncle," Heine replied, with unwonted self-control, " but, you see, my trade is to write verse ; the King of Bavaria also writes verse, and he spoils my trade. I can't just let that happen without saying anything."

Heine carefully avoided any semblance of a quarrel with the irritable invalid. But Salomon had his two sons-in-law at his elbow—Dr. Halle, the husband of Therese, and Moritz Oppenheim—both of whom had often been victims of their cousin's bitter tongue. They avenged themselves for past affronts by exciting the ill-humoured old man against him.

After Mathilde's departure Heine stayed on at Hamburg to settle his affairs with Campe. His publisher possessed a genius for non-committal silence as soon as the question of money was broached. At the beginning of the summer, when Heine, worn out by his eye trouble, had begged Campe to send him money enough to enable him to undergo treatment in Switzerland, Campe had not even replied to his letters. In conversation, however, he was always overflowing with joviality and friendliness. Heine particularly wanted to conclude his business with the publisher before *Germania, A Winter's Tale* appeared, for he knew that the publication of that book would close Germany to him for ever. But Campe had every reason to keep him waiting.

" The horizon darkens, my business affairs are in a bad way," wrote Heine to Mathilde. And again he poured out the same entreaties and the same effusions of affection : " *Meine liebe Frau,* I love you madly." But he also suffered the same tortures, for Mathilde never answered his letters. " *Mon Dieu,* the very thought that you are in Paris without me makes me tremble. My poor lamb, alone in Paris, in that capital of hungry wolves. . . ." His anxiety was all the greater because he had reason to know what passion burned unsatisfied in his young wife. Already before leaving for Hamburg he had written to his sister Lotte : " For years I have not slept with my wife—how, then, do you expect us to have children ? " He did his best to reassure Mathilde : " Don't grieve your poor husband, he will turn out to be, for all your teasing, a phœnix." He would not even allow Mathilde to go to visit her sick mother, who knew nothing of her daughter's return. Heine preferred the watchful care of Madame Darte to that of the old peasant woman. Anxiety concerning his own safety increased the nervous tension in which he was living. " I have been alarmed by a warning from high quarters, and am making ready to leave," he wrote to Marx. " I am suspected of having taken a greater part in *Vorwärts* than I can flatter myself to have done. But, frankly, that sheet does show genius in the art of irritating other people and of compromising itself. It is to be hoped that nobody in Paris invents any calumnies against me ! " The last remark was almost prophetic. He did not then know that as early as April 1844, and again in August of the same year, warrants for his arrest had been issued in the various States of Germany. The Paris police had obligingly provided a description of him for the purpose of these warrants : " Heine, man of letters, fifty years of age, average height, pointed nose and chin, pronounced Jewish type ; he is a debauched individual whose diseased body shows exhaustion."

Heine returned to Paris in the middle of October. His arrival was the occasion for a wild outburst of joy on the part of Mathilde and himself. " We are intoxicated with happiness at being together again," he wrote to his mother. " We look at each other with eyes full of love ; we laugh and joke and kiss ; we talk of you ; then it all begins again—the laughter and kissing—and the parrot joins in and squawks madly." But scarcely had he regained the normal tenor of his life than he learnt that his apprehensions concerning *Vorwärts* had been realised. And when this blow fell, while he was still grieving over his separation from Marx, Heine fell a victim to one of the worst disappointments of his life.

Towards the end of December he received news of the death of his uncle, and it upset him greatly, even though he had been prepared for it. " This man has played a great part in my life," he wrote to his sister ; " and how kind he has been to my poor old pussy cat ! " he added, thinking of his mother. He was not much concerned about the financial aspect of the matter, for he relied upon a half-promise made to him by his uncle at the moment of his departure from Hamburg. But within a week a letter came from his cousin Karl Heine, drily informing him that a few days before his death his father had made a new will, by which Heinrich would only receive a lump sum of 8,000 marks. The letter continued that he, Karl, would be prepared to grant his cousin an annual allowance on condition that everything which Heinrich wrote about Salomon Heine should be submitted to him in manuscript before publication. Heine read this letter through, pale as a ghost, unable to believe his eyes. The shock and the resulting fit of violent indignation were too much for his weakened constitution, and he fell to the floor in a dead faint. Mathilde and little Weill rushed to pick him up, and, with cries of alarm, carried him to bed.

On regaining consciousness Heine began to weep ; the only tears, said Weill, that he ever saw him shed. He wept at the thought of the old man's thrust at him from the grave, at his own weakness, and at the dark prospect of a poverty-stricken future. As for Mathilde, she had understood just one thing—that they were faced with penury. The thought paralysed her. For two whole days she did not budge from her place by the fireside, sitting with tightened lips and staring, unseeing eyes, dumb and threatening, her dull mind churning over thoughts which horrified her husband.

It was less the disappointment itself than Karl's insolent attempt to dictate what he should write which roused Heine to a paroxysm of rage. It brought out all the worst that was in him, spurring the embittered malice of his nature to blind revolt.

The attack which had laid him low the day on which the news arrived was an apoplectic stroke ; it weakened his intellectual faculties, and, as he slowly recovered, there was at first nothing left in him but intense hatred. He cast aside the last remnants of restraint which he had always preserved hitherto. The man who had never yet mentioned the name of a woman with whom he had relations, dared to write to his old friend Detmold that he had been the lover of Cécile Fould before her marriage with Karl Heine, that it was he who had arranged the marriage, and that, owing to his having quarrelled with them, the Fould family was exciting Karl Heine against him. He threatened a lawsuit against Karl, but Salomon's heirs did not even deign to reply to his letters. Karl Heine was enjoying his revenge. Was it really his wife's old lover whom he set out to destroy, or was he merely settling accounts with the insolent companion of his youth who had so often shown his contempt for him? In either case the peaceful citizen of Hamburg, who, according to Heinrich Heine, cared only for women, cigars, and material comfort, ferociously indulged his hatred of the tormented genius. It was the beginning of one of those distressing family conflicts which are the most obstinate and bitter of all quarrels, because each side knows too well the hidden weaknesses of the other. On one side was ranged the law, strength of possession, and the respect which great wealth can always command. On the other side there was nothing save anxiety for the future, and the poisoned darts of calumny.

Heine prepared to throw mud at his Hamburg relatives: "They are not used to it," he wrote cynically; "whereas I can put up with waggon-loads and feel all the better for it—like a flower on a dung-heap." First he arranged for the publication of articles containing insinuations against Dr. Halle, whom he suspected of being the brain behind the intrigues against himself. But at the same time his customary underestimation of the intelligence of others led him to send emissaries to Halle bearing hypocritical letters of friendship. He evolved a whole plan of campaign which was as malicious as it was absurd, and he brought his friends into action for the furtherance of his schemes. Then suddenly he abandoned the whole affair, and, except that he still remained obdurate with regard to the supervision of his writing, he declared himself willing to make any promise and any apology so long as he got his allowance and was left in peace.

The reason for this sudden volte-face was Mathilde. It was by far the most difficult period which had occurred in their life together since their marriage, and the woman showed her egoism to the full. " My domestic Vesuvius, which has lain dormant for three years, has begun to spit fire," Heine wrote. The Hamburg affair had excited Mathilde to desperation. Her husband was at his wit's end, and confessed it in a letter to Detmold : "'Contemnere mundum, contemnere se ipsum, contemnere se contemni,' that is what we were taught by the old monks. I too have come to the same conviction by disgust ; disgust at life, contempt for men and for the Press—by my illness—and by Mathilde."

After some months he was ready to accept the conditions which Karl Heine had at first laid down—that he should publish nothing against his family. But the *amour-propre* of the indignant relative demanded that the poet's humiliation should be complete. Prince Pückler Muskau had intervened on behalf of Heinrich Heine, and Karl wrote to him in a tone of insolence induced by his consciousness of greater wealth : " I am not cruel—I am not even unreasonable in the matter of money, but there are things which must first be wiped out by repentance and good behaviour." It meant nothing to him that Prince Pückler Muskau expressed the opinion that every German should be proud that his country possessed such a genius as Heine. More than two years elapsed before the miserable business was settled—two years of emotion which proved disastrous for Heine's health. " When one thinks back over the circumstances," he wrote, " it is just a cowardly assassination which has been committed. Dull mediocrity and vicious jealousy of genius have waited twenty years to enjoy their little hour of triumph. At bottom it is just the same old story all over again."

The matter was finally settled about the beginning of 1847. The allowance would be paid, and Heine promised to write nothing against his family.

But the poet's voice was to rise later, from beyond the tomb, in accusation against his relatives. Their name was not mentioned, as he had promised, but this cry from the dead was the more poignant because of the determination with which they had tried to stifle it :

Es gab den Dolch in deine Hand
Ein böser Dämon in der bösen Stunde—
Ich weiss nicht wie der Dämon hiess—
Ich weiss nur dass vergiftet war die Wunde.

" An evil genius in an evil hour put the dagger in your hand. I do not know the name of that genius, but I know the wound was poisoned."

The drama of the family conflict appeared in the guise of poems on historical themes, such as the gloomy ballad of the " Spanish Atrides," and in verses paraphrasing the biblical curse : " And his name shall not be spoken." It rises, too, in this cry of impotent despair :

Wenn ich sterbe, wird die Zunge
Ausgeschnitten meiner Leiche ;
Denn sie fürchten, redend käm' ich
Wieder aus dem Schattenreiche.

Stumm verfaulen wird der Tote
In der Gruft und nie verraten
Werd' ich die an mir verübten
Lächerlichen Freveltaten.

" When I die, my tongue will be cut from my dead body, for they are afraid lest I return from the land of shadows and talk. . . . My dead body will decay, silent in the tomb, and never will I betray the crimes committed against me."

The years in which Heine exhausted himself in this ridiculous campaign of calumny against his relations were years of torment. He was ill, a nervous wreck, and Mathilde nagged incessantly. He came to distrust all his old friends, yet he snatched avidly at any help that was offered him. Work was out of the question ; he could think of nothing but the wrong which had been done. In the complete isolation which threatened him at this period he found his only consolation in the companionship of a young friend who had no cares of his own—Ferdinand Lassalle.

Lassalle was scarcely twenty when he came to Paris, as a student of philosophy, to do research work in the libraries for his book on Heraclitus. He was the son of a rich industrialist of Breslau, and had been expected to enter his father's business. But even as a child he had been possessed of inordinate ambition, and had left the technical school to work for a degree, with a view to following an academic career. It was his ambition which had led him to change his Jewish name of Lassal, borrowing the adopted form from a French family that was well known at the time of the Revolution. The same reason caused him to embrace Protestantism, despite his deep sympathies with his race and the day-dreams of his childhood in which he had seen himself heading the fight for liberty on behalf of the oppressed Jews.

He was tall and slender, with a long thin face, a high forehead, and curly hair. His appearance was enhanced by the intelligence of his large brown eyes and by his shapely mouth. Ferdinand Lassalle seemed to possess everything that was necessary for the fulfilment of his dreams. Men of learning such as Boeck and Humboldt saw in him a boy who was wonderfully endowed with talent ; the study he was making in recondite Greek philosophy promised to give extraordinary results which would launch him on his career.

But his temperament and his own realisation of his exceptional qualities led him to interest himself in the most advanced ideas of his time. When only fifteen he wrote in his diary, with all the disarming presumption of youth, with regard to Schiller's *Fiesco* : "Although at present I am revolutionary, democratic, and republican by conviction, I feel that had I been in the position of Count Lavagne I should have acted as he did. I would not have been satisfied merely to be the first citizen of Genoa, and I too would have stretched my hand out towards the crown. If my analysis of my state of mind is correct, it is clear that I am just an egoist. Had I been born a duke or a prince, I should have been an aristocrat to the backbone. But, since I am only a plain bourgeois, I shall one day be a democrat."

Heine was immensely attracted by this distinguished young man, imperious though he was, as full of high spirits as of ideas, quick-witted and amusing, and as definite in his judgment as he was imperturbable in his actions. Before this vision of triumphant youth, Heine, usually so little inclined to bow to the opinions of others, betrayed an admiration which was almost humble. Comparing his own attitude with that of the young man's domineering insolence, he felt himself to be irresolute and sentimental, hedged about with the vain scruples of another generation. His feelings are well expressed in a letter which he wrote to Varnhagen : " Herr Lassalle is so pronounced a child of the new generation that he will not even listen to an explanation of the renunciation and modesty with which we came to terms with our world, more or less hypocritically. This new generation means to enjoy life and show its worth in the open, whereas we of the older generation prostrated ourselves before the invisible; we sought shadowy kisses and the perfumes of blue, ghostly flowers. We renounced much and lamented it, and yet, perhaps, we were happier than these thick-skinned gladiators who so proudly march to death in battle."

" Compared with you I am but a humble insect," wrote Heine to Lassalle. And again : " You have the right to be high-minded, the rest of us are but usurpers of that divine right, that heavenly privilege."

There is a warmth of emotion in his admiration for Lassalle which no other friendship ever excited in Heine. " He is a young man of quite exceptional intellectual quality, full of the deepest scientific ideas, and possessing the widest knowledge, coupled with the most acute faculty of perception, that I have ever encountered ; the ripest gift for expression is combined in him with an activity of mind and an intelligence of action which is amazing." To the same degree in which Heine's relations with Marx and his wife had been of a conventional nature, consisting of family visits and the sharing of family troubles, so did his relations with Lassalle tend rather towards the hidden side of his life. The handsome boy already possessed that power of fascination over women which was to be the cause of his tragic end, and Heine, who had given up his former dissolute way of living, began, in his company, to frequent the world of easy virtue again. In spite of his affection for Lassalle (he once wrote to him : " I am very fond of you ; it is impossible not to be ; you torment a person incessantly until he does become fond of you "), or perhaps on account of this affection, Heine was consumed with anxiety for the future of the unruly young man. One day he predicted for him a great future in Germany, and Lassalle asked him : " What do you mean by a great future ? " Heine answered with a laugh : " To be killed by one of your own disciples."

In 1846, Lassalle went to Berlin, charged by Heine with the mission of interceding in his unpleasant family conflict and of persuading Varnhagen to rouse public opinion on his behalf. At this time Heine's anxiety for his young friend even transcended the obsession of his quarrel. " Knowing your character, I am full of petty bourgeois fears in your behalf," he wrote. It was at that period that Lassalle first met Countess Hatzfeld, an event which was destined to change his whole life. Heine was constantly warning him, and wrote again and again in his letters that he " was thinking with the greatest concern about him and his future." Nevertheless the enthusiasm with which Lassalle made the cause of Countess Hatzfeld his own ended by destroying their friendship. Lassalle would not forgive Heine for not using his pen in her behalf, but, in spite of all the services Lassalle had rendered him in his family quarrel, the poet persisted in maintaining that it was a matter for Sue rather than for himself. The abrupt termination of their relations by Lassalle did not kill Heine's affection for him, quick though he usually was to take offence. Several years later we find him writing to his friend's father in the warmest terms : " My poor

Ferdinand Lassalle, my heart melts when I think of him and when I see the richest gifts of nature in process of annihilation by this demon of self-destruction which is in him."

The affection which he felt for Ferdinand was extended to his sister, Friederike Friedland, who arrived in Paris accompanied by her husband shortly after her brother's departure. " She is exceptionally intelligent, and bears the most delightful resemblance to yourself," he wrote enthusiastically to her brother. He found the young woman to be a passionate admirer of his works. Friederike Friedland was married to a company promoter, who was full of new ideas and audacious projects, and who was obliged to live an expensive life in order to acquire the necessary prestige for the fulfilment of his schemes. His wife sought relief from the world of business by devoting her attention to intellectual matters. She was herself an amateur writer, and she burned with a desire to know the celebrities of the literary world. She spent a great deal of time with Heine, deep in those brilliant, intimate conversations of which he so well knew the secret. " Often we understand each other in a twinkling," he used to say. Heine as a rule did not care for ambitious women, but for Friederike he mobilised all his most celebrated French friends. In March 1846 he gave a dinner-party in her honour, to which were invited Balzac, Boyer, Gozlan, Gautier, and others, and later he undertook to collect the autographs of famous men for her album.

Fascinated by Friederike, he even went so far as to believe her husband to be a genius, and entrusted him with a sum of money to be invested in a gas company at Prague. This venture led to his loss of faith in a man so optimistic that he believed " in everything and everybody, even in himself." When all the money he had invested was gone, because the gas company went bankrupt, he heaped abuse on Friedland's head, and even went so far as to use his friends in order to slander the unfortunate speculator publicly, until he got back a portion of his money. His affair with Friederike ended with her departure for Germany. But for Heine it was more than just a few months' courtship paid to a pretty woman, it was the last of the long series of amorous adventures before he became totally incapacitated by his disease. It is the note of irrevocable loss in it which caused the pathetically persistent memory of Friederike. Years after she had gone he would recall her picture : " Not a night passes in which her little face does not appear to me. How white a skin, how warm a heart."

His disease began to make rapid strides. During the winter of 1846 his doctors, Roth and Sichel, told him that he would not recover. At first he refused to believe it, and was determined at least to seek relief for his eye trouble by consulting the now famous Berlin doctor, his old friend of early days, Dieffenbach. He planned a visit to Berlin, but first tried to make sure of his personal safety. This time the Prussian Government was informed about the measures which had been taken against " the man Heyne, accused in several instances of *lèse-majesté* and incitement to disobedience, and who in consequence is liable to arrest immediately upon setting foot on Prussian soil." Alexandre von Humboldt intervened warmly on his behalf, but the Prussian authorities nevertheless refused to give Heinrich Heine a safe conduct, and the great scientist notified him of the refusal and begged him not to risk the journey.

Having been refused permission to go to Germany, Heine, on the advice of his doctors, tried to check the spreading paralysis by spending the summer of 1846 at Barèges. He could no longer swallow meat, his throat was partially, and his lips entirely, paralysed, and he had great difficulty even in speaking. His left eye was closed, and only a little light filtered through the right eye. Condemned to remain idle he became a prey to despair. His only consolation was the high spirits of Mathilde, who threw herself whole-heartedly into the amusements of the little spa, dancing and making innumerable excursions into the surrounding mountains. The only unhappiness she knew there was when her parrot escaped and flew away ; then she ran crying and screaming through the village until some soldiers, touched by her distress, went off in pursuit of the bird, and eventually brought it back to her in triumph. " Stupidity is the happiest gift of the gods," wrote Heine later to his mother, when speaking of Mathilde.

He began to lose weight rapidly. On his return to Paris he seemed only the shadow of his former self, and his clothes hung about his bony frame pathetically. His stiff and haggard features were entirely changed by the beard which grew in profusion now that he was no longer able to shave. This bushy brown beard, flecked with white, and the large blue spectacles which protected his eyes, increased the impression he gave of being a ghost from another world. Friedrich Engels encountered him in the street, after his return from the Pyrenees, slowly groping his way along with hunched back and head turned to the ground. Engels recoiled in horror from the sight, and wrote in great agitation to Marx: " What an appalling tragedy to see so precious a being die by inches ! "

The rumour of his death had already appeared in the German Press, and several papers printed his obituary. He himself knew that at best he had before him only a few more years of suffering. But he was strangely calm and resigned. He complained little, during the long winter of inactivity, of the hours of silence to which his paralysed lips condemned him, and of those empty evenings spent with Mathilde, who sighed, " What a German conversation ! " At night a persistent cough racked his chest. But, in spite of all, his mind remained alert, and he even kept his sense of humour. Once when a new doctor was examining him, and asked, so as to test the extent of the paralysis, if he could still whistle, Heine replied : " Not even at a piece by Scribe ! " " All the pretty women turn to look at me when I pass in the street," he wrote to Caroline Jaubert. " My closed eyes (the right eye is now only one-eighth open), my sunken cheeks, my unkempt beard, and my unsteady gait all help to give me a most killing appearance ! I assure you that as a half-dead body I am a huge success. I devour all hearts, only I cannot digest them."

At last it was over—that terrible winter which he himself

was surprised to survive—and with the spring came some relief. He had recovered his speech and could again communicate with his fellows. The summer was spent in the country at Montmorency, where he had already stayed in 1845. This time Mathilde rented a charming house in the Châtaigneraie, which had a large quiet garden shaded with trees. Mathilde had remained a countrywoman, and was delighted to find herself again with a garden in which to work. She had regained her good humour and her energy, and was busy about the place from morning till night, laughing her childish laugh, watering the flower-beds, and picking the fruit and flowers. The silence of the country was a relief to Heine after the noisy apartment in the Faubourg Poissonière. The shade of the trees was good for his half-closed eyes, and his lungs breathed in the sweet scent of the acacias. During the long summer evenings he would sit out under the stars, listening in silent melancholy to the song of the nightingales. Every Sunday the omnibus brought out visitors to the little house. Alexandre Weill came regularly, and often there would be Théophile Gautier with Signora Ernesta, Alphonse Royer and his wife, and a few Germans, amongst them Heinrich Seuffert, the correspondent of the *Augsburger Allgemeine Zeitung*, and Alfred Meissner the young poet from Prague, whose young and cheerful enthusiasm Heine especially welcomed. Visitors to Montmorency found the same lavish hospitality as before, for Mathilde had not yet learnt to husband their slender means, and Heine's plaints at her extravagance echo dolefully through all his letters. There was the same profusion of champagne and other wines. Heine himself could no longer distinguish between them, but Mathilde considered them indispensable for her comfort. As a climax to her satisfaction a small country orchestra took up its quarters in front of the house, attracting both Parisians and villagers. Stately quadrilles were danced by the girls in their bonnets and abundantly petticoated skirts, and when some student from the city tried to show off, by dancing the new and fashionable *cancan*, the children who had crowded round would clap and shout.

For Heine these summer months were like a truce accorded him by his illness. His mood was one of superficial gaiety, interspersed with the shadow of his former caustic humour. The friends who came to see him always had some anecdote or *bon mot* to take back with them to Paris. One day the young journalist Seuffert related in disgust how he had been to see Rachel, the great French actress, at her home, but had only succeeded in meeting her parents. Heine answered, in his curious half-joking, half-serious way : " You were wrong to try to see Rachel at home, dear friend. You should see her in the theatre, where she is great and beautiful. At home you will find only a thin and sallow-faced woman, wholly lacking in distinction and almost lacking in intelligence. Your story reminds me of a man who went into a side-show at a fair to see something advertised as a ' miracle of nature,' a cross between a rabbit and a pike. He paid his penny and went inside, but could find nothing but the ordinary inhabitants of a menagerie. After hunting round for some time, he went up to the proprietor of the booth and asked where he kept the miracle of nature. ' Well,' said the man, ' we haven't got it here at the moment, but you can see the parents which produced it, both the rabbit and the pike.' You too, Seuffert, wanted to see a miracle of nature, and were only shown an old Jewish couple who had produced it. . . ."

The autumn rains began early that year, and at the beginning of September Heine's paralysis spread suddenly to the stomach and legs. He was no longer able to leave his bedroom, in fact only with great difficulty could he struggle from his bed to a chair by the window. Montmorency proved to be " the same disappointment as Barèges last year," he wrote to his doctor. " My fate drags onwards to its end. I bear it with calm and dignity."

But it was not the end ; it was only the commencement of a long martyrdom. The winter which followed that golden summer in the country was particularly trying and painful for him. Twice after his return to Paris he changed his apartment, moving first from his old quarters in the Faubourg Poissonière to the Rue de la Victoire. But his bad luck followed him—as he said—or more probably the incompetence of Mathilde was to blame. The new rooms were dark and gloomy, and the chimneys smoked. Directly underneath there were stables, so that the whole house resounded day and night with the coming and going of horses and the shouts of their grooms, until his splitting headaches almost drove him out of his mind. He was also plagued by financial worries. The treatment he was obliged to undergo was expensive, and his condition prevented him from earning anything. Half-way through the winter a new method of treatment, suggested by a Hungarian doctor, seemed at first to work miracles. This Dr. Gruby was a tiny little man, a mixture of genius and quack, who was enjoying great popularity in Paris at that time. Much of his treatment was based on suggestion, and women who suffered from nervous troubles spoke of the marvellous cures he had effected. Heine was induced by such stories to believe in Dr. Gruby, and hope came to him again.

But the emotional crises which he had to endure were deadly for his health. First of all there were the tantrums and nerve storms of Mathilde, who, in one of her fits, bit into pieces a glass of water which had been brought her. Then the sudden upheaval of the February Revolution. At that particular moment Heine was staying in Dr. Faultrier's clinic in the Rue de Lourcines, where he had been sent by Dr. Gruby in order that he might escape the gloom of his own apartment. On the evening of the Revolution, Heine had driven with Mathilde to Gruby's, where they were invited to dinner. The cab which should have called to take them home again was broken up on its way by the revolutionaries, to help form a barricade, and the sick man had great difficulty in regaining the clinic.

The news of the Revolution came as no surprise to Heine, who had predicted it long before; he had foreseen the inevitable fall of a regime which was incapable of understanding the new times and the movement they engendered. But when the event actually happened he was overcome by what he called "this world disaster, this madness of God."

He did not think that the dream of a republic, which was firing all minds, could be realised in practice. " The republic is nothing more than a change of name, a mere revolutionary handle. Where do you expect men to find their republican virtues, since they are the same men who, until now, have thought of nothing but making money, of intriguing for soft jobs, of driving in their coach and four, or of having a box at the theatre ? " A bitter smile would contract his lips as he answered his own question : " No ! Better give up the idea of a republic—for lack of republicans."

Later he was to ridicule fiercely the members of the Provisional Government. "The very title 'Provisional Government' was a sign of their hesitancy, and straightway robbed them of the good they might have done for the people who trusted them, who had put them into power and protected them with a bodyguard of three thousand men. . . . There were abject creatures among them who recalled the amateur actors with whom Shakespeare makes such play in the *Midsummer Night's Dream*. The miserable wretches had only one fear, which was that their fooling should be taken seriously, and Snug the joiner proclaimed in advance that he was not really a lion, only a provisional lion . . . that the public need not be afraid of his roars, for they were only provisional roars."

Heine had some cause for personal resentment against the new men who came to power, for the Revolution brought with it a disaster which affected him both materially and morally. The *Revue Rétrospective*, or the *Secret Archives of the Last Government*, was a publication issued by Paulin. In its endeavour to prove the corruption of Guizot's Ministry it printed in full the list of those who had received money from the Secret Fund, and Heine's name was amongst them. This revelation discredited Heine for ever in Germany. His glory as a poet was definitely tarnished by the shame of his having received money from France. Even if admiration for the author of the *Buch der Lieder* managed to survive the wave of patriotic indignation, all his political works, his social convictions, and, above all, his efforts to bring about a *rapprochement* between France and Germany, remained under the shadow of suspicion. After the revelations of the *Revue Rétrospective* the *Augsburger Allgemeine Zeitung* hastened to publish a defence of its late correspondent, stating, as its opinion, that Heine had not been paid for what he wrote, but for what he did not write. With good reason Heine called this clumsy statement " the defence with a bear's paw."

The general effervescence of the period made his own inactivity all the more intolerable. " It is hard indeed to be chained to my couch at a time when everyone else is on his feet and things are moving," he wrote to his old friend Dubochet. " The news I hear from my own country increases my distress. At this moment, when I should be pursuing my whole life's work to the fullest extent, I am condemned to lie idle. I cannot even answer my friends, who, as usual, turn to me and cry for help. Our friends have the upper hand in Germany. The so-called ' National Party ' surpasses itself in absurdity and brutality. Their bluster is incredible. They think only of assuming to themselves the chief rôle in the history of the world, and of rallying the lost tribes under the banner of nationalist Germany. If you do not hasten to give them back Alsace, they will not hesitate to demand Lorraine also. God knows where their uncouth pretentions will stop ! They want war, and in this they are in sympathy with our princes, who ask nothing better than to be able to direct upon the foreigner all the warlike ardour and unruly sentiments of their rebellious subjects. From the Rhineland I have received news which is very depressing. The most devoted friends of France, men who have worked for twenty years to destroy the Prussian influence in the Rhenish provinces, to-day no longer dare to struggle against the wave of nationalism, and have even hoisted the colours of the German Empire."

In this state of mind it was more than ever necessary for him to escape from the solitude which weighed him down. " I see nobody ; I speak to nobody," he lamented. With a great effort he summoned such strength as he had left to drag himself from his bed in order to see a few of his friends once again.

He first went to visit Gautier, whom he had not seen for several months. But, when he appeared, Gautier entirely failed to recognise him in the stranger who held out his hand and addressed him by his Christian name, a human skeleton with a long beard who faintly resembled Géricault. At length, when a characteristic witticism revealed his identity, Gautier cried : " It's the devil, or else it's Heine."

Heine also went to see Caroline Jaubert. He had himself carried up from the cab to her apartment on the second floor. But even this effort was too much for him, and no sooner was he laid on a couch in the *salon* than he was overcome by a terrible bout of cramp which contorted him from head to foot. The only thing which would disperse the atrocious pain of these seizures was the application of hot cones of morphine to the spinal column. " The Little Fairy " did her best to help him in the painful treatment, trembling all over, and with tears in her eyes. It was Heine himself who sought to console her as soon as he was able to speak. " My disease is incurable, *chère amie*," he said, " and I have come here to make you promise that you will never desert me. If you do not take your oath upon it, I will have myself carried away at once and frighten you again as I did just now." And he continued to joke : " What a fine hero I should have made for a novelist had I died under your roof. . . ."

He left her as he had come, carried in the arms of a porter. He knew it was the last time he would be able to visit his faithful friend. Just before leaving, he said to her : " You see me calm and self-controlled, but there is one thing which I find almost too hard to bear, that is when I receive letters from my mother. I write to her very often, but have not told her of my condition, and she tells me in every letter that she thanks God daily for preserving her beloved son in good health. And God can let that happen without remorse ! He is certainly a barbarian God, like the god of the ancient Egyptians ; a Greek divinity would not treat a poet thus. He might strike him with a bolt from the blue, but, to let him languish miserably, inch by inch . . ."

Heine went out once more into the world of men. It was in

the spring ; the sun shone and a soft breeze played about him as he dragged himself slowly along the street, stopping from time to time to rest against a wall or to clutch at a gate for support. Life surged all around him, the good life he had known so well. Gasping and nearly blind he heard the rustle of dresses as they passed, and the gay laughter of their wearers. Presently he tottered slowly through the courtyard of the Louvre and dropped, with a sigh of relief, on a bench in one of the galleries. As he recovered his breath in the cool interior a beam of light enabled even his poor eyes to see that he was before the statue of the Venus de Milo. As he drank in the beauty of the marble body his own past came up before him—his worship of love, and his lifelong passion for beauty. Then the contrast between his brilliant past and his awful present swept over him like a cloud.

" Life has done with me for ever," he murmured ; " the life I have loved so well." Suddenly he slipped from the bench and fell in a heap on the marble floor.

When they picked him up he was completely paralysed. No sooner had he regained consciousness than he muttered, with the shadow of his old smile : " And the goddess did not stretch an arm to help me ! You know her misfortune ? Her divinity, like my humanity, is reduced by half ! "

CHAPTER XI

TWILIGHT IN THE RUE D'AMSTERDAM

Keine Messe wird man singen
Keinen Kadosch wird man sagen
Nichts gesagt und nichts gesungen
Wird an meinen Sterbetagen.

(*Romanzero*)

THE SCENE IS NO. 50 RUE D'AMSTERDAM. A narrow, winding staircase leads up to an apartment on the second floor facing on to an inner courtyard. The door is opened by a mulatto woman with pock-marked face and head covered in a bandanna. Long conversations take place in whispers between visitors and the servants in the little kitchen. No, Monsieur is not seeing anybody—Germans least of all ! The sick man's room is only separated from the entrance to the apartment by a tiny antechamber, every word spoken in an ordinary voice can be overheard. The noise of a world about its business rises from the courtyard—the sound of women gossiping and quarrelling ; the distant rattle of carts on the cobbles, in the street ; a carpenter and his apprentices clatter in with their tools, and begin to hammer and saw. Through open windows on other floors the clumsy, conscientious fingers of little girls are heard strumming exercises on the piano. " It is a sordid, noisy, nerve-wracking little hole," wrote Heine, to his brother Max. " I chose it out of an exaggerated sense of economy."

A greenish light filters through the heavily curtained windows, and a large screen half hides the pile of bed-clothes. Gradually, as the eye becomes accustomed to the darkened room, other things are distinguished : in a corner is a large black arm-chair : a writing-desk stands by the bed, and the white paper on it reflects back the little light there is.

A curious contrivance, made of ropes in the shape of handles, hangs at the head of the bed—a complicated and probably useless apparatus for exercising the muscles of the invalid's right arm, which are not yet entirely paralysed. The room is pervaded by the acrid smell of burnt flesh—a suffocating odour which is never entirely absent, for the treatment consists in frequent cauterisation of the nerves of the back ; and, in addition, a sore has now opened on the nape of the neck which is kept powdered with opium.

On the mattresses lies a thin and wasted body, scarcely larger than a child's, so shrunken that its outline can hardly be discerned beneath the counterpane. And on the pillows a white face whose sharpened features stand out against the darker hair. The forehead is smooth, and the temples have sunken little, but the swollen eyes are hidden behind heavy lids. Two flecks of white hair running downwards to the chin mark the soft brown beard which almost hides the stiffened mouth. Illness has chiselled this emaciated face with the delicacy of a Gothic sculptor, and from the yellow ivory of its features has drawn a head of Christ. " Yes, it is the very image of the Lord. He too was a Jew," said Heine, when somebody remarked upon the semblance of his portrait by Kietz to that of the traditional Christ.

When he is not speaking the face seems like a death mask, but from time to time it comes to life and moves. The left hand slowly raises an eyelid, and the glassy stare of the blue eye transfixes whoever is present. The hands still move in spite of their half-paralysed fingers, and they are still beautiful : " Small hands, soft and slender and as white as a wafer," Gautier said. The voice alone is unimpaired ; sometimes it is reduced by weakness, but its warm deep tone remains, and its inflexions still catch every nuance of the emotions which move it.

In the darkened room, so plainly the habitation of suffering that the visitor is instinctively awed into speaking in whispers, this voice seems the only thing really alive. It is so pure of tone and clear that it hardly seems to be associated with the wasted frame lying on the bed. It almost seems like a voice from some mysterious beyond, or like a voice in a dream. It is in this voice that the flame of life still gutters up. It seems to attract strange figures to the little room, as moths are attracted by a candle. Few of the visitors are old friends of Heine's. Germans returning from Paris tell how they sought in vain for his address. For the most part, those who find their way there are creatures, not merely from the margin of society, but from the borderland between sanity and madness. So in fairy-tales does it occur that ordinary human beings pass unseeing through the fairy kingdom, whilst its mysteries are revealed without effort to the eyes of children and of mad people.

Nevertheless Heine was not neglected. " I receive visits almost every day, and hear all that is passing in the world," he wrote ; " and that means a great deal in Paris, where one is forgotten in six weeks." He urged each visitor to come again soon to see him : " You are only a few steps away from here. If you miss this opportunity of seeing me, you will soon have to make the uncomfortable journey to Montmartre Cemetery, where I have already hired an apartment with a view overlooking eternity."

Those who did come usually returned. Between them they seemed to form a synthesis of his life, as if all its heterogeneous elements arrived to group themselves around the bed of the dying man. The Judaism of his childhood was much in evidence in the shape of a little man named Weill, a former chanter in a synagogue, who insisted upon intoning for hours " the ancient lamentations of Israel in the desert, in their original purity, as they had been handed down by tradition." When the little Jew began to wail the monotonous chants in his harsh, metallic voice, the poodle, Minko, would utter a yelp, and dive beneath the bed as though he had been kicked. Soon the little Jew would forget his old ambition to become the poet of Alsace, forget that he had been a writer on the Catholic *Gazette de France*—forget everything, and ignore his audience. Even the squawking accompaniment of the parrot could not break his trance. He felt himself to be again in the crowded synagogue lit by candles, the interpreter of the lamentations of a multitude who sobbed and beat their breasts as they implored the mercy of their God.

To the sick man on his bed the dreams of early youth called up by the chanting served as a gentle drug. And when Mathilde came bursting into the room to beg M. Weill not to sing so loud, asking, in astonishment, what he was singing, Heine would reassure her by saying that they were "old German folk-songs," and, as best he could, smile his old mocking smile.

Other shades of the ghetto visited Heinrich Heine in his retreat, and amongst them was his clown and parasite, the poet journalist Louis Wihl, who had been expelled from Paderborn after the Revolution of 1848. He, too, was a weird-looking creature, all beard and shoulders, and with an enormous head placed squatly upon a stumpy body with hardly any neck at all. He would come creeping in at almost any hour of the day or night. "He is the most persistent person you can imagine," Heine complained. But Wihl's visits amused him all the same, and he would smile mischievously as he listened to the flood of comment from this innocent plunged so suddenly into the "centre of civilisation." Wihl spoke only a broken French, and that with difficulty, but his obvious bewilderment at his surroundings touched even Mathilde's heart, and his comical helplessness roused her maternal affection.

"The gloomy rabbi," as they called him, was a romantic individual to whom the strangest adventures happened in Paris. In the most prosaic circumstances imaginable he had been suddenly transformed into a comical Romeo—a Romeo whose Juliet had red hair and a sallow complexion. Louis Wihl owed the great romance of his life to his rheumatism. One day he went to M. Jacquard's shop at No. 16 Rue Saint-Jacques to buy a woollen vest. He was served by the wife of the proprietor, who had hurried, with flushed face, from her kitchen behind the shop. When the bargain was being concluded they were interrupted by the arrival of a plainly excited M. Jacquard, also from the room behind the shop, who began to whisper hurriedly to his wife. Having made his purchase, Wihl gathered up his parcel, and was preparing to leave when he found that with the package he had been handed an invitation to dinner! Nothing loth, the little man accepted, and soon found himself seated at table with an unknown company of middle-class French people. Unfamiliar as he was with the ways of the world, he felt this unexpected invitation could only be due to a desire to honour in his person the poetic art of Germany, in gratitude for which he proceeded to guide the conversation of the outfitter and his friends to the subject of the spiritual *entente* between neighbouring peoples. Only much later was he to learn that M. Jacquard, about to seat himself at table, had discovered to his horror that they were thirteen, a most unlucky number with which to celebrate his birthday. But that fact for the moment was unknown to little Wihl, whose soul expanded under the influence of good food and wine, and whose wit soon adapted itself to his company. The superstition of the dealer in underwear had already plunged Wihl into an atmosphere in which he seemed to be living a dream. He felt no surprise at all when, at the end of the banquet, a lady seized his hand and drew him aside into a corner to whisper in his ear, with warm conviction : " Monsieur, I feel sure that we were born under the same star. I cannot believe that we could have met here in this way except by a stroke of destiny. I shall think of you often during these coming days ; and, I pray you, think of me too. I am held a prisoner by wicked guardians, but I hope to come back in four weeks' time. Shall I find you here ? " There was hidden in the soul of Louis Wihl such an untapped wealth of fantasy that it never even occurred to him not to take the strange adventure at its face value. He swore discretion and fidelity to the mysterious lady, and went forth into the streets of Paris, strutting with pride. Having walked awhile and calmed his feelings he found his way to the bedside of the sick poet, who took delight in listening gravely to the most startling confessions and confidences of his strange visitors.

The Juliet of little Wihl was a poor woman from a mental

home who, on that particular day marked out for grotesque happenings, had obtained permission to visit her family. Between madness and eccentricity there is a bond ; whilst she no doubt dreamt of the encounter behind the walls of her asylum, Louis Wihl was holding forth at length to Heine in a flood of sentiment.

" He is mad himself," Heine said of Wihl, " but he has lucid moments when he is only stupid." And sometimes when Wihl had stayed too long, and it had been impossible to make him keep quiet, Heine would say to the next comer : " My hcad is buzzing, and you will find me idiotic. A friend has just left me and we exchanged ideas."

But not all the crazy folk were harmless who stumbled up the narrow stairway to where the brain-alone kept watch over a shattered body. The most alarming of these phantom visitors was Gérard de Nerval, translator of Heine's *Intermezzo* and his *Nordsee*. A German friend said of Gérard de Nerval that he was " perhaps the only man whom Heine ever sincerely loved and to whom he confided his most intimate woes." There was nothing about the French poet to proclaim his abnormality, except the haunted look in his pale blue eyes. There were moments when those eyes would, without warning, become fixed in a terrible glassy stare, and he was already undergoing treatment at the clinic of Dr. Blanche. Mathilde was afraid of him, which is not to be wondered at, since, in his crises, he had more than once thrown himself upon her with gnashing teeth. In his lucid intervals he was full of great schemes, and wanted to return to Weimar, where he found his poetic talent confirmed, Goethe having expressed enthusiastic admiration for his translation of *Faust*. He was working on his translation of Heine's poems, and at any moment, anywhere, would fish a piece of paper from the mass of books and pamphlets which always stuffed his pockets and begin to scribble on it in his small cramped handwriting. He was always ready with a wealth of argument, and used it to explain his lapses into madness and to justify, with some semblance of logic, the plunges which his brain was forced to take. But these peregrinations into the depths passed more and more beyond his control, and he was haunted by the fear that one day he would return no more to the surface. Whenever his mind was properly under control he would always appear in the little room in the Rue d'Amsterdam, and then would take place long, strange conversations between the paralytic, waging a hopeless fight against the inferno of pain which racked his body, and the man of healthy appearance who was already vowed to madness.

The moments Heine found most bearable were at dusk when, sometimes, they would prop him up with cushions in a chair, like a marionette with a broken back whose limbs fell all awry. There he would sit facing his friend, and talking. But, even so, such excursions often proved too much for him, and he would have to be replaced in bed, with livid mouth, and body drenched in sweat. He took drugs in large quantities to ease his pain—for years he had taken seven grains of morphine daily, four times the usual maximum dose.

In the intervals between their attacks, when both were able to talk, the two men would struggle with pathetic haste to exchange ideas before one or the other of them fell again. It was as if each clung desperately to the multi-coloured strands of life which still connected them with the world of the living—that world in which both had once so passionately dissipated his portion. It seemed almost as though they consciously adopted a tone of mocking cynicism, as if to drive tragedy from the room and the fear which possessed them from their hearts. Together they would recall the gayest scenes of their past lives, and evoke together the memory of such people as Mlle Clélie, an actress at the Ambigu, who had been one of Heine's mistresses in far-off days. " That little cat who talks more amusingly than anyone about her love-affairs " still came to see her one-time lover, bustling suddenly into the room to chatter frivolously before rushing off again on her gay round. When too long a time passed without her coming, Gérard would be sent to remind her that " her poor Henri waits impatiently to see her."

But it was not only the past which occupied the attention

of the two friends, portions at least of the present belonged to them, and they had work to finish, which obliged them to summon up their last remaining energy. Heine would thrust the manuscript of his poems into de Nerval's hand, urging him the while to get on with the translation. But he quarrelled as violently as ever about the words employed by the translator, indignant at every alteration necessitated by the foreign language. Fretting about his own inability to rewrite his works in French, his annoyance relieved itself in abuse of the falsifiers of his thought.

"A thousand years from now I shall be damned by reason of this horrible translation," he would scold. "'See, gentlemen,' the Professor of Ancient Literature will say in some New Zealand university, 'the period in which men still spoke various languages gave birth to a type of creature who behaved towards writers as the monkey behaves towards man. They were called translators. The task of this sub-human species was to render intelligible the work of a poet to those who could not read the poet's language. They usually behaved as monkeys do when they mimic the behaviour of men. Now in a certain country which was called Germany . . . there existed a minor poet named Heine, who betrayed obvious signs of softening of the brain by the manner in which he mimicked his own work and gesticulated so as to make them intelligible to the French.' That is what will happen, Gérard, and you will be largely to blame."

But Gérard calmly let the storms blow over, and would listen to the most appalling denunciations with a smile. Their quarrels over such matters had lasted too long for any offence to be taken. De Nerval also found in Heine the most clear-sighted critic of his work, for he still continued to write. He began a poem describing the martyrdom of doubt which assailed Jesus on the Mount of Olives, and compelled him to undergo a moral crucifixion before the physical.

He recited his poem to Heine in the presence of another witness, a young German journalist named Martin Cohn, who signed his published chronicles of a visit to Paris with the pseudonym A. Mels. This young man relates how he himself sat riveted to his chair, quite overcome by the intense atmosphere of suffering which pervaded the little room, and how de Nerval, as he declaimed, was carried away by the passion of the sentiment evoked, until he sank down in a semi-stupor. So moved was the young German that at first he scarcely noticed when de Nerval stopped, nor that his head hung downwards strangely and the fingers of his hands were jerking convulsively as though pulled by wires. Soon Heine realised that something was wrong, and, to see, lifted an eyelid with his finger. At once he murmured shortly to the visitor, " Ring."

Mathilde came to the door, and Heine, still holding his eye open, pointed at de Nerval. A short interval of anxious silence until she returned, accompanied by a thick-set individual, in whom the visitor recognised the *concierge* of the house. The man showed no surprise, and seemed to know what to do as though accustomed to it. Taking de Nerval by the hand he several times repeated the words he had been taught, treating the poet like a little child : " Do you want to help your best friend ? " De Nerval resisted like a hunted animal, shouting, " I don't know you." But the other took no notice of him, and went on : " I am sure you do. M. Alexandre Dumas has sent me. He has been taken ill near by, and has asked me to take you to him." The summons of a friend pierced even through the fog of madness in this man to whom friendship spelt lifelong service. He rose suddenly. " Dumas ill ? " he cried, in the hoarse voice which came to him during his attacks. Then he seized his hat, and rushed away, blind and deaf to all around him, a prey only to his fears.

As he went Heine's head fell back upon the pillow again, his hands stretched motionless upon the counterpane. The glassy eye remained open under its swollen lid, and the grief written on the motionless features was so overwhelming that the young visitor would gladly have offered all his clumsy strength if by so doing he could have alleviated the sick man's suffering. " And to-morrow," murmured Heine, " the poor fellow will awake and remember nothing of all this. Do you call that madness ? The pretext of the sudden illness of a friend, whom he loves like a brother, has often served me at such times. My *concierge* will take him to Dr. Blanche's clinic. To-morrow he will be about again, unless the malady has advanced greatly during the past month."

Gérard de Nerval was an almost constant visitor throughout the years in which Heine lay in his noisy prison. He was revising and polishing his translation of the poems, until at length the day arrived when he could come no more. On a misty winter morning, January 26th, 1855, they found his body in the Rue de la Vieille-Lanterne, one of those sordid back streets in which poverty and crime live cheek by jowl. He had hanged himself from the bars of a vent-hole, his feet swung above a sewer, and his body was leaning against the filthy wall. Théophile Gautier, one of his most faithful friends, hurried to the place as soon as he heard of the discovery, and relates how he found a carrion crow, hopping from stone to stone above the corpse, uttering his hoarse caw. The thought that came to the mind of the last of the romanticists was of Edgar Allan Poe and his raven : " Nevermore."

Other visitors marked for death found their way to the Rue d'Amsterdam. One of them was Delphine de Girardin, who summoned her last strength to make the journey. Heine welcomed her with the words : " Ave Delphina gratia plena, moriturus te salutat." It was many years since Madame de Girardin, then a radiant blonde beauty, had hailed the birth of romanticism by leading the applause at the stormy first performance of *Hernani.* At the time she visited Heine her wonderful complexion had changed to a deadly pallor, but in other respects her beauty had withstood the ravages of the incurable disease from which she was dying. One day a friend, who had met her at Heine's, asked Mels from what she was suffering. Mels replied : " I put the same question to Heine, and he answered that she was dying because she was a true poet."

But, side by side with this world of shadows who hovered in the twilight of the sick-room, there existed another world, the world of Mathilde and her friends, which, with boisterous vitality, redressed the balance.

The atmosphere of the sick-chamber, where poignant horror almost stifled each visitor from outside, had no effect at all on Mathilde's high spirits and sturdy nerves. It was not that she was indifferent to the agony which Heine was enduring, nor was she insensible to the tragic fate which had overtaken him in his prime, for she loved him passionately. It was as though she had an inexhaustible capacity for accepting life as it came—a fund of resignation which did not allow her compassion to run so far as to suffer in sympathy. She adapted herself to the awful drama which was being played out before her eyes as though, by ignoring it, she could deny its existence. Her obstinate, simple faith refused to let her believe that he was incurable. "God can work miracles," she would reply, with the conviction of a child, when the doctors tried to break the truth to her. She believed in miracles, and she had to believe in them if she was to keep her own appetite for life intact.

For Heine this wild cat, with her sudden explosions of hysteria, had proved "a source of bitterness which often overwhelmed him," even before his illness had laid him low. At first, when he had taken to his bed, her violent outbursts continued to turn the small apartment into an inferno of noise and argument. Heine always found an indulgent word for this *bonne enfant*, but even he was forced to admit that his angel of fiendish caprice had a disastrous effect upon his nerves. But, as the years went by, she slowly acquired the patience of a nurse and learned to keep her own health independent of the suffering she tended.

The Paris *grisette* to whom Heine had been bound by physical subjection was at heart just a little French bourgeoise, with all the deep-rooted convictions of her childhood still in her, and the prejudices which generations of peasant ancestors had helped to form. It was these principles, and the narrow dogma of her religion, which enabled her to accept without question, as a natural duty, the adversity which had overcome them. The quiet heroism which had kept her steadfast by the sick-bed was but the development of that wild passion which, on her first night of love, had caused her to swear to Heine that she would never leave him. Henri was "her man," and she remained by his side, faithful as women of her kind know how to be, even to a lover in prison. Weill himself, who, after his quarrel with Mathilde, did his best to blacken her in order to excuse himself, even Weill insisted that she was faithful to Heine with a dog-like devotion which neither Heine's infidelities nor his long years of illness ever shook. It was from this devotion that her sense of duty was born, unexpected in such a selfish woman, yet so deeply engrained that it enabled her to subdue her riotous passions.

It was her pride to remain the centre of the sick man's life, as she had been when he was well. She was only jealous of those who could rob her of this privilege—of the doctors and nurses, for example, whom Heine seemed to consider too important. She had no qualms about admitting women visitors to his side, and felt no jealousy of the friends who came to see him. Henri belonged entirely to her ; it did not occur to her to be suspicious of friendships which existed only in the spiritual sphere ; such things were trifles and quite incomprehensible—in fact, slightly ridiculous—to her. But within her own sphere she defended her interests with vehemence. She boxed the ears of Dr. Wertheim, and forbade him the house, when she overheard him say that the attention which was being given to Heine left much to be desired. Just as her crazy extravagance did not prevent her from harbouring the illusion that she was a good housekeeper, so she was ambitious to become such a good nurse for Heine that no other woman could hope to excel her. Pretty Mariette, who looked after Heine with such care, was ruthlessly dismissed. But she tolerated the dreadful old mulatto woman, whom Heine, as he wrote to Dr. Gruby, "feared more than Napoleon's enemies feared the Old Guard."

Her confidante Pauline and the mulatto took turns in nursing, but it was Mathilde herself who sat beside his bed throughout the night. He forgot the pain more easily, and slept better, when she held one of his hands in hers, and her quick eyes shone with proud possession when the deathly face sent her a half smile of gratitude.

Ever since the night in which Heine, then already half paralysed, had dragged himself from his room only to sink fainting at her door, to be carried back to bed in her strong arms, she had denied herself all other pleasures than good food and dresses. She was getting fat, the disappearance of her good looks distressed her, and she sought to make up for it by wearing expensive clothes. She often went walking with Pauline in the Champs Elysées, and would return chattering enthusiastically about all she had seen. The variety and movement of the streets always enchanted her; she was ever in the front row of any crowd which gathered, and even mixed in street fights, to the great distress of the poor invalid at home. She talked to her Henri of all the little insignificant things which happened, speaking more to herself than to him. Then she would dash off to hold a conversation with her parrot or the cat. She was always restless, always talking, and, when not actually in the room, the sound of her high-pitched voice would come to him through the walls. Heine would interrupt a conversation in order to listen, smiling, to the echo of her voice in the distance. He told Caroline Jaubert—" the Little Fairy," as Mathilde called her—that " this voice had recalled his soul at a moment when it had definitely set forth on its flight to the unknown." It was the cord to which he clung as he sank in a fit of despair, or in the confusion of his opium dreams; her piercing voice gave him the illusion of still belonging to the world of the living.

But he paid dearly for her devotion, and heavy were the sacrifices he had to make to her world of boisterous good health. To please Mathilde he invited her friends to visit her, and Alfred Meissner speaks of the little room which was proudly called the " *salon* " as being full of " a display of plates, glasses, and bottles out of all proportion to its size and their financial status." Mathilde's friends were such people as " Elise with the Flaming Eyes," and her husband Arnaud, a circus owner. Meissner has carefully recorded some of their conversations which are comical to a degree. The circus owner was one of the major trials of Heine's life during this period. This " Barnum of the Hippodrome " looked like the classic adventurer from southern lands, pale-faced and dark-haired. Wearing a broad-brimmed, long-haired felt hat, and swinging a gold-mounted cane, he would lounge to the door of the sick-room. " How are you, Heine ? " he would ask loudly, with the manners of one who feels that wealth permits him to tap the whole world on the shoulder. " My God, you look like a dead man. In all my life I never saw anyone have such trouble in dying." Then he would sigh about the weight of worry on his own shoulders, or sing the praise of his own acumen. The hippodrome enabled him, when times were good, to earn ten thousand francs a day. " I have become poet ; my brain produces the most amazing ideas ; the show is the *Arabian Nights* over again. You may well say I stuff the Parisians with marvels." The booming voice went on, droning its imbecilities, the boasting speech punctuated with loud taps of the cane against the bed-cover, each tap resounding like a blow in the sick man's splitting head.

To vary the recital about the wonders of his circus the ignoramus proudly displayed his knowledge by giving details. He spoke of Sancho Panza—" Sancho Panza, you know, is a character in a Spanish novel "—of naked women ; real houris—" for you must know, my dear Heine, that the women who people the Mohammedan Paradise are called ' houris.' " Then he would burst into his coarse laugh : " What a shame that you are ill, Heine. You could have had some fun in my circus, *mon vieux*." He believed himself to be a model of altruism in devoting part of his precious time to the cheering of this ruin of a man. He visibly swelled with pride at his own magnanimity, and the more he thought of his unselfishness the more devastating he became. " My job calls for more head-work than a poet's. And the risk there is in it ! When you write something that doesn't suit you, my dear Heine, then you have only spoilt a piece of paper. But for me it's different. If one of my ideas does not come off, I may be ruined." His latest effort was "a fête at Pekin." "You must know that Pekin is the capital of the Chinese Empire, and the mandarins are what you might call the aristocrats of the country. . . ."

The invalid listens helplessly, muttering curses in German under his breath. At last he can stand no more, and when he speaks his voice is trembling with hatred : "You heard this creature explaining to me where Pekin is, and what mandarins are. He and his ten thousand francs ! Go and ask Julius Campe what he earns with a single edition of my *Buch der Lieder*. . . ." Then he falls back on the pillows, exhausted, murmuring : "An individual as healthy as that must be half a brute."

Visitors to the sick man in the Rue d'Amsterdam grew more rare. "I have lost my friend Balzac ; that cat, George Sand, has not been near me since my illness," Heine groaned. "One after another my friends desert me, and those who remain only confirm the old proverb, that in adversity one's friends can be counted on the fingers of one hand."

In his loneliness he had already acquired sufficient objectivity to be able to add, with the bitterness of remorse : "But that proverb is double-edged, it accuses those who use it as well as those against whom it is used. It reminds me only too well that I have been short-sighted in my choice of friends."

This admission was, however, only a part of the process of reviewing his past standards which he underwent at this period. The great conversion from atheism which took place on his sick-bed was fundamentally different from the conversion of so many sceptics in the hour of death. With Heine it was not a question of returning to God on any conditions, for it was not in his nature to make a clean break with the past, or radically change his opinions. Among his contemporaries Alfred Meissner was the most perspicacious observer of the poet's life and character, and he has summed up in a sentence Heine's deeper intellectual attitude when he says : "He invariably looked at both sides of a question."

The great struggle between reason and sentiment took place in him during the long silent nights when he lay sleepless. Tortured with pain he asked why he was suffering. He demanded justice from above, the intervention of a personal God. When at last the dawn came to dissipate the nightmares of his solitary agony his lips smiled at the thought of his violent arguments with God. He tried to withstand the pressure of this evolution by appeal to his old gift of irony, but his mind returned to the problem again and again until, during these years of sickness and isolation, it came to occupy the centre of his spiritual existence. His evolution began by a simple revolt against the cruelty of destiny : " It is a tragedy such as is rarely encountered in the annals of human suffering, an unheard-of misfortune, terrifying, mad." Heine would accept no illusions as to his condition ; he steadfastly refused that opium of the incurable. He had the courage to admit to himself that there was no hope of improvement for him, and that " this abominable disease will become still more abominable as the end approaches." In order to live at all despite this absence of illusion, and not to be utterly crushed by the inexorable cruelty of his fate, he found it necessary to fit his own suffering into the general scheme of things, to give it the meaning of a trial and thus make it part of the mysterious designs of Providence.

But for all this, his religious crisis did not arise solely from " despair of the flesh." The " February Revolution " of his ideas, as he called it when writing to Laube, corresponded to the evolution of the times—the external conditions of life were being transformed at the same time as his own inner convictions. Even though his critical sense no more than partly allowed him to abandon himself to an idea, and though he was always held back by his instinct for seeing both sides, nevertheless he felt the need of a goal towards which he must strive and of a faith in which he could sincerely believe. Bound as he was to the period in which he lived, he plunged with his whole heart and mind into the struggles of his day on behalf of art, and on behalf of political and social liberty. But during the period of reaction which followed after 1848 he was constrained to part company with his times—his "Fatherland in history," as he called it—for there was no longer any place for the fighter for human liberty which he would have gone on being even had the soldier not been a paralytic tied to his bed. The *coup d'état* of December 2nd only confirmed Heine's prophecies, both in regard to the insecurity of the republican regime and the strength of the Napoleonic legend which survived in France. When Laube visited Strasbourg in 1836 he had not heard a single voice raised in favour of Louis Napoleon, only jokes and ironical remarks about him: "A new Napoleonic regime in France was considered as an impossible figment of the imagination. Heinrich Heine was at that time the only man who believed in a possible resurrection of the Napoleonic faction. A poet! and a pretentious poet at that, people said, when they spoke of his poems on Napoleon." Three years later when Laube made the acquaintance of Heine in Paris, he was amazed to hear him discuss so seriously a question which appeared merely ridiculous. But Heine persisted, telling him to go back to the provinces and listen to what the peasants were saying amongst themselves: "You call me a dreamer, but I dream with my eyes open and they see things. I tell you that only the bugles are lacking. When the trumpets sound the call they will be the trumpets of the resurrection, and the remnants of the Grande Armée will arise with all their descendants crying, 'Vive l'Empereur!' They will be there in their millions—the masses will see to that. The masses need something tangible round which to rally, and the standard of Napoleon is the only one there is. Constitutional shades of difference are too subtle for the peasant; he believes only in what he can see and his God must be a visible God."

The *coup d'état* gave Heine the personal satisfaction of having proved a sound prophet. It did more, for he saw in the return of a descendant of Napoleon some compensation for the defeat of Waterloo. Heine expressed his views on this subject when he wrote his *Confessions of a Poet*, in 1854: "It was not only the French and the Emperor who were defeated at Waterloo. The French certainly were fighting in defence of the homeland, but they were at the same time Crusaders of the Revolution, and their Emperor fought not only for his crown, but for the flag of revolution of which he was the bearer. He was the banner-bearer of Democracy just as his opponent, Wellington, was the flag-bearer of Aristocracy on the field of Waterloo. And the bad old cause of injustice, of falsehood, and the spirit of servility triumphed. It was liberty, equality, fraternity, truth, and reason—it was all humanity—which lost the Battle of Waterloo. . . . I do not need to explain that not until December 2nd, 1852, did the French people obtain full satisfaction by the staunching of the old wound to their national pride. . . . With all my heart I welcome this triumph, having felt so bitterly the earlier defeat."

But when he sent the long fragment entitled " Waterloo " to Campe, memories of the wars of liberation, in which he had been a volunteer, awoke in the heart of the publisher, and he wrote indignantly to Heine : " You appear to forget that you are a *German* writer. You insult the whole German people to its face, and you do so in defence of the French ! " When Campe insisted, Heine was forced to suppress the passage, profoundly though he himself felt the truth of it. It marked a return to the convictions of his childhood—he had turned full circle, and arrived back at his starting-point.

Thus it came about that, being no longer able to take part in questions of public interest, which had always held his eager attention, Heine was driven back upon himself, and sought in himself the answer to the riddle of existence. And this last research, so passionately undertaken, led him to the conception of a personal God.

" At the risk of being accused of softening of the brain, I will no longer conceal from you the great event which has taken place within me ; I have deserted German atheism and am about to join the company of ordinary believers," he wrote to Mignet.

From time to time his old irony would reappear : " If I could go out on crutches," he sighed one day to Meissner,

" do you know where I would go ? Why, straight to church." And when Meissner protested, incredulous, he went on : " Certainly I should go to church, where else should one go on crutches ? Of course, if I could go out without crutches, I should prefer to stroll along the gay boulevards and amuse myself in the Bal Mabille."

In his most sincere moments he denied that his conversion had to do with his illness. " The religious upheaval which has taken place in me lies entirely in the spiritual sphere," he wrote to Campe. " It is far more an act of reflection than of sentiment, and my illness has had little to do with it, of that I am quite convinced. Great and terrible thoughts have had possession of me, but they were flashes of light, not the phosphorescent reflections from a decaying sentimentality." Pathetically he continued to insist that his new faith was born of lucidity of mind. " Those who know me and see me can bear witness to the fact that my mind is not enfeebled and that my faculties are as intact as ever," he said to Alfred Meissner, seeking his confirmation. His lips hardly moved, and his face stiffened with the effort of forming the words, but his voice was clear and persuasive. " Believe me, my friend, it is Heinrich Heine on his bed of suffering who assures you, after long years of meditation, and after having read and digested all that has been said and written on the subject in every country, that he is convinced that a God exists who judges our actions, that our soul is immortal, and that there is another world in which virtue is rewarded and vice punished."

The personal God in whom Heine came to believe in spite of himself was the God who tormented Job, the same pitiless Deity whose avenging shadow had lain across his early childhood. He would remark sarcastically that " neither priest nor rabbi introduced him to God," but it was nevertheless to Jehovah that he returned ; his paganism ended by submitting to the faith of his ancestors. Heine would only admit this to his very closest friends, and then only to those of his own blood and faith. This Judaism, which he concealed so carefully from Mathilde, remained one of the few things which were sacred to him, a fact with which Campe, in a fit of temper, had once taunted him.

Once, during his illness, Heine dictated a letter to his brother Max, in which occurred the passage : " During my nights of agony I compose beautiful prayers, which I do not dictate." Then he added in his own hand, so that one of another faith should not see the confession : " Prayers which are all made to the God of our fathers." This was no mere return to an old tradition, for to him that tradition had been feeble even in childhood ; it was the instinctive part of his character which led him to Jehovah, the God who demands an eye for an eye and a tooth for a tooth. For Heine, that strict accountant of his own loves and hates, there could be no other God than He whose law was that of retaliation.

But the faith of his fathers was unable to supply him with one of the assurances of which he stood in need, namely survival after death. He pondered and argued on that question incessantly with himself during the intervals in his lonely nights when opium had brought some relief from his intolerable pain. " All my reason, all my knowledge, tells me that belief in individual survival after death is crazy. There is no trace of the idea in the Old Testament—Moses was too sane a man for that. It was the vitiated sect from which sprang Christ and Christianity which discovered immortality, along with ascetism. By my reason I am convinced of our disappearance into nothing, but my sentiments revolt at it. I cannot convince myself of it so long as I still *exist.*" Lost in these contradictions he no longer knew what position to adopt—until one day there came to him a visitor whom he hailed as the arbiter of this debate within him.

It was on an afternoon in the autumn of 1851 that Immanuel Hermann Fichte, son of the great philosopher and himself a philosopher of theism, came to see him. It was twenty-nine years since he had met Heine, and he had been trying, ever since his own arrival in Paris, to discover where he was living and had at last succeeded. Accompanied by his son he crossed the noisy, littered courtyard and climbed the narrow stairs. At the door of the apartment Fichte handed in his card. As the visitors waited they heard an agitated voice giving orders, followed by the sound of things being hurriedly put in order ; then at length they stood beside the motionless body under the thin counterpane, and looked down upon the emaciated countenance of the poet.

With his usual movement of the hand Heine raised the lid of his right eye in order to see his visitor. Fichte shuddered with pity and horror. " I found the poet's hands and mouth of a noble beauty," he writes. " It would be difficult to do justice to the finely cut lips, soft and yet vigorous, which are so perfectly arched to form that magnificent mouth." At first their conversation dragged, for Heine did not often have occasion to speak in German, and the after-effects of drugs still clouded his brain. He had to grope for scientific expressions, the titles of books escaped his memory, and he could not properly formulate his thoughts in words. " He was like a man awakened from a deep sleep who needs a few moments to collect himself before being able to concentrate his attention on the things around him." Soon, however, his faculties returned : he spoke of Socialism, of the insecurity of the Republic, of Pierre Leroux and of Proudhon, whom Fichte had just visited in his cell in the Conciergerie.

But another question was in Heine's mind under all this talk of present-day matters, and suddenly he found words to utter it : " Tell me in all sincerity whether or not you believe in our survival after death ? This problem pre-occupies me more and more since I have been tied to this bed of suffering." Who, after all, was better equipped to dissipate his doubts than Fichte, who had long studied the whole question of the relations between reason and faith, philosophy and religion, and who had published a book on the very problem which was tormenting Heine: "*The Idea of Personality and of Individual Survival?*" But Fichte knew, precisely because the blunt question concerned his own deep studies, that a plain yes or no would not satisfy Heine, and so, while answering " Yes," he was careful to add that there was scarcely time to analyse the philosophical proofs of immortality. But Heine would not accept such a summary dismissal of the subject. At last he had found someone capable of giving a rational answer to the enigma which puzzled him. "A purely physiological and psychological study," said Fichte, " divorced from any other consideration, irrefutably confirms individual survival after death." Heine seized eagerly upon this crumb of rational assurance. Here at last was something tangible to which in his doubt he could cling. He struggled to retain the sentence in his mind in order that this newly acquired guarantee of immortality should not escape him again.

Fichte was so touched by the obvious joy shown by the invalid at his answer that he continued his disquisition. To the affirmation of survival after death, which Heine so passionately wanted to hear, he added another concerning prenatal existence, of which Heine had no need and at which his individualism revolted. Heine possessed no faculty for abstract thinking ; he was accustomed to give plastic expression to his thoughts and to reduce them to clearly defined form. That he should be asked to consider himself a mere link in an eternal chain was so contrary to his instincts that his faith in the immortality of his soul came near to being lost again. This was noted drily by Fichte's son, who seems to have been quite impervious to the pathos of the scene.

But Heine would not give in so easily. Before him sat a man who seemed to hold clearly in his head the answers to problems which he himself could only obtain at the price of nerve-racking struggle. That man would shortly rise and go out again into the wonderful world of healthy, happy creatures, whilst he, Heine, would be left alone to struggle with his doubts and would never see his visitor again. There was no time to be lost, and, like a child, he did not hesitate to lay bare his desire in all its simplicity. He had discovered his personal God, now he wanted to have his God's existence confirmed by someone in authority. There were still too many things which puzzled him, for example all this subconscious mental activity of which he was so often aware and which attracted him so irresistibly. In that respect the son of the nineteenth century was seeking to open doors which the twentieth century was only to succeed in pushing ajar. He feared that this obscure world would be thrust aside as man's civilisation advanced, and that in the end the growth of human reasoning power would entirely obliterate it. For Heine that world contained a medley of ecstatic moods, in which visions, premonitions and manifestations of disembodied spirits moved and spoke to him. Could Fichte, in this all too short visit, shed some light on the confusion and contradictions of his own mind on this subject? . . .

It was a strange consultation which was held there between the hale philosopher and the paralytic abandoned by the world of the living and clinging, therefore, all the more eagerly to the world of the invisible.

When at last the door had shut behind the visitor whom he would never see again, Heine in solitude began to put some kind of order into the wealth of new ideas which had been given him. He was engaged upon the concluding chapters of a work at which he had laboured for two years—his *Romanzero*—and he still had a few pages to write so as to bring the book to the necessary length. Working with a speed of assimilation worthy of a journalist, he employed his colloquy with Fichte for the purpose, and wrote to the philosopher to tell him he was using his information "all hot." The passage on Swedenborg was also the result of newly acquired knowledge obtained at second hand and revised. It is possible that he felt this himself, for he adopted an ironical style, and embellished the dialogue with anecdotes of his own invention. He even speaks of his return "to the ancient superstition, to a personal God," in a tone which wavers between conviction and ironic pleasantry.

It was with mixed feelings that Professor Immanuel Hermann Fichte read the interpretation of his philosophical ideas in the preface to *Romanzero*. He remarked that "a waggish laugh seems to break out in almost every line of this confession, and a mocking voice murmurs 'all this is only joking.' But yet we know from Heine himself that this time it is serious." *Romanzero* does contain a new note of gravity—the first onset of his illness; the exhaustion which came from his degrading quarrel with the family ; the effects of his loneliness, of which he himself was not at first fully conscious, and the echo of old conflicts. The book still bears the imprint of his art, but already new characteristics are to be seen which were to become still more pronounced by the suffering of his last years. It contained three years of his work, a medley with connecting thread that is not easy to discern. Heine wrote to Campe of *Romanzero* : " You know that order is one of my chief characteristics." But it was a meagre harvest for three years' work. Heine did not possess the form of egoism common in sick persons for whom the body becomes the centre of the universe. " I string out a good many verses," he wrote at a time when his suffering was worst, " amongst them some which soothe my pain like magic incantations when I murmur them over to myself."

Few of these poems written in his hours of pain have survived. He had not always the strength to write them down, and used to wait until morning in order to dictate them to his secretary. And when dictated he often found them unsatisfactory. His mind worked so much through the faculty of vision that he only reached auditory perfection with the help of his eye ; to appreciate the quality of a poem he had to see it written down. With his mania for generalisation he attributed this originality to some special quality in the German tongue : " Our language is made as much for the eye as for the ear. It is plastic, and in verse the writing is as decisive as the sound."

Even when the half-blind man did succeed, with great toil, in noting down the poems which came to him during the night, they were not infrequently destroyed as bits of paper of no value by the women.

But technical difficulties were not the chief obstacle. While he was fighting with disease, his energy was sapped by the daily struggle to obtain money on which to live. " A spell has been cast upon my finances," that is his constant plaint throughout his life. He had no moment's respite from this worry, and there is hardly one of his letters in which it does not occur. He spared none of his visitors the details of his present poverty and his fears for the future. Karl Heine regularly paid the allowance, won with so much difficulty, though it is true that he had tried to reduce it. Campe, too, paid over the monthly sum due under his contract; but money ran through Mathilde's fingers like water. His illness accounted for much of the household expenses, even the "Old Guard" was paid at the rate of five francs a day. "It is expensive enough to live in Paris, but it is still more expensive to die there," Heine sighed. Truly he bought his domestic peace at the price of gold—that "*chère paix*" of which he spoke with such bitter irony. To others he made every excuse for Mathilde, and attributed her reckless extravagance to pure kindness of heart. But to his mother he wrote: "Mathilde gives me endless trouble by her incurable thriftlessness. She is really the cause of my greatest worries. This craze for spending is truly awful."

The household lived literally from hand to mouth. On one occasion the rent was forgotten until the very last moment. The faithful Pauline had to ransack every drawer in the house. But when the necessary amount had been collected from odd corners it was found that there were only a few sous left to live on. "Nobody can say I am not a poet after that," Heine would remark when telling the story.

Whenever there was no more money at all in the house, Heine would try to extract some from friends. He would use any means to gain his end, sometimes even going as far as blackmail. He threatened Karl Heine indirectly at the same time as he was writing him letters of self-abasement. To Rothschild he wrote letters which varied between the grossest flattery and the tone of the professional beggar.

To follow Heine's zigzag path in his efforts to get money is soon to come upon inelegance and even trickery. The most astonishing thing about his elaborately constructed webs of intrigue is the fact that they were so crude and blatant that the most dull-witted could not be deceived by them. Mathilde, with her common sense, was right when she once answered a friend who was exclaiming at Heine's subtlety: "Lui! il fait semblant d'être malin." In all practical matters he did indeed only " pretend to be shrewd " ; he was, as Campe bluntly said, " pitifully stupid " as soon as he had anything to do with financial matters. His contempt for those who did succeed in that respect was such that he judged them to be more stupid than the most stupid amongst them ever could have been.

Heine's excuse for his constant appeals to others for financial help was that the inadequacy of his own preparation for the battle of life gave him the right to expect compensation. This point of view—that art should be an exclusive profession in which the successful artist should be placed above monetary cares—was far in advance of the period in which he lived. In this respect, also, Heine was born too soon ; the harsh criticisms so often levelled at his memory on account of his financial shortcomings leave out of account the difference of opinion on such matters between his times and our own. His importunate appeals to Campe were the logical outcome of his view as to the nature of artistic work. He saw in Campe the usurer of his art, the pedlar of the fruits of his mind. But if Heine envisaged the relations between a successful author and his publisher in the light of the next century, Campe, for his part, did not even rise to the level of his own period.

The dissensions between Heine and Campe are perhaps the darkest chapters of his difficult years. There were endless arguments, more painful even than the friction with his family in Hamburg, certainly more unnecessarily cruel for the sick man than the bargainings of Karl Heine about his allowance. Neither Salomon nor Karl had ever pretended to possess any realisation of the unique value of the artist. Campe, however, knew it, not only by the pecuniary success of his earlier publications, but also by his instinctive *flair* for artistic work of high quality.

During three years Heine wrote long letters to Campe telling him of his suffering and his worries ; and during the whole of those three years, from April 1848 to July 1851, they remained unanswered. Considering Campe as the most reliable of his friends, he entrusted him with the mission of breaking the news of his illness to his sister, who did not realise its gravity. He implored Campe to help him, tried to arouse his curiosity as a publisher, begged and threatened in turn, but all in vain. Campe paid the bills which Heine was entitled to draw upon him, but remained barricaded behind his wall of silence. Heine recalled the moral debt he owed him : " You are seriously affecting my literary interests, already you have caused me irreparable loss." That Campe recognised the truth of this is shown by a letter which he wrote to Adolf Stahr : " In not replying to his letters for three years I deprived literature of several books. I deplore that, for nobody lost more by it than myself." The only reason he gave for his silence was that " Heine had allowed himself to write things to me which irritated me." For having treated in such heartless fashion a man who was virtually dying, a poet for whom he had the greatest respect, a man whom he called his friend and one whose charm cast a spell over him each time they met (" Heine is an absolute angel, who recognises and is careful not to offend my sensibilities "), Campe could find no better excuse than this arrogant pretension : " I merely claim the right to act after my own fashion when the fancy takes me, just like anybody else."

Then suddenly, as if his spite had spent itself or he had judged the lesson sufficient, he appeared one day in the Rue d'Amsterdam. Breathing heavily, but smiling broadly, his corpulent person appeared at the door of the second-floor apartment. The servant who opened to his knock recognised by the high-buttoned redingote, white silk scarf, and unusual hat that here was one of those Germans to whom her instructions were to refuse admission : " Monsieur is so ill ; he can see nobody, it is useless to announce you."

" Mademoiselle," replied the smiling Campe in his flowery old-fashioned French, " there is no rule without its exception. Be so kind as to hand him my card."

Campe made no allusion to the gulf which had been opened between them by his long silence. After years of separation he picked up the conversation where it had been dropped at their last meeting, and proceeded to fill the small, dark, room with his comfortable vigorous personality, as though his presence there was in itself the most eloquent of explanations. Not a muscle of his face moved as he noted the appalling physical change which had come over Heine in so short a time. Campe certainly demonstrated the toughness of his nerves by remaining unmoved in the presence of such terrible suffering. He behaved towards Heine as though he was dealing with a man in ordinary health, and the invalid, who was usually only too well aware of the effect of his appearance upon visitors, was able for a few moments to entertain the illusion that he was still as other men were.

The first question which came to his lips was, " How is my mother ? " It is not the poet who speaks, the poet who for years had been waiting the opportunity to appear again before his public ; it is not the man consumed with worry for whom the presence of Campe is an augury of better times : it is the stricken son who still plays at being in good health for the sake of his old mother. Campe gave him warm greetings from all the family, though his tough gaiety was surely a poor conductor of the finer sentiments. Then, without further delay, he came straight to the reason for his visit : " In Germany, just now, we are liable to have our houses searched, and I should like to know, if such a visit were made to Heinrich Heine in Paris, whether something might not be found."

As an experienced man of business Julius Campe knew that generosity sometimes paid for itself. He offered Heine 6,000 marks for the collection of poems to be published under the title *Romanzero*. Twelve thousand francs appeared a fortune to the man who, shortly before, had been obliged to borrow 600 marks from his mother. He was unable to restrain his joy : " The great Goethe never received so much for all the poems published in his lifetime ! And a poor invalid like myself, who is not even an Excellency, can win such a victory over the old fox ! "

For nine days Campe was constantly with Heine. He discussed the smallest details of the coming book with him, and then departed, happy and satisfied. "Everything has been settled splendidly between us, and in an atmosphere of friendship and affection," he announced complacently.

Heine himself was not sure of the exact worth of *Romanzero*. His capacity for judging it had been affected by the difficulties encountered in its production—material as well as spiritual difficulties. He had been obliged to dictate the whole work to young Hildebrand, "that Schlemihl," who watched with intelligent sympathy over the painful birth of the new work. "My new poems possess neither the artistic perfection, the spiritual substance, nor the richness of my earlier works; but the subjects are more colourful, and perhaps, too, the method with which they are treated renders them more intelligible to the general public." Campe, however, knew better. He had the poems read aloud to him by his readers, and as they read a smile of satisfaction spread across his face, and his lips repeated the words in silence. "There is not a gourmet in the most exclusive restaurants of Hamburg," said Rudolf von Gottschalk, "who derives more voluptuous pleasure from the finest oysters and the best of wines than does Campe from the verses of the *Romanzero*." When the reading was over, Campe slapped his leg gleefully, declaring that the new book was both "real genius and a good investment."

If the book is read with knowledge of the conditions in which it was written, it seems as though all the pleasures which Heine had been forced to abandon—colour, travel, adventure—had returned to his mind with redoubled intensity. Much that, to normal sight, is lost in the detail of the everyday scene, appeared to this half-blind invalid with all the clearness of things passionately loved, now lost for ever. The malady which kept Heine a prisoner in semi-darkness turned him into a painter. Behind the closed eyelids such vivid pictures had been formed that, once read, they remain for ever in the memory; as, for example, the impression of Spanish breastplates digging into the naked flesh of the Indians in the hand-to-hand fighting of the Mexican War . . . or the scars, "monuments of pleasure," which enabled Edith Swan-Neck to recognise the corpse of King Harold.

To this new faculty of vision was added also a new form of sensibility, expressed by an intense sense of pity and a glorification of suffering. In spite of all differences the Romances harmonise with the Hebraic songs by reason of the tragic end common to both. *Romanzero* is the hymn-book of the underdog, the chronicle of creatures who have failed and been sacrificed. Each of the Romances contains the lesson which Heine puts into the mouth of the King of the Moors :

Nicht allein der Triumphator,
Nicht allein der sieggekrönte
Günstling jener blinden Göttin,
Auch der blut'ge Sohn des Unglücks.

Auch der heldenmüt'ge Kämpfer
Der dem ungeheuren Schicksal
Unterlag, wird ewig leben
In der Menschen Angedenken.

" Not the triumphant victor alone, not alone the favourite, victory crowned, of that blind goddess, but the blood-stained son of misfortune, and the heroic fighter who was defeated by tremendous fate, will live for ever in human memory."

With this book Heine became the singer of grief, as he had in the *Book of Songs* been the singer of love. And to paint sorrow he used sumptuous colours, just as he had done before for love. Only now he used them more simply and directly, and with more striking effect. Just as generations of young lovers found themselves portrayed in the *Book of Songs*, so victims of fate were to find in *Romanzero* a confirmation of the tragic verdict that it is the best who succumb and the wicked who triumph.

There is no more sentimentalising over trifles. The easy tears of Heine's youth are dried, and stark tragedy stares dumbly from every sentence ; timeless wisdom of unchanging value stands before us in every simple phrase :

Hat man viel, so wird man bald,
Noch viel mehr dazu bekommen.
Wer nur wenig hat, dem wird
Auch das wenige genommen.

" Those who have much will soon have much more, those who have little will be deprived of even that little."

" Never in living memory has a book known such success from the first moment of publication, and it is a volume of poems," wrote Meissner enthusiastically. Julius Campe had not been deceived ; he had scented the amazing novelty of the work, and it was that which had appealed to the public beyond his wildest dreams.

But for the invalid of the Rue d'Amsterdam the success of *Romanzero* brought only a brief respite. He was overcome with longing for the open country, for green fields and sunshine. But Mathilde did not wish to leave the city, for her the animation of a great town had become a necessity of life. She too was living very much alone, since her quick temper had brought about a break, not only with Alexandre Weill, but also with her old friend Elise Arnaud. When at length she gave way to the entreaties of her invalid, there remained no money to enable them to move to the country ; financial troubles again beset them.

Once more Heine made application to Campe, feeling himself justified in doing so by the success of *Romanzero.* But he only revived their earlier quarrel in still harsher form. He charged the clumsy Max to bring pressure to bear upon Campe, and to this end thought out an absurdly cunning scheme in which his other brother Gustav, the editor-in-chief of the official *Wiener Fremdenblatt,* was to have played the part of possible rival to Campe. But Gustav was not content to play second fiddle to anyone. He seized the opportunity of a chance visit to Hamburg to enter into personal negotiations with Campe. The stolid business man was treated to a lively display of flowery eloquence, and, when he retreated behind the letter of his contract, Gustav replied : " What is a contract ? " He seized the end of his cravat, knotted it to the right, and said : " That is a contract." Then he untied it, and knotted it again on the left, exclaiming in triumph, with a fatuous smile : " And that is also a contract, adaptable as you could wish."

Campe parried the childish diplomacy of the " brotherly congress " with weapons no more honest than their own. It was always Heine's misfortune to awaken meanness in others by his own attitude. Campe avenged himself indirectly by slandering the poet to his friends, and by inspiring attacks upon him in the Press by people whom he later disavowed. Years passed thus in useless conflict.

It was now six years since Heinrich Heine had been carried up to the miserable little room in the Rue d'Amsterdam. Friends fell away, and solitude embraced him more and more. His agony was proving too long drawn out : " The precious sympathy of my contemporaries melts as time passes," he remarked, with a disillusioned smile. When Berlioz on one occasion found his way to him, Heine exclaimed : " What, somebody to visit me ? Berlioz was always original ! "

Paris in the summer of 1854 was desolate and deserted. Another wave of cholera from the south threatened the city. The rich fled to Baden-Baden or the banks of the Rhine, and the fell disease swept the streets clear of all but a few poor wretches, for the most part already marked for a horrible death. But the sick man realised but little of what was happening outside. He was hard at work preparing a collection of his political correspondence published under the monarchy of July. It seemed as though death did not know how to capture this man, who yet was only half alive.

One day the house in the Rue de Milan which backed upon that of Heine, caught fire. Inside on the courtyard, behind drawn blinds, the danger was not at first noticeable. Suddenly the crackle of flames was heard through the walls, and the room became filled with a stifling cloud of smoke. Mathilde wrung her hands and screamed for help—if the fire spread but a little farther the paralytic would be burnt alive. Neighbours hurried to their aid, and the invalid was carefully carried downstairs, on his mattress, and laid on the floor of the *concierge's* dark little room, to wait until the fire was overcome. He soon found himself surrounded by a crowd of curious people, craning their necks to see the " man wrapped in his shroud " about whom a legend had grown up. But the chattering curiosity of the crowd of idlers became stilled at the sight of the agony-ridden face with its closed eyes, and, with hushed voices, those who had come to stare asked what help they could give. For the space of a few minutes Heine found himself once more in the heart of the French people. When the fire had been quenched, there were many more strong arms than were needed to bear the wasted body back to the room, which closed once more upon him like a tomb.

A voice still lived amidst the solitude. The unspoken word of the poet rose the more strongly as life died down within him. The eternal question of the reason for life's injustice obsessed the tortured brain, and expressed itself in words of such harsh bitterness that they wound the reader :

Woran liegt die Schuld? Ist etwa
Unser Herr nicht ganz allmächtig?
Oder treibt er selbst den Unfug?
Ach, das wäre niederträchtig.

Also fragen wir beständig,
Bis man uns mit einer Handvoll
Erde endlich stopft die Mäuler—
Aber ist das eine Antwort?

" Whose is the guilt? Is not our Lord almighty? Or does he work the mischief himself? Oh, that would be too despicable. So we ask continually until our mouths are stopped with a handful of earth at last. But is that an answer? "

Heine himself knew the effect of his words : " German poetry has never uttered such things ; it has never done so because no other poet has ever been in such a situation."

" Yes, I know, it is beautiful, horribly beautiful," he

smiled at Meissner with his bloodless lips, as the latter was going through his last poems. " It is like a wail from the tomb "—a spasm of cramp shot through his brain, and a terrifying pallor took all semblance of life from his features. " One who is buried alive cries in the darkness " ; pain strangled his voice and great drops of sweat stood upon his forehead, but his will-power forced out a few more words : " It is a corpse which speaks, or—or "—the voice dropped still lower, to an almost inaudible whisper—" or the grave itself. . . ."

CHAPTER XII

THE PASSION FLOWER

"The motto of my life is: 'Never more.'"
(From a conversation with Fanny Lewald)

"I AM ENJOYING a moment of triumph," wrote Heine to his publisher in September 1854. "My article in the *Revue des Deux Mondes* [" The Confessions of a Poet "] has caused a great sensation. As the editor of the review said to me, no essay has ever made such a stir."

This echo from the outside world came as an immense consolation to the lonely man. In April 1855, when he published the French edition of the collection of essays entitled *Lutèce*, he wrote with satisfaction and, perhaps, a touch of bitterness to Philarète Chasles : " *Lutèce*—the book of which all Paris talked for eight days . . . imagine engaging the attention of Paris, the centre of the world of fashion, for a whole week ! But you know it is a prodigious honour for a poor German who tended pigs in his own country ! "

But for these last literary successes Heine would have been completely lost to view. A German visitor who searched all Paris to find him at the time reported that he " had the impression Heine was already dead in so far as society was concerned." Plenty of people knew his old addresses, but he had moved too often and the *concierges* were not helpful to those who wished to find him. The well-known men of letters of the day did not know him—a new generation had risen to fame—and as for his old friends, their consciences were uneasy at their neglect.

" I perceive that in this light-hearted country everything is subject to mortality, and friendship here is by no means lifelong," Heine wrote bitterly to Michel Chevalier, whom he once called the best and noblest of his friends.

It was a great event for him when, one day early in 1855,

Béranger came to see him. They had not met for twenty-four years, and the old man of seventy-five had come in on foot from Le Marais, in spite of the winter cold and fog. He arrived " as full of life as a Paris street-arab," and a woman friend who chanced to be with Heine was amazed at his vigour and pretended not to believe that Béranger was more than sixty. " The reply the singer made to her cheered me for a whole day," wrote Heine to Alexandre Dumas, " for in that half-mournful, half-mischievous tone he has he drawled : ' You are wrong, madame, and if it were possible for you to allow me to produce proof, I should most certainly prove to you that you are wrong and that I really am seventy-five. . . .' The wicked old rascal ! " Heine added. The story so amused Dumas that he went about repeating it to all and sundry, until finally Béranger himself heard it. At first he was much annoyed, but in the end his pity for the solitary invalid made him forgive him and he went again to see him.

The Great Exhibition of 1855 brought many German visitors to Paris, some of whom remembered Heine's illness and sought him out. Amongst them were Adolf Stahr, who had one day nicknamed him " the dying Aristophanes," and his wife, the novelist Fanny Lewald, who was one of the first feminists in Germany.

On a November afternoon Fanny came alone to see the poet. She found his condition much changed for the worse since their last meeting four years earlier. She remarks upon the trembling of the hand which raised the fallen eyelid and the racking cough which shook his paralysed body. In this talk with her he did not make his usual effort to be amusing to a visitor in order to prove that he was still the same Heine. He could always talk more easily with women than with men, and to Fanny Lewald he spoke openly about his condition. " It is impossible for anyone to imagine my state. The motto of my life is : ' Never more. . . .' Have you ever thought how cruel those words can sound ? " Overcome with pity, Fanny Lewald did not reply, and Heine continued in his low, weak voice : " Never to walk again ! Never again to see ! Never, never ! " His voice rose almost to a cry. " It is like a roller coming slowly towards you, nearer and nearer, crushing everything that lies in its path until all at once it is upon you, and all is over."

But the end towards which his poor life dragged in terror and revolt did not come upon him " like a roller," by a steady decline of his physical and intellectual strength, as had seemed likely in the Rue d'Amsterdam. A sudden revival roused him from his torpor, as if a reflection of his former life had fallen across the darkness of his agony, only to be snuffed out again in eternal night.

It happened several months after he had left his uneasy tomb in the Rue d'Amsterdam. A great deal of diplomacy had been necessary to persuade Mathilde to leave the centre of Paris, and it had been necessary also to find money for the removal. But at last, in April 1854, Heine was installed near the outskirts of the city, at No. 51 Grande Rue des Batignolles. It was a house with a large sunny garden perfumed with flowers. The invalid lay out of doors in the sunshine ; his eyes were closed against the light, but his waxen hands slowly opened and shut, as though to catch and seize the life-giving warmth around him. For Mathilde the big house was at first like a new toy ; she filled it with her usual busy clatter, and when he called to her she would answer : " Meine Frau est très occupée . . . " so that he smiled, content. But hardly had they settled than she tired of the place ; the house without others in it weighed upon her and she felt too far from her beloved Champs Elysées. Two months later the sick man was again transported across Paris on a stretcher. But this time he refused to be immured in a room over a courtyard ; he wanted sunshine, and to be away from the noise of neighbours. They settled in an apartment on the fifth floor at No. 3 Avenue Matignon. The small bedroom had a balcony shaded by an awning and protected from the wind, and there, on warm autumn days, they spread his mattress. He would have his head raised on cushions so that he could see a little of what happened in the street below. The daylight hurt his eyes, but in spite of this he borrowed glasses from Mathilde in order the better to observe the tiny square of life which was visible to him through the railings of the balcony. For years he had been unable to look upon passers-by, and he watched eagerly the ladies in crinolines who came to buy cakes from a baker's boy standing opposite. " And then a little dog came trotting along and cocked his leg against a tree. After that I gave the glasses up and did not wish to see any more, so much did I envy that dog."

" The dying Aristophanes " had no more desire to see or hear ; he shut himself up in himself with the poor remnants of life still remaining in his body. All through the winter months he worked at the revision of his *Vermischte Schriften*, his last work. Everyday life went on as usual while he suffered so tragically. An atmosphere devoid of all sentimentality, and almost cheerful, reigned in the apartment and astonished his visitors.

Erstorben ist in meiner Brust
Jedwede weltlich eitle Lust,
Schier ist mir auch erstorben drin
Der Hass des Schlechten, sogar der Sinn
Für eigne wie für fremde Not—
Und in mir lebt nur noch der Tod!

"All vain and worldly joy is dead in my breast. Dead is also my hatred of evil and even the sense of my own or of others' distress. And death alone lives in me ! "

And just at this moment, as he sought in vain to rouse his failing strength, life returned to him, bringing with it all its joys and all its torment.

In June 1855 a young woman climbed the stairs to Heine's apartment in order to leave some music composed for his poems by one of his great admirers, Baron Vesque von Puttlingen of Vienna.

She handed the parcel to the servant and was about to go when Heine, overhearing a conversation outside, rang the bell impatiently and told them to bring the lady in.

He was accustomed to receive visits from women ; they

were more faithful than his men friends. Caroline Jaubert often came to see him, looking more than ever like a little porcelain figure. Sometimes, too, came Princess Belgiojoso, who had just returned from her long stay in the Orient. But Cristina had changed much ; she had never recovered from the horrible wound on the neck which her oriental servant had given her. Her head now hung down upon her chest, like a broken flower. Age and troubles had destroyed her mysterious divinity ; she was now a sister in suffering, like Heine himself ; a creature hounded by life.

There came also to the poet's side a whole procession of fallen aristocrats—German princesses turned bigot after a life of gaiety, who bore their illustrious names like notice-boards amid ruins. As Heine said, he received the whole "princely demi-monde," and he sarcastically remarked that he was surrounded only by *déclassés*.

The young woman who came into his room on that June afternoon, knocking herself, as she entered, against the screen which protected his bed, seemed to him the very essence of life in comparison with the way-worn faces to which he was accustomed. She also held, for him, the charm of the unknown, the fugitive grace for which his roving eye had ever sought in earlier days, as he walked along the boulevards or under the arcades of the Palais-Royal. Now, more than ever, he had need of the admiration which the unknown evinced, with conviction and yet withal so discreetly ; he felt the effect of her presence in every fibre of his broken nerves. When at length she took her leave, he asked her to come again to see him, using one of those seductive little phrases the secret of which he knew so well and which had always proved so irresistible to women.

The stranger came more and more often ; the miracle of an unknown woman in his life had again been realised. He knew nothing of her, neither where nor how she lived. Only later did she tell him something of her story, a mixture of scraps of experience and melodramatic romance the truth of which seemed to be demonstrated by its obvious gaps. He did not even know her name, for the name she bore at the moment was only one of many pseudonyms adopted by her in the course of her life.

In this year of 1855 she was known, however, as Elise de Krinitz; "a fine-sounding Prussian name; the French particle fits it marvellously," as her ex-lover Alfred Meissner sarcastically remarked. To Heine, in the darkness of the sick chamber, she appeared almost a young girl. Little brown curls threw fleeting shadows across her vivacious features, and drew attention from their irregularity and the contrast between the queer little upturned nose and her large mouth and big, strong teeth. She had transparent blue eyes, quick and intelligent, eyes which seemed to have seen much and were therefore not easily cowed. In general her appearance reflected the inner tension in which she lived, always watchful for the effect she was producing. When she smiled, she had the charm of gentle melancholy, but on the rare occasions on which her looks were uncontrolled her face seemed tired and almost haggard.

"She had no particular charm of feature," says Alfred Meissner, "Heine made the lady's acquaintance ten years later than I had done, and in the meantime the seduction of her beauty had gone." When, as Elise de Krinitz, she came into Heine's life, she claimed to be of Swabian origin, and he once wrote to her that she had the dainty grace of a Swabian buttercup. But her Swabian origin is denied by all who knew her. One day she said she was born at Dresden. When she died she was registered as coming from Hungary, but it seems that she was a native of Prague. One of her friends knew her as Mlle von Belgern, but later, when she had become the mistress of Taine and wrote the widely read story of her life, she used the name Camille Selden.

She had made the acquaintance of Heine's faithful friend, Alfred Meissner, in a train between Paris and Le Havre in 1845, and had fallen a victim at once to the charm of the young Austrian's artistic appearance and delicate manners. Even then she had lived abroad so long that she spoke her native German with a slight French accent; the encounter with Meissner awoke chords in her memory. But the affair lasted only a few hours, for Meissner was leaving France, and the unknown lady, who called herself Margot, gave him a little ring as a souvenir by which to remember her. Four years later Alfred Meissner came across her again in Paris. She appeared suddenly in his room in the modest hotel in which he was staying in an outlying quarter, and threw herself laughing into his arms.

She was the personification of the woman who abandons herself entirely to the affair of the moment, living with such intensity in the present that neither past nor future seems to exist for her. But her happy prattle ceased immediately as soon as her impatient lover sought to penetrate her mystery. With smiling tenacity she would lapse into silence, refusing to betray even her name to him. Meissner had been much intrigued by her, and kept asking himself what could have brought her to him. He surmised that she had been abandoned by her lover, or that she had run away, perhaps, from a respectable family, or from her husband.

Meissner returned to Austria ; years passed, and the joyous adventure had faded almost from his memory. Then he found himself again abroad, this time in London, a voluntary exile from the persecutions of Austrian reaction. Passing one day down Regent Street at the time of day when it is filled with well-dressed women bent on shopping expeditions, he suddenly saw Margot. She was stepping out of a magnificent carriage, the door of which was held open for her by a footman in livery. She was accompanied by an imposing old lady, and was moving across the pavement to a jeweller's shop when Meissner barred her passage, with arms outstretched and a happy cry of surprise. The young woman eyed him with icy pride : " You are mistaken, sir. I do not know you." Margot was absorbed in a new rôle, and had adapted herself to perfection to another stage in her varied career.

The joy of acting combined with an atmosphere of mystery was the element in which Camille Selden chose to live. She detested and feared the curiosity of those who might seek to ferret out her past. When, after the death of Heinrich

Heine, she decided to forsake her incognito and to bask in the glory of having been the last love of a great poet, she still strove desperately to maintain intact the veil which shrouded her earlier existence. It was almost with a note of horror that she implored Karpeles, the biographer of Heine, " to protect her from indiscretions."

She too had something of the hunted animal in her. The constant contrast between the surrender of herself and her flight is to be explained by her origin as well as by her temperament. She was the illegitimate daughter of a governess, one of those poor women who live on the fringe of others' lives, surrounded by luxury in which they have no part, moving from one strange home to another until they come at last to lose their own identity, ending their days the prey to vain and shadowy regret, unless some big adventure has chanced to sweep them for a moment from the mediocrity of their existence. As the daughter of such a woman Camille Selden had early known the bitterness of a false position, and the pitiful struggle to acquire at least some semblance of respectability. When she crossed the threshold of Heine's sick-room, an acute observer might have seen upon the face of the " Swabian buttercup " the traces of a life of wide experience.

Part of the story of her life she told to Heine in the course of long afternoons spent at the bedside of the man " whose body was a battlefield of pain." She told it gently and with the restraint and dignity which she thought she owed to her aristocratic descent and to the great tragedy. When she was eighteen years old she married a Frenchman, who, after a few months of passionate love-making, and when her dowry had been spent, wished to get rid of her, and to this end employed a means more common in cheap novelettes than in everyday life. He took his wife to London, where she was sent on a visit to a distinguished-looking house, which, after her husband's departure, she discovered to be a private mental home. She was so overcome that for several weeks she was deprived of speech. Like many another of Heine's *déclassées*, she would talk about her first tragedy ; but of her later adventures, amongst which her meeting with Meissner was perhaps only an episode, she would say nothing. They were more difficult to clothe with romance, or at least she could not draw from them the tender picture of herself which she wished to give the dying man.

Nor does it matter whether she was a martyr or a mere adventuress. Neither her past nor her future are important. What matters is that in the little time she dwelt in Heine's life she fanned its last spark into flame, becoming at once his last despair and his last great enchantment.

Though already apart from life, his physical suffering reminded him only too well that he still belonged to the world of the living. His great fear throughout his last years was that his disease would reach his brain. He read every book on medical science which he could procure ; he had studied endless tomes on the physiology, anatomy, and pathology of his complaint, and at the end could state with a sorry smile : " My studies have served me little. At best I shall be able to give lectures in Paradise to prove to my audience that the doctors on earth know little about curing diseases of the spinal column." He was intensely interested in other cases similar to his own. When Caroline Jaubert returned from a visit to Thierry, he deluged her with questions. " Can he sleep ? Does he eat ? How does he work ? " But above all, in an agony of suspense : " Has he really still retained all his intellectual faculties ? " The fear of madness choked him ; all those witty sallies which he displayed to visitors were perhaps nothing more than an effort to prove to others, and to himself, that his mind was not impaired.

In meinem Hirne rumort es und knackt,
Ich glaube, da wird ein Koffer gepackt,
Und mein Verstand reist ab—o wehe !
Noch früher als ich selber gehe.

" There is a stirring and a cracking in my brain. In my head are noises as though a trunk were being packed there. I fear my reason will go, alas, before my body has gone."

He was slipping then towards the deepest pit of all his suffering ; his life was so bare of joy that he no longer even dared to express the hopes with which he had still played during the first years of his illness.

Noch einmal, eh' mein Lebenslicht
Erlöschet, eh' mein Herze bricht—
Noch einmal möcht' ich vor dem Sterben
Um Frauenhuld beseligt werden.

" Once again, before my life's light is extinguished, before my heart breaks—once again, before I die, let me be blessed by love of woman."

This joy to which he aspired, whilst hardly daring to hope for it, came about at the same time as a last supreme revolt against his destiny. Instead of the dreamy tenderness, " the gentle warmth of friendship between souls," which he had thought to bring him the last miracle, he became aware of an acute sharpening of his senses and a sudden return of physical desire, in awful contrast with the utter impotence of his body. As Mouche leaned towards him (he called her thus on account of a seal she always used, in which a fly was engraved) his paralysed fingers would tremble with desire to caress her. His letters—he wrote often to her in the intervals of her visits—are short and abrupt, but burn with passion. Most of them are in French, and often they end : " Je pose une empreinte vivante sur les traits suaves et quelque peu souabes," and then the cry, " If I were a man, that sentence would end in less platonic fashion." Mouche listened to the words he murmured to her in the darkened room—words of passion, stifled with emotion. Overcome with pity for him, she could only strive to make him understand that love which was restricted to the spiritual sphere was also beautiful. But the dying poet would not listen. In bitter self-mockery he mumbled in reply :

Worte, Worte, keine Taten!
Niemals Fleisch, geliebte Puppe,
Immer Geist und keinen Braten
Keine Knödel in der Suppe.

" Words, words, no deeds ! Never any meat, dear doll ; always spirit and no roast, no dumplings in the soup."

He awaited the coming of Mouche with the impatience of one who has nothing else in the world to wait for and who is acutely conscious of the fact that time is slipping by. The intervals between his crises grew shorter and shorter, and more and more often was he obliged to write his desperate little notes begging Mouche to postpone her visit until the morrow on account of the pain he was enduring. But when she did not appear at the expected moment he would fall into a frenzy of impatience, starting up automatically at each ring of the bell, only to fall back again, panting and exhausted, upon the pillows. During one sleepless night which followed upon such an afternoon of waiting he wrote:

Lass mich mit glühnden Zangen kneipen
Lass grausam schinden mein Gesicht,
Lass mich mit Ruten peitschen, stäupen—
Nur warten, warten lass mich nicht!

"Let me be pinched with glowing tongs, let my face be cruelly flayed, let me be whipped with rods, only do not let me wait!"

This last revolt of the pain-racked body seemed to revive every sensual memory, even those of his childhood. It was as if the spirit of passion had descended upon his bed of torment, so that the dying brain could think of nothing but his past sensual pleasures. The verse written during this last ghastly resuscitation is the most coarsely outspoken that he ever wrote. It had often been possible before to reproach his disrespect for the conventional moral code; but now he surpassed himself in audacity of language, as if to make up for the lost years in which his body had failed to respond to any appeal of his senses. Gone was the ascetic martyr of the Rue d'Amsterdam, who had destroyed poems in his desire to weed all poisonous plants from his garden; gone was the poor sick Jew who sought return to his God, and resigned himself to the incomprehensible designs of Providence. Once more the eager pagan in him was awake, panting hoarsely in the stanzas of "Citronia" and the "Teleology." "I am a dead man athirst for the most living of life's pleasures."

This revolt used up the remnants of his strength. There were other, more domestic difficulties, too. Mathilde was jealous. Mouche was not accepted by her with the stolid calm which greeted other women visitors of Heine. Her woman's instinct told her that this " secretary " whom he averred to be so necessary to his work was merely a disguise for the dangerous enemy who would snatch what remained of her Henri's love away from her. Mouche, she felt in all her bones, was not of that class of intellectual friend whose presence she tolerated with indifference. The sick man's acting did not deceive her at all. His general disquiet, the feverish impatience with which he waited for the bell to ring, the very tone of his voice, all said too plainly that her long and undisputed sway over him had ended. She defended her position by every means her shallow brain could think of. With her inborn distrust of all that was foreign, she tried to persuade Heine that Mouche was a Prussian spy, recalling his former fears about hirelings of the reactionaries. She went off into fits of temper, and implored him to send the young woman away. But for Mathilde, Heine now felt no more than a little tender indulgence and an almost paternal consideration for her future. That spectre still haunted his long nights of insomnia ; he saw his poor, helpless lamb wandering unprotected in that worst of deserts, the great city of Paris, " the angels' hell, the paradise of devils." But all his solicitude was no more than the ashes of his past love for her.

Mathilde lived on in her own house like a queen dethroned. She would not deign even to reply to Mouche's friendly greeting ; an evil look would come to her face as soon as she heard her enemy's step approach, and she would at once leave the sick-chamber. She who in former times had so strangely tolerated infidelities which were far less platonic, had, in the course of her years of supremacy, acquired her own ideas concerning her rights as a wife, and those she clung to with a childish but fierce tenacity. She felt the power of Mouche upon her husband and she did not dare to forbid her the house, as formerly she had done with visitors whom she disliked. But outside the sick-room

Mouche was not admitted. Despite all Heine's supplications or his angry demands, Mouche never once stayed to eat at their table ; that last symbol of her rights at least Mathilde defended successfully. The two women continued to confront each other in the small apartment, and the atmosphere around the dying man was charged with hatred. In the book which Mouche wrote after Heine's death her sole comment upon Mathilde is : " It would be idle to seek to transform into the heroine of an idyll one whom the poet himself never wished to make an idyllic personality."

The atmosphere of tension was relieved by a visit which Heine had long awaited, but which nevertheless would have been more welcome to him at any other time—that of his sister Charlotte, who was accompanied by Gustav. With tense nerves, Heine awaited her arrival, and before the bell began to ring he despatched Mathilde to bring his sister to him, so that not one moment of her precious company should be lost !

The passing years had dealt kindly with Lotte ; she still retained the look of dainty grace which her brother so admired. She appeared so young, in fact, that Béranger, who met her one day at the poet's bedside, enquired if she was the new reader-secretary, Mouche, whom literary circles already spoke of as his last consolation. " Certainly not," said Heine, slightly embarrassed ; " you must have a fly in your bonnet, *cher maître*. This is my sister."

For days and nights together Charlotte remained at the sick man's side. Heine believed that some magnetism flowed from her delicate fingers, and under her touch his pain seemed to find relief. She was not dismayed by the enmity which lay within the narrow walls of the apartment. But Gustav augmented the tension which already existed between Mouche and Mathilde, for he saw in the latter the source of all his brother's troubles, his financial difficulties, and even his illness, and he made no effort to conceal his feelings. " Come quickly," Heine wrote to Mouche ; " my brother's eloquence is stunning me." Charlotte did her best to bring conciliation to the house, to quieten Mathilde and make Gustav hold his peace ; her sympathy was all with Mouche, whose tragic story had won the heart of the woman who was herself so sheltered from life's troubles. They felt themselves united, too, by a common sorrow—the conviction which both had of Heine's approaching end. Mathilde herself had been hardened by watching through so many years of suffering and did not realise that death was near. But the sick man himself was aware of it. He entreated Charlotte to stay, begging one day after another of her company. He tried hard not to frighten her, for he saw that grief at his condition and the incessant friction between the other three were making her ill. He forced himself to smile, but in spite of himself a murmur escaped his lips :

" We shall never see each other again, Lottchen."

At last the news of the illness of one of her children recalled her to Hamburg. The year 1855 drew to its end. Mouche came back to her place at the bedside. One day, as she sat there, Heine seized her arm, gripping it tight in his bony fingers. " Forgive me," he whispered, while his mouth was twisted with pain ; " it will soon be over. Death comes nearer and nearer with great strides, and when I feel him so close to me, as I do now, I feel I must cling to life, even if all I cling to is only a rotting beam."

More and more often he became delirious, and his dreams wandered beyond the boundaries of the visible world. In those dreams he saw his father, as he had seen him as a child, sitting before a mirror, his pink face all smiles, in a cloud of powder while his hair was being done. He tried to run towards him to kiss his hand, but as he touched it he started back in horror : " The fingers were dead branches and my father himself became a leafless tree, covered thick with hoar-frost." Sometimes he saw himself dead and lying in a marble coffin ; flowers nodded their heads about it, flowers which bore the faces of women known long ago. Above his head hung the flower which people say was born of the blood of Christ on Golgotha, and which they call passion-flower. This flower seemed to be Mouche, who smiled at him the disturbing smile which had re-lit the flame in his listless body.

From portions of such dreams, from memories of his talks with Mouche in which he had recapitulated the struggles of his life, was formed his last great poem, dedicated to Mouche. As if urged on by fear of the eternal silence which would follow, he sought to give it the clearest, most vigorous expression of which he was capable. This poem clearly bears the character of his artistic testament. It is the last long look which the dying man throws back across his life, the register of all his efforts and his aspirations. Seen from the threshold of the grave, the meaning of life appears again to Heine to be an eternal struggle between the Greeks and the Barbarians:

O, dieser Streit wird enden nimmermehr,
Stets wird die Wahrheit hadern mit dem Schönen,
Stets wird geschieden sein der Menschheit Heer
In zwei Partein : Barbaren und Hellenen.

" Oh, this conflict will never end, which Truth fights with Beauty; the army of mankind will ever be divided in two parties—Barbarians and Greeks."

He himself has no longer the strength to struggle in the great battle of life.

O Tod! mit deiner Grabesstille, du
Nur du kannst uns die beste Wollust geben ;
Den Krampf der Leidenschaft, Lust ohne Ruh',
Gibt uns für Glück das albern rohe Leben.

" O death, with thy graveyard stillness, only thou canst give us the purest joy. Vain, crude life gives us, for happiness, the stress of passion, pleasure without rest."

It was a cold, wet afternoon in February 1856. Mouche had not been to see him for some days ; she had had a chill and did not dare go out of doors in such miserable weather. When she did at length drag herself from her bed to climb, with aching limbs, the five floors up to Heine's apartment, she was received with a flood of reproaches. She did not understand his impatience nor fully realise his anguished state of mind. But for some reason she felt suddenly overcome with grief, and threw herself on her knees at the bedside, shaking with sobs. A light but feverish hand passed softly across her forehead and caressed her hair. Then presently came the old imperious words, but this time in a voice which shook with weakness. " Good-bye till to-morrow. Do you hear me? Don't be late."

As Camille Selden crossed the Champs Elysées, hurrying home through the driving rain and icy biting wind, she did not know that she had said farewell for ever to Heinrich Heine.

He lay almost alone through those last grey days. Only Caroline Jaubert braved the inclemency of the weather. She came for the last time on February 13th, carrying her eternal little umbrella in her tiny hand. Her painted doll's face in its frame of white hair was the last face from the outside world to smile upon him.

On the Thursday evening he was seized with a sudden convulsion, which they took to be a stomach disorder unrelated to his disease. The vomiting lasted throughout the night, and in the morning they fetched the nearest doctor, since his own Dr. Gruby could not be found. When Gruby himself arrived on Friday evening, he prescribed ice compresses, which brought the sufferer some temporary relief. With a trembling hand Heine raised his paralysed eyelid, and his look searched the face of the little doctor. " Tell me the truth," he muttered, half choked with pain. " Is it the end? " The doctor dropped his eyes before the rigid gaze which pierced him through. Gently he pressed the dying man's hand between his own and gave a questioning look at the door. " No," Heine whispered, " let Mathilde sleep." The shadow of a smile passed across his face and faded again. The big child would learn of her misfortune soon enough.

Still the hours dragged on, and still he lived. His mind was filled with thoughts of Mathilde and of his mother. He reproached himself for not having written more to his mother while he could still write. His last thought of all was a financial worry. There was no money in the house. Mathilde lamented the fact on waking; her eternal plaint was not hushed even in the presence of death. Heine's lips could scarcely move, but a sound came from them, a feeble murmur of consolation: " Ne pleure pas; tout s'arrangera.

There will be money; little Zacharie will come presently with a sack full of silver crowns." They took the mumbled words for delirium.

But on the day after the funeral, which was paid for by a friend, a strange little dwarf, dressed all in black, came to the desolate apartment and, with a low bow, said that he was M. Zacharie from the publisher Michel Levy. Held in his hand was a canvas sack containing the money due for the French edition of Heine's works.

Only the nurse, Catherine Bourlois, whom he called "La Dame Infortune," was with him through his long last night. When she saw the end approaching, she called Pauline. Mathilde was sleeping peacefully in the next room, worn out by tears. All sign of life had already gone from the waxen face, though the lips still shaped the words of a letter to his mother. He was fully conscious, and awaited the end with his senses alert. A few minutes before it came they called Mathilde. As she entered the room the nurse said in a harsh voice, "All is over." There came the death-rattle, a last shudder shook the body, and his head fell back.

The next day Mouche came at her usual hour. She stared uncomprehendingly at the Christ-like head which lay upon the pillows, then stooped to kiss the cold hand with her lips and fled. Mouche was alone again, back in her solitude, from which her love-affair with Taine would soon draw her, but only to overwhelm her with fresh tragedy. "Heine dead," she wrote in later years; "the parts we played were interchanged; henceforth he was the living, I the dead."

"I request that my funeral shall be as modest as possible, and that the expenses shall not exceed those of the simplest citizen," Heine had written in his will. On February 20th, at eleven o'clock, a small group assembled before the house in the Avenue Matignon. An hour and a half before the funeral, Mathilde had left the apartment. It was said that she did not leave alone.

Karl Marx, in the letter to Engels in which he speaks of Heine's death, recalled some lines the poet had written long before:

Um Sechse des Morgens war er gehenkt,
Um Sieben ward er ins Grab gesenkt;
Sie aber schon um achte
Trank roten Wein und lachte.

" At six in the morning he was hanged, at seven he was lowered into the grave. But at eight o'clock she drank red wine and laughed."

" He had foreseen exactly what came to pass," said Marx. " His body still lay in the house as, on the day of the funeral, the sweet angelic Mathilde waited at the door for the *maquereau* who was to fetch her."

The day was overcast and cold. A biting wind whipped the faces of the mourners as the coffin was carried out, a coffin far too large and heavy for the wasted body. The way to Montmartre Cemetery seemed long, and the humble procession attracted no curious crowd.

An occasional passer-by removed his hat respectfully, then replaced it quickly and hurried on. Only a few people followed the hearse, most of them Germans, with a sprinkling of those friends who had remained true through the last years. Théophile Gautier followed now as he had followed the living poet in the golden days of his arrival in Paris.

At the cemetery the coffin was unceremoniously lowered into a temporary grave. No speech, no song or hymn accompanied the gravediggers in their work. But amidst the silence there came the heavy sobs of a man. Alexandre Dumas wept aloud for his friend, his great mulatto face and thick lips puckered like a child's.

Like so many other foreigners who had fled to Paris in their exile, to be lost in the end amongst the multitude of those who sleep in its great cemeteries, in a tomb watered by the tears of a few friends, Heinrich Heine found peace at last.

THE END